III. THAT THE SCOTCH DESERTED THAT LARGE LAME WOMAN (AND, ACCORDING TO THE SCOTCH, THAT PARAGON OF ALL THE VIRTUES), MARY STUART, IN HER HOUR OF DIREST NEED.

IV. THAT IT WAS THE SCOTCH WHO SOLD CHARLES I. (AND A STUART) TO THE PARLIAMENTARIANS FOR £400,000.

V. THAT THE STUARTS WERE THE WICKEDEST AND STUPIDEST KINGS EUROPE HAS EVER KNOWN.

VI. THAT THE SCOTCH ARE IN POINT OF FACT QUITE THE DULLEST RACE OF WHITE MEN IN THE WORLD, AND THAT THEY "KNOCK ALONG" SIMPLY BY VIRTUE OF THE SCOTTISH SUPERSTITION COUPLED WITH PLOD, THRIFT, A GRAVID MANNER, AND THE ORDINARY ENDOWMENTS OF MEDIOCRITY.

VII. THAT IT WAS A SCOTCHMAN WHO INTRODUCED THISTLES INTO CANADA, AND THAT, VERY LIKELY, IT WAS A SCOTCHMAN WHO INTRODUCED RABBITS INTO AUSTRALIA.

It is a nice question whether any "proper child of Caledonia" has debunked the historical bases of national self-esteem with more devastating effect (Crosland is a Southron); but surely it's not because the Scots have failed to try.

The Scots, in fact, have been poking fun at themselves for many long years, and their complaints about fellow countrymen have aimed at, and hit, every conceivable target. Often the heart of the joke is an intellectual exchange; a moment of awareness—the stupid answer, at which we are expected to laugh, is deceptively shrewd—nips in the bud any tendency to condescend. *Punch*, that quintessential periodical of British humor, has often implied that the Scots lack a sense of humor; but a statistical count once showed that three-quarters of the jokes appearing in its pages

Although the legitimate Stuart male line ended with the death of Bonnie Prince Charlie and his brother Henry, cardinal of York, a nineteenth-century "pretender" named Charles Sobieski Stuart enjoyed a certain notoriety by claiming to be a descendant of Prince Charles and his unhappy bride, Clementina Sobieski of Poland.

The romantic image of Scotland was spread abroad by photographers such as George Washington Wilson of Aberdeen. They captured the essence of Sir Walter Scott's romanticism in visual terms. Here is the forbidding coast of the island of Staffa, home of Fingal's Cave.

contributed by those not on the permanent staff came from Scotsmen, and that Charles Keene (1823–1891), the well-beloved staff illustrator, spent over half his time memorializing Scottish foibles. In its twenty-five volume *Library of Humor, Punch* devoted two full volumes to Scottish jokes.

Understandable resentment exists over one staple of British humor: the notion that the Scots are more penurious, nay, downright stingy, than they need to be. Perhaps this irritation at the widespread currency of a national stereotype is shared more by expatriate Scots than by those who have stayed in Scotland and is regarded by sensitive souls as a slur on Scottish honor. Willingness to laugh at the outcry of a man with a ruffled temper—"As sure's ma name's Tammas Paterson, I'll hae the law o' ye, though it should cost me hauf-a-croon!"—may come hard at times. But there is no question that the Scots cultivate this image.

The most popular Scottish entertainer of this century, Sir Harry Lauder (1870–1950), delighted his homeland with his routines, songs, and off-the-cuff remarks about an unwillingness to spend money, long before he made his debut in London in 1900 and the first of his more than forty tours of the United States. In each of his four books, Sir Harry explained how useful to the development of his stage personality was the humor implicit in a tightwad's perspective, and how, on occasion, he could not resist the temptation to play offstage the role of a Scottish miser.

Lauder wrote most of his own songs, including "I Love a Lassie," "Roamin' in the Gloamin'," and "It's Nice to Get Up in the Mornin'." For millions who saw him personally onstage or in films, or who saw those who imitated him (for example, Fred Astaire and Bing Crosby), the kilt, glengarry, and crooked stick are inseparable from memories of his love of all things Scottish:

> There's a wee hoose 'mang the heather,
> There's a wee hoose ow'er the sea,
> There's a lassie in that wee hoose

Waiting patiently for me.
She's the picture o' perfection,
I wouldn' tell a lee;
If ye saw her ye would love her
Just the same as me.

The music-hall comedian may have been responsible for making per-manent in the popular imagination more images of Scottish life than the work of an entire tourist board.

The point is probably clear by now that popular images of Scotland possess an element of truth and satisfy various preconceptions or needs of the audiences that sustain them for many generations, and over several centuries, in all the lands to which the Scots have emigrated, as well as in Scotland itself. It is true that homogenizing influences are at work.

The true Lowland Scots is dying out, despite the best efforts of writers who banded together under the rubric of the Scottish Renaissance; elementary schools on the same model as England are replacing the old parish schools; cheap books and newspapers circulate the same junk on both sides of the border; "grim, doctrinal" Scottish theology interests fewer and fewer Scots; and, perhaps as serious as any other change, the Scots are becoming more temperate. But the Scots are different from the English and will remain different. There are as many Scots to put the lie to any generalization about the land and the people as there are elements of any other national population waiting to deny the validity of stereotypes that affect them. Three unrelated generalizations (not stereotypes) are worth noting before we move into more detailed consideration of Scottish culture, because they affect our understanding of the people.

19

Well fortified against the North Sea's blasts is Lybster Harbor, Caithness.

With the restoration of Highland dress in the army, the bagpipes reappeared, and their wailing cry was heard over the guns of Waterloo, piercing the air over the noise of the battle. These bagpipes were played at Waterloo by George Mackay, and at the entry of George IV into Edinburgh in 1822 by James Mackay.

(1) The physical features of the land have helped to shape Scottish character. "Places affect people, and people affect places," one historian has written. "It is pointless to speculate on how much the lovely grandeur of Scotland's mountainous north and west affected the highly distinctive Highland character." The physical terrain may, in fact, be the most important influence operant over the past two millennia. With a total area (including water enclosed by land) of 30,411 square miles, Scotland exercises jurisdiction over 787 islands, and has, in its 33 counties, a population of 5,230,000 (1971 census). One-third of it lives in the Clydeside area (centering on Glasgow). As in other highly industrialized economies, population is unevenly distributed: 75 percent in the Central Lowlands, which have only one-seventh of the country's area. The average density of population, 900, is more than four times what it is in the rest of Scotland (170 per square mile). Because of emigration patterns in the past, there are probably four times as many outside the country who can legitimately claim Scottish blood.

But Scotland, despite its superb beauty almost everywhere one travels through either the Highlands or the Lowlands, is a hard place to make a living. The discovery of North Sea oil has simply underscored the historic truth that Scotland has few natural resources: the surrounding seas are of limited value to commercial fishermen; the best stands of timber have long since been stripped away; and peat mosses have never turned into a fuel of much interest to the outside world. The minerals of the Central Lowlands, particularly coal and iron, contribute to the wealth of the major cities, Edinburgh, Glasgow, Aberdeen, and Dundee; but there is very little elsewhere to hold Scots to the land.

Reviewing the reasons why the Scots have fled from their native land —some 1,912,000 between 1900 and 1971 alone—involves us in larger considerations of history, religious oppression, economic dislocation, enclosure acts, and eviction notices that will be discussed more fully in subsequent chapters. But the reality confronted by all generations of Scottish men and women is that only a small fraction of the soil is suitable for agriculture, and opportunities outside Scotland have seemed too good to be ignored. Leaving the land was never a decision to be made lightly; it came, usually, after bitter experience with poverty, enforced unemployment, the diseases that strike those in weakened health, and anger at the indifference of the wealthy and those charged with the responsibility of governing. As a consequence, the Scots have developed a well-earned reputation for wariness, and for their doctrine that life is a hard—or dour —experience, more to be endured than enjoyed.

(2) The Scots are first-class fighting men. This maxim is worth a book in itself and can be generously documented. The twelve regiments, known as Jocks to non-Scotsmen, consist of Highland and Lowland soldiers in a mixture that can never be dissolved into its components. They protected French kings and earned the praise of Froissart, the medieval historian. They were in Joan of Arc's army. They were conspicuous in all of Louis XIV's great campaigns. They fought their way across the Continent with Napoleon and served in all corners of the world, sometimes hiring themselves out as ferocious mercenaries to the Russian czar and other foreign rulers. They distinguished themselves at Blenheim, Fontenoy, Fort Ticonderoga, Waterloo, Balaklava, Lucknow, the battle of the Somme, Tobruk, and in the Peninsula Wars and Korea, to name only a few of the battlefields in which they were engaged. For a nation with a small population, the number of Scots volunteers before conscription insured a steady flow of soldiers toward the war fronts of the Great War is truly astonishing: five hundred thousand by the end of 1916. Of these, one hundred thousand died.

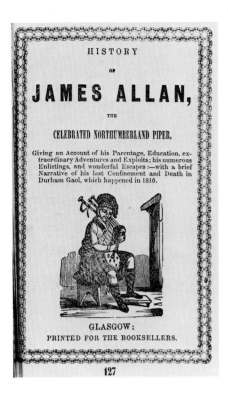

HISTORY
OF
JAMES ALLAN,
THE
CELEBRATED NORTHUMBERLAND PIPER.

Giving an Account of his Parentage, Education, extraordinary Adventures and Exploits; his numerous Enlistings, and wonderful Escapes:—with a brief Narrative of his last Confinement and Death in Durham Gaol, which happened in 1810.

GLASGOW:
PRINTED FOR THE BOOKSELLERS.

127

ROB ROY,
THE
Celebrated Highland Freebooter;
OR,
MEMOIRS
OF THE
OSBALDISTONE FAMILY.

GLASGOW:
PRINTED FOR THE BOOKSELLERS.

2.

The title pages of two nineteenth-century chapbooks printed in Glasgow.

(3) Scotland will remain Scottish, a distinctive cultural entity within the United Kingdom, even if devolution proceeds no further than the delegation of limited powers to an elected assembly (voted on favorably in Parliament in 1978). It is understandable that the grim unemployment figures of the 1970s—over 150,000—should lead to equally grim reflections on the disparity between Scottish and English gross domestic product (the former is only 8.5 percent of the latter, and, on a per-capita basis, only 91.3 percent of the U.K.'s G.D.P.). Moreover, Scotland has lost much of its economic independence during the past century as more and more of its large companies were sold to, or were squeezed out by, American and English firms. The fact that major political decisions are made in London is inescapable in any consideration of Scotland's future.

Even so, the Scottish world is more than a matter of sentiment and tartans, marmalade, Balmoral, Burns's birthplace, and what the Reverend Sydney Smith once called "Calvin, oatcakes and sulphur." There is a recognizable Scottish character. Those who have tried to define it speak of its pragmatism, honesty, homeliness, concern with logic, a love of independence (never destroyed by the Union), and democratic fervor, applying not merely to forms but to the spirit of egalitarianism. It is true that Scotland has pursued lost causes and damaged its own interests by romanticizing selfish and irresponsible heroes and heroines, some of whom did not share the national faith. But looked at in another light, this excessive response to rhetoric, fluttering pennants, and physical beauty distinguishes the Scots from the English. Moreover, the Scots are remarkably homogeneous, despite the heavy influx of Irish immigrants during the nineteenth century. There is a pride of race among the Scots, both at home and abroad, that cannot be diluted by appeals to "a common heritage," or even by loyalty to the reigning sovereign of Great Britain. The Scot thinks well of himself, as Wallace Notestein has written:

... In his heart he believes that no people since the Athenians have so much to their credit and he might, in a pinch, leave the Athenians out. He is British, yes, and he will sing "There will always

The river Tay at Perth.

be an England" but he murmurs to himself, "As long as Scotland is there."

Scotland is there, for him, even if it has become merely a northern province of Britain. He remains a Scot, a citizen of what has been no mean nation. Upon his face and in his speech and in his way of doing things and even of thinking is written his character, a fixed and definite character that has come out of long national experience.

Walter Scott's lines, in *The Lay of the Last Minstrel*, may serve as an even more eloquent restatement:

> O Caledonia! stern and wild,
> Meet nurse for a poetic child!
> Land of brown heath and shaggy wood,
> Land of the mountain and the flood,
> Land of my sires! what mortal hand
> Can e'er untie the filial band,
> That knits me to thy rugged strand!

The true Scot has demonstrated the truth of Scott's implicit answer. "The filial band" remains as strong today as it ever was.

2

From the Beginnings to 1058

Leslie Alcock and Alexander Morrison

FROM THE BEGINNINGS
TO 1058

*by Leslie Alcock and Alexander
Morrison*

Scotland is divided into three major
physical regions: the Southern
Uplands, the Central Lowlands, and
the Highlands. The Southern
Uplands form a dissected plateau
reaching heights of over twenty-five
hundred feet, drained to the east,
south and north. The Lowlands,
forming only about 15 percent of
Scotland's landmass but containing
about 75 percent of its present
population and most of its industry,
are penetrated by the estuaries and
main valleys of the Clyde, Forth,
and Tay, which were major routes
for early inland colonization. The
Highland zone is the least populated,
although low-lying areas reach far
north along the east coast and in
even smaller patches at the heads of
sea-lochs and on the western coast;
the Grampian Mountains, in places
over four thousand feet high, have
some of the oldest and hardest rocks
—granites, schists, and greisens—in
Britain, and the whole region shows
evidence of erosion, uplift, dissection,
and glaciation.

The successive stages of glaciation
over the British Isles during the
Pleistocene geological period formed
the characteristic Scottish Highland
landscape of lochs and glens, and
left fertile deposits in the Lowlands.

THE NORTHERN PART of Britain was covered with ice several
times during the last geological period, the Pleistocene. During at
least one of these Ice Ages, the ice front reached as far south as the
Thames Valley, and Scotland would have been even more drastically
affected by a thick and heavy ice-covering. The effects of this series of
glaciations can be seen in the denuded landscapes of the Highlands and
Southern Uplands and in deposits of clays, sands, and gravels left by the
melting ice as drumlins and moraines in many parts of the Lowlands.

Today we can talk of man's presence in Britain in terms of hundreds
of thousands of years. He may never have been present in sufficiently large
numbers to warrant any great expansion toward the north during the long
cultural period we know as the Palaeolithic, or Old Stone Age, and
evidence for his presence even in the northern half of England is very
sparse due to the destructive effects of successive glaciations. There is no
undisputed evidence for Palaeolithic man in Scotland and, on present
knowledge, he seems to have been a postglacial arrival.

Most dates mentioned in the first half of this chapter are those
obtained by the radiocarbon technique, in which the surviving radio-
activity in organic materials was measured and the date of the death of the
organism ascertained. These dates are normally published with a standard
error (e.g., 8000 plus or minus 50 or 100 b.c.), which indicates that there
is a statistical probability that the man, animal, tree, etc., died within
that time range. For simplicity, the standard errors will be omitted, but it
should be borne in mind that a time-span of anything up to several
centuries is involved rather than an exact date. It is now known that
radiocarbon years are not the same as calendar years, and that in some
prehistoric periods there may be differences of several centuries between
them. Where necessary, the convention has been adopted of showing
radiocarbon years in lower case (b.c. or a.d. and calendar years in small
capitals (B.C. or A.D.).

As might be expected, the final stages of the last glaciation affected
Scotland to a greater extent and to a later date than regions farther south.
With the gradual decay of the ice sheets coupled with the retreat of the ice
front, Britain was probably entirely free of ice before 10,000 b.c. However,
glacial conditions returned to Scotland for a period during the Loch
Lomond Readvance, when the ice again reached as far south as the
southern end of Loch Lomond and the vicinity of the Lake of Menteith in
the upper Forth Valley. Eventually the final retreat began, and the ice
disappeared by about 8000 b.c.

Deglaciation had left a bleak and watery landscape to be slowly
recolonized by forest. It was during this postglacial period that the first
human groups ventured into Scotland. Their culture period is known as
Mesolithic, signifying groups of hunters/fishers with a material culture and
economy not unlike that of the later Palaeolithic period, but adapted to
the changed and changing environments of the time-span between the end
of the last glaciation and the coming of the first farmers.

The origins of these early colonists are inadequately known, but a
northward spread from England seems most likely. Groups in England with
a Mesolithic form of culture are known from shortly after the end of the
late glacial period. The routes northward may have been mainly coastal,
avoiding densely forested regions. There were a greater number of lakes
and swampy areas than exist at present.

Evidence for Mesolithic occupation in Scotland dates from a time
when the sea level, relative to the land, was rising. This had begun by the
mid-seventh millennium b.c. and, over the next two thousand years, the
sea invaded many coastal areas and penetrated into river estuaries and
valleys, depositing marine sediments and forming shorelines higher and

farther inland than those of today. The early groups were simple hunters, fishers, and food-collectors, whose seasonal campsites have been found mainly on the seashore, lakeside, or riverbank. Many of their artifacts have been found close to the "raised beaches" created by the higher sea levels already mentioned. Their tools, weapons, and other implements were made of stone, flint, bone, or wood, and they must have led a mainly nomadic existence.

A good example of coastal location and activity is the site at Morton Farm on Tentsmuir Sands, Fife, which shows evidence of intermittent occupation by hunter/fisher groups over a number of centuries. Postholes and other evidence indicate the use of very simple shelters or windbreaks, some of quite small dimensions. A number of radiocarbon dates for the site lie between 5000 and 4000 b.c. On the west coast, Mesolithic sites with a somewhat earlier dating are known from the island of Jura. These are remarkable for their large quantities of small, finely worked flints, which probably served as arrowheads and as barbs for spears and harpoons.

Elsewhere, the Mesolithic occupation of Scotland is represented by a number of shell middens on the island of Oronsay. Dates for these sites range between 4000 and 3000 b.c., and similar groups, or the same groups pursuing different seasonal activities, occupied caves on the mainland around Oban. Bone and antler implements associated with whale remains have been recovered from the carse clays of the Forth Valley west of Stirling, suggesting the presence of hunters/fishers.

A densely forested and watery environment presented Mesolithic man with problems of movement and transport, but the coastal, riverbank, and lakeside regions offered good routes as well as an abundance of fish, game, and wildfowl. Mesolithic sites are few and the population can never have been very large. But man's effect on the landscape, his role in changing the environment, had already begun, but at a low level of technology and only to a limited degree.

The rising sea level probably reached its maximum height about 4000 b.c., after which it was outstripped by the continuing recovery of the land from the weight of glacial ice. Temperatures were somewhat higher than at present, and the dominant vegetation was a mixed oak forest with elm, lime, and alder. By the middle of the fourth millennium b.c., the first groups of people practicing agriculture and having domesticated animals were arriving in Scotland as part of the greater diffusion of Neolithic culture, when man was becoming sedentary, able to grow his own food, and no longer completely reliant on hunting and fishing for his livelihood. From this period dates man's earliest deliberate alteration of the environment—fields cleared for crops and pasture—on an appreciable scale.

These earliest farmers seem to have avoided low-lying areas or river valleys, where the soils were marshy or formed of heavy clays, difficult to work with the simple and light implements of the period, and likely to be covered with a thick and tough deciduous forest, which would be hard to clear with the Neolithic polished stone ax. The preference would be for the less densely forested sand and gravel terraces, hillslopes, and upland soils, which were better drained and lighter to cultivate. Traces of their settlements or habitations are relatively rare on the Scottish mainland, but recent discoveries have added greatly to our knowledge of the period. Excavations at Balbridie, on the south bank of the Dee, in Kincardineshire, have revealed the foundations and postholes of a large rectangular wooden building measuring about eighty-five feet by forty-two feet, which may be the earliest substantial architectural structure so far discovered in the British Isles. Associated with these remains were traces of barley and shards of a type of pottery hitherto accepted as characteristic of the

Early Neolithic period in the Orkney Islands. Radiocarbon dates give a range from the late fourth to the early third millennium b.c.

In general, traces of settlement amount to no more than a few postholes or pits, with perhaps a scattering of pottery shards or flints. In the north, however, particularly in the Orkney and Shetland Islands, the almost treeless environment forced the use of more durable materials for building, in particular the Caithness flagstone. Its use in building ensured the survival of many prehistoric structures, one of the best known being the Late Neolithic village of Skara Brae, on the mainland of Orkney, which was occupied between about 2500 and 2000 b.c.

The main evidence for the distribution of these Neolithic peoples is found in the remains of their burial places, the chambered tombs. These communal burial vaults had chambers constructed of great stone slabs or boulders, covered over with a cairn of smaller boulders which greatly exceeded the actual burial area in size. Fashions ranged from the segmented chambers under long cairns of the Solway and Clyde regions to the passage graves of the Orkney-Cromarty-Hebrides groups of which the finest example must be the great tomb of Maes Howe, on the mainland of Orkney, covered by a mound 24 feet high and 115 feet in diameter.

The Stenness stones, a rough circle of tall, slender, balanced slabs, overlook the Loch of Stenness on Orkney Island. Though the Stenness circle is similar in pattern to dozens of other ancient stone monuments in Scotland, Ireland, England, and Brittany, its meaning and function remain unknown, but it seems clear that most such sites were sacred places consecrated for the performance of rituals related to nature—to enhance fertility of crops, herds, and individuals, to promote or restore health, and to ameliorate weather.

Apart from the ritual involved in death and burial, Neolithic communities in various parts of Scotland constructed circular open sanctuaries enclosed by a ditch and outer bank. These have been termed "henges" after the first stage of construction at Stonehenge, and their distribution suggests that, apart from their ceremonial function, they may also have served as regional gathering places. The labor and building materials necessary for the construction of these sites and the chambered tombs suggest some form of social organization, but evidence for the stratification of Neolithic society is not obvious from the archaeological record in Scotland, unless we accept the idea that communal burial in the chambered tombs was a privilege reserved for particularly important families.

In the late third millennium b.c., changes in burial rites and the introduction of copper metallurgy heralded the incursion of a new and different culture group, named from their distinctive pottery forms, the Beaker folk. Their burials are found in single graves under round barrows or cairns, but there may be more than one grave under a barrow. In Scotland the burials are often in small stone slab coffins or cists, usually no more than about four feet by two feet, in which the body was laid in a crouched position and accompanied by grave goods such as the characteristic beaker, stone battle-ax, barbed and tanged flint arrowheads, and occasionally a metal object such as a tanged copper dagger or knife. There was an undoubted cultural interchange between the Beaker folk and the indigenous Late Neolithic groups, and the traditions of both were affected. It was probably the Beaker peoples who modified the native henges and embellished them with standing stones. While they introduced a form of single burial, the Beaker folk were not averse to adopting local customs, and there are many chambered tombs with secondary Beaker interments; indeed, some later Neolithic chambered tombs were not constructed until after the coming of Beaker culture.

By the early second millennium b.c. an alloy of copper and tin was being introduced for weapons and other implements. Gold and copper were available in various parts of Scotland, but the use of tin implies a movement of materials by way of trade or exchange. In the Early Bronze Age, the range of manufacture was limited to flat axes, halberds, rivet-handled daggers, and objects of ornament or decoration. Many of these have been retrieved from burials, but quantities of metal objects were now being buried in hoards, perhaps by itinerant bronzeworkers. It is possible that at this stage of economic and social evolution few communities were wealthy enough to have their own smith, so that the traveling specialist may have been a necessary arrangement.

Early Bronze Age groups have often been labeled according to the types of pottery associated with their settlements or burials. Beakers have already been mentioned, and these continued in use to overlap with food vessels, so named from the theory that they contained food offerings for the dead, and cinerary urns, which contained or were inverted over cremated remains. There were, however, no fine distinctions, and all three forms of pottery have been found together, suggesting perhaps variations in function and fashion rather than cultural differences. There was strong continuity from the Neolithic period, in pottery styles, in some farming techniques, and in certain traditions of burial and ritual. Near Kilmartin, in Argyllshire, a region with a dense concentration of prehistoric monuments, a Neolithic chambered tomb became the focus for a linear cemetery of Early Bronze Age cairns, stretching north to south over a distance of about three miles.

The custom of erecting circles of standing stones continued, no longer simply as additions to henges, but as separate monuments without banks and ditches, and related to the alignments of standing stones with which they are combined in the magnificent site at Callanish on the island of Lewis. There is good evidence to suggest that many of these lines and circles had astronomical sighting functions, and some are laid out on quite accurate mathematical principles, but complete interpretation is impossible. Within some of the stone circles on Machrie Moor, on the Isle of Arran, were burials in cists accompanied by food vessels. Another manifestation of Bronze Age ritual is to be seen in the cup-and-ring-marked stones. These designs appear on the stone slabs of cist burials, occasionally on standing stones, and most often on rock outcrops and boulders. The true significance of these is not known, but they seem to have embodied something more than mere decoration.

After the middle of the second millennium b.c., it becomes difficult to trace continuity in certain elements of earlier Bronze Age culture. The use of open-air circular sanctuaries, the erection of stone circles and alignments, and the manufacture of most forms of Early Bronze Age pottery seem to have ceased. Most frustrating to the archaeologist is the discontinuation of burials with grave goods, those aids to dating and indicators of changes in fashion or ritual. Later burials seem to consist of cremation deposits, occasionally accompanied by a plain, undistinguished urn. Only the metalworking tradition appears to continue without interruption.

One suggested reason for the cultural break is climatic deterioration, whereby increasing wetness and cloud cover might have forced the abandonment of sites involving "sky-oriented" rituals or ceremonies as well as the elaborate forms of burial which were probably closely associated with them. Such a climatic change might also have caused a move away from upland settlement and agriculture, with a consequent population disturbance and pressure on land necessitating the construction of defended settlements. A suggestion of a change to a more water-oriented religion is to some extent borne out by the many finds of Middle and especially Late Bronze Age metalwork seemingly deliberately deposited in rivers and bogs.

By the Late Bronze Age, the leaf-shaped slashing sword had appeared. It was a longer weapon than the rapier, with the weight in the blade. The ax had developed to a socketed form with loops, and the spearhead was now riveted to its shaft through a socket. During this period there was a floruit of sheet-bronze working which produced some fine buckets, cauldrons, and shields. Continuing the idea of votive offerings was the discovery of a ring of five or six bronze shields in the parish of Beith, in Ayrshire. These shields date from the eighth century B.C.

The Late Bronze Age may have been a period of movements of peoples or wide-ranging cultural contacts. The proliferation of the heavier leaf-shaped sword suggests increasing aggression, and the fortification of hilltop sites had begun by this time. A displacement of population may have been caused by incursions farther south, and some retreat into cultural backwaters probably occurred, continuing well into the second half of the first millennium b.c. A Bronze Age settlement at Jarlshof, on Sumburgh Head, Shetland, had a group of stone-built "courtyard houses" whose architectural style had Neolithic origins. The inhabitants' way of life had changed little in a thousand years: they raised sheep and cattle, grew barley, fished, collected shellfish, and hunted wildfowl. Their tools and weapons were of stone and bone. At a late stage in this occupation, a bronzesmith, probably from Ireland, arrived and began to manufacture leaf-shaped swords and socketed axes. The local Late Bronze Age had begun, but iron was already in use on mainland Scotland.

The beginning of the Iron Age is often described as an invasion of Celtic peoples, groups speaking a language ancestral to Welsh, Irish, and Scottish Gaelic, and having cultural origins at least as early and as distant as the Urnfield period in the central European Late Bronze Age. This statement involves a much discussed and disputed combination of linguistic, historical, and archaeological evidence. To cut across the argument, it might be expedient to agree that the bringers of iron probably were Celts, but that they may not have been the first such groups in Scotland, and that some form of proto-Celts may have existed among the Bronze Age peoples already discussed. The initial incursions were unlikely to have been "invasions" anyway, but rather movements of small groups displaced from more southerly regions and bringing elements of new material culture piecemeal rather than in discernible stages. The introduction of ironworking cannot be located in time with any certainty, and exotic objects of iron were in use in Scotland long before manufacturing began. A socketed ax of iron was recovered from a pre-hill-fort settlement on Traprain Law, East Lothian, suggesting that local smiths were using the new material, but in forms controlled by continuing Late Bronze Age traditions.

Unlike earlier prehistoric periods, little is known about death and burial in the later first millennium b.c. Much of the archaeological evidence for the period consists of settlements, fortifications, and remains of material culture. Habitations in many parts of Scotland, and particularly in the west and north, consist of the ubiquitous hut-circles—the stone foundations, or low stone-walled huts with internal wooden posts to support a roof which almost reached to the ground. They cannot all be classed automatically as Iron Age, but excavation has shown many of them to be of this period on the evidence of pottery or radiocarbon dating.

In the southeast of Scotland, in the counties of Roxburghshire, Peeblesshire, and spilling over into Lanarkshire, are the remains of what have been described as unenclosed platform settlements, with origins possibly in the later second millennium. They consist of groups of up to a dozen circular timber-framed houses, usually on a hillslope. Small areas of the hillside had been scooped out and the material formed into a level platform on which the house was situated. The houses may be loosely clustered or strung out along the hill contour, but usually there is no enclosure. Elsewhere, settlements were enclosed by a timber palisade, and this type also has a concentration in the southeast, but a palisaded site underlying a stone-built fort at Craigmarloch, near Kilmacolm, Renfrewshire, has been dated in the late seventh to early sixth century b.c.

Another type of defensive habitation site occupied in southern Scotland in the Iron Age and into very much later historic periods was the crannog. This was an artificial island constructed by sinking boulders, logs, and brushwood offshore in a loch, river estuary, or marshy area until the top rose above the surface of the water. On a timber foundation platform on top of this, a large hut would be constructed, often with space for cattle brought from the shore for protection. The crannog might be linked with the shore by a causeway of wood or stones, which in some instances would be hidden just below the surface of the water.

That the "rural, tribal, hierarchical and familiar" Celts were horse- and chariot-riders is well supported by the archaeological record of many finds of horse gear and trappings. A fine example is the bronze ornamental cap for a chariot pony from Torrs, Kirkcudbrightshire, dated to between 250 and 200 b.c. It is interesting to note that Ptolemy in his list of tribes notes a group in the area of present-day Argyllshire as the *Epidii*, or "people of the horse."

The need for protection against internal warfare as much as, if not more than, against external invasion produced the large numbers of

A stone from Invergowrie in Angus (left), dating from the early tenth century, bears a bold and lifelike depiction of a warrior refreshing himself from a bird-head mounted drinking horn like the one on the Torrs "cap."

This ancient artifact, a pony cap known as a chamfrain and two drinking horns, was wrongly assembled into a fanciful headgear after being found in a bog at Torrs in Kirkcudbrightshire in 1820. Typical of the work done by Celtic tribes about 250–200 B.C., the bronze is finely worked with repoussé and engraved decoration in La Tène style.

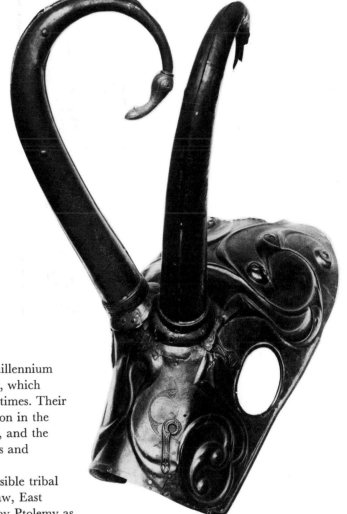

fortified sites which are the main record of the later second millennium b.c. on the Scottish landscape. The major form is the hill-fort, which probably developed from the palisaded hilltop sites of earlier times. Their distribution in Scotland is mainly easterly, with a concentration in the southeast. Drystone is the main material of their construction, and the walls were surrounded by outer defenses of one or more banks and ditches.

A number of hill-forts are large enough to be seen as possible tribal capitals, or *oppida*. In this respect, the hill-fort of Traprain Law, East Lothian, has been suggested as the capital of the tribe listed by Ptolemy as the *Votadini*, or *Otadini*. Its forty-acre area contained a settlement and workshops where the products included metalwork and glass bangles. The fact that it continued to be occupied and to function after Roman occupation of the region suggests some sort of client relationship or collaboration with the Romans.

One of the most imposing hill-forts in the northeast is the White Caterthun, north of Brechin, in Angus, which lies at a height of almost a thousand feet above sea level. This has one of the most impressive surviving walls, in some places possibly originally forty feet in thickness, but the defenses as a whole seem to be unfinished. In the southwest, a large hill-fort at Walls Hill, in Renfrewshire, just over eighteen acres in area and with traces of circular timber-framed houses, may have been a center of the later-named *Damnonii*.

From the first century B.C. until about A.D. 200, the inhabitants of the far north of Scotland and the islands in the North Sea built circular stone towers known as brochs. At right is the broch at Mousa in the Shetlands. The brochs were situated in commanding positions along the coast and utilized a circular form to enclose the maximum space within their defensive circle. These buildings may have been as large as 50 feet in diameter and 45 feet high. Within double walls, up to 15 feet thick, were cells and stairways.

Originally the broch at Jarlshof (opposite) resembled Mousa broch, and may have been as tall. After the period of effectiveness of the broch, wheelhouses were built from its stones. These were divided by radiating interior walls into paved and roofed-over compartments surrounding a central hearth. Later these houses were used as stables.

In the west of Scotland, on the coasts and islands, the main fortified site was the dun. These were usually circular, built of drystone with a rubble core to the walls, and between about thirty-five and fifty-five feet in internal diameter. The interior may have been roofed, or left as an open courtyard area, approached by an elaborate passage through walls up to fifteen feet in thickness. Their small size suggests a much smaller social unit than in the larger hill-forts, perhaps in many cases single families. Many were located strategically on the coast or on hilltops controlling routes or passes; others seem less securely placed, easily approached or overlooked by nearby hills and seem to have been constructed more for reasons of prestige than for defense.

The Western Isles offer a wide range of habitation of the period from the mid-first millennium b.c. to the mid-first millennium A.D. Many are particularly adapted to climate and availability of building materials, often partly subterranean to avoid the Atlantic winds and rain. Apart from a number of duns of the type already mentioned, there are variations on a type of roundhouse or wheelhouse, stone-built and subdivided internally by stone pillars or piers supporting the roof and leaving an open area in the center. A wheelhouse at Drimore, South Uist, had an ironworking furnace, part of an iron ploughshare, bone objects including an awl, netting needle and fish gorge, stone querns and mortars, and Hebridean Iron Age pottery. The structures showed five phases of occupation and modification.

In the far north, a type of fortified refuge related to the hill-forts and duns, but having a shorter life than either of these, was being constructed from the first century B.C. This was the broch, a circular drystone-built tower of up to fifty feet total diameter and rising exceptionally to a height of about forty-five feet. The walls were hollow above a certain height in most examples, the double wall casing being linked by cross slabs. Within the walls were cells and also stairways, possibly leading to a parapet walk on top of the wall. The walls were up to fifteen feet thick and enclosed a central area thirty to forty feet in diameter. The only entrance was through a long narrow passage which had door checks and a socket for a bar to hold the door in place. Between the door and the interior there might be one or two small guard cells to protect the passage.

Brochs are concentrated mainly in Caithness, Orkney, and Shetland, areas with ideal building stone, but there is a spread into Sutherland and some of the Hebrides. Many are situated in commanding positions at the heads of valleys or overlooking the sea, often associated with an area of cultivable land. The best-known broch is probably that of Mousa, in the Shetland Islands, mainly because of its surviving height, forty-three and one-half feet, and well-preserved condition, although it is not typical of brochs in general. The site of a broch at Dun Mor Vaul, on the island of Tiree, had been occupied for some centuries before the broch was built. A date from the primary floor in a wall gallery of the broch is in the first century b.c. to first century a.d. range. The finest examples are in Orkney and Shetland, with sites at Jarlshof and Clickhimin showing the broch as only one phase of continuing occupation, often to be followed by a fairly open, seemingly nondefensive type of settlement.

It has been suggested that the brochs were a short-lived response by the northern Iron Age peoples to a threat from aggressive neighbors to the south, probably by sea as well as land. If this is so, then the danger seems to have passed by the end of the first century A.D., the latest date assumed for broch construction.

33

In A.D. 43 there occurred one of the major events in the early history of Britain: the invasion of the southeast by Roman forces under the emperor Claudius. After the initial bloodshed of the conquest, many of the

material benefits of Mediterranean-style civilization were introduced to the southern part of the island, including town life, a good system of roads, new standards in domestic architecture, sanitation, and an abundance of consumer goods, both luxuries and necessities. There were spiritual benefits too: a measure of peace, the concept of Britannia as a unified entity, and, in the fourth century, the introduction of Christianity as the official religion.

Few of these benefits, however, reached Scotland, where the Roman period may be seen as a mere interlude, a minor disturbance of established ways of life. This is because northern Britain was always a frontier zone, at the far limits of Roman military lines of communication. Presumably, too, the Romans deemed that there was little in the way of natural resources to make conquest and occupation profitable in the face of vigorous hostile tribes and rugged terrain. In this, surely, they undervalued Scotland's mineral resources, especially the lead of the Southern Uplands, as well as the rich cornlands of the east.

There were three major military events which left their mark on the Scottish landscape. The first wave of conquest did not reach the north until A.D. 80, when the Roman governor Agricola, having subdued north Wales and northern England, advanced through the Southern Uplands to the Forth-Clyde isthmus. In four seasons of campaigning, he outflanked the Grampian Mountains (The Mounth) and advanced to the shores of the Moray Firth. He brought some of the Highland tribes to a pitched battle at Mons Graupius, defeating them heavily. He established a forward line of forts along the edge of the Highlands from Loch Lomond to Strathmore, backed up with a system of roads and forts leading back through the Southern Uplands. But pressure elsewhere in the empire made it impossible to consolidate this advance, and after his governorship ended, his whole system was gradually dismantled.

Nonetheless, a military presence was retained in the Southern Uplands. In the 120s, this came to be based on the great barrier of Hadrian's Wall, across the Tyne-Solway isthmus, with one of its forward posts in Dumfriesshire. Then in the 140s and 150s there was, once again, a forward policy. Inspired by personal ambition rather than by any strategic considerations, the emperor Antoninus Pius advanced his forces to the Forth-Clyde line, where he built some sixteen or more forts, linked by a barrier of turf and timber and by a military road. Out in front of the Antonine Wall, a road and forts extended to the lower Tay Valley—altogether a more modest advance than that of Agricola. But this system did not long outlive Pius himself. In the mid-160s there was, once again, a retraction to the line of Hadrian's Wall.

Despite this, the Romans retained an interest at least in southern Scotland. By a mixture of bribes and punitive campaigns they endeavored to keep the northern peoples cowed, if not friendly. Between A.D. 208 and 212, the emperor Severus and his son Caracalla mounted a more weighty campaign, at least up to the northern end of Strathmore, where the Mounth comes down almost to the sea. The construction of a fortress in stone on the Tay suggests that a permanent occupation was intended; but Severus's death put an end to such plans. Thereafter, the empire was on the defensive throughout its northern frontier in Europe.

What was the impact of all this on the natives? We have one Roman verdict, in the account of Mons Graupius given us by Tacitus. Into the mouth of Calgacos, leader of the Caledonians, he put the words: "They—that is, the Romans—create a desert, and call it peace." But this was scarcely a fair verdict, because the benefits of *pax Romana*, the Roman peace, can clearly be seen, at least south of the Forth-Clyde line. In the Southern Uplands, the defenses of the small fortified settlements were deliberately demolished, and houses overflowed the original ramparts. This must surely imply peace and sufficient prosperity to cause a rise in population. The inhabitants also benefited from Roman manufactures and trade goods, including superior pottery and enameled bronze trinkets. For the first time, too, coins were used, albeit in small numbers. Elsewhere in southern Scotland, high quality metalwork, both iron and bronze, was also reaching the wealthy inhabitants of the crannogs.

North of the isthmus, Roman pressure over the centuries led gradually to the political consolidation of a number of separate tribes into a single nation, the Picts. The name, *Picti* in Latin, meaning Painted Men, suggests that these northern folk, alone among the inhabitants of Britain, had retained the Iron Age practice of painting or tattooing themselves with blue woad or other dyes. The Picts first appear in historical records in A.D. 267, when they were described, along with the *Hiberni* or Irish, as enemies of the Britons. From then on, for some five centuries, they remained the most formidable military power in northern Britain. Yet this reputation, securely founded in historical sources, is curiously at odds with the archaeological evidence for the early Picts and their immediate ancestors. They appear rather as peaceful farmers, living either in large circular houses of wood, or smaller figure-of-eight plan houses with unmortared stone walls. In either case, they stored foodstuffs in large underground chambers or souterrains.

In the far north and west, peoples whom we may describe as peripheral Picts lived in rather different settlements. It appears that, during the second century A.D., the brochs went out of use even more suddenly than they had originally appeared. Some may merely have been abandoned to decay, others may have been deliberately demolished, but in either case they were used as stone quarries for the building of nondefensive houses. What caused the sudden abandonment of the brochs is uncertain, but the descendants of the broch builders continued to enjoy a rich material culture, with plentiful pottery, pins, combs, and other objects of bone, but some scarcity of metalwork.

Throughout the fourth century, from the Hadrian's Wall base line, the Romans continued to patrol parts of southern Scotland and to influence the area politically by diplomatic gifts. One index of the creation of a definite pro-Roman party is seen in the personal names of rulers in the following century, for a number of these are Celticized versions of Roman names. Tribal magnates based at Traprain were presented with silver belt-suites of the kind worn by high-ranking Roman officers, as well as with a costly set of Mediterranean silverware. But against the Picts north of the Forth, bribes were of no avail. In A.D. 367, a "barbarian conspiracy," or anti-Roman alliance, was formed between the Picts, Irish, Anglo-Saxons, and others. The Roman defenses were overrun, and leading generals were killed or captured. With difficulty, the Roman position was temporarily restored, but further Pictish wars followed. By now, however, barbarian pressure on the Continent and internal economic and social collapse had so weakened the empire that the province of Britain had to be abandoned to seek its own salvation. The last word lay with the Picts, for it was their pressure which led the Britons to employ Anglo-Saxon mercenaries for their defense. This action, crucial for the emergence of England, was also of high importance for the ultimate character of Scotland.

With the ending of Roman military power and influence in the early fifth century A.D., we enter the most formative period in the national development of Scotland no less than of Britain as a whole. In A.D. 450, the land that was to become Scotland was inhabited, so far as we can tell, by two Celtic peoples: the Britons to the south of the Forth, and somewhat overflowing the Clyde to north and west; and the Picts over the rest of the mainland, and into the northern and western isles. To the south there was no border, and the Britons of the Southern Uplands merged imperceptibly in speech and material culture with the inhabitants of modern Cumbria and Northumbria. Indeed, the border was not to be defined for many centuries. During the course of the sixth century, two new dynastic elements were injected: on the west, that of the Scots from northeast Ireland, and in the southeast, that of the Angles from south of the Humber. Over the next three centuries, these four political groups formed shifting alliances and enmities in an unsuccessful struggle to dominate the whole of northern Britain. We will survey them briefly in turn.

The Britons formed part of a wider nation who were known to the English as *wealas*, Welsh, that is "foreigners," but who called themselves *Cymry*, "the fellow-countrymen"—a name which survives in modern English Cumbria as well as in a Welshman's name for his own country, *Cymru*. More specifically, they came to be known as *Gwyr y Gogledd*, "the Men of the North," for they bore the brunt of English hostility and conquest in the north, and tales of their heroic deeds were preserved in Wales long after they had lost their independence. One of their poets, Taliesin, celebrated the victories of his patron, Urien of Rheged—roughly Dumfries, Galloway, and Cumbria—in his battles against Aethelfrith, king of Northumbria. But the major poem was that known simply as *Y Gododdin*—the name of the people who inhabited southeastern Scotland. In the Roman period, their capital had been Traprain Law, but in the sixth century it was on Castle Rock, Edinburgh. From there, they dispatched a mounted force of three hundred warriors against the Angles, with the poet Aneirin as one of their number. But it was a doomed expedition. Only Aneirin and two companions survived, and the poem is in fact a collection of elegies for fallen heroes.

No trace of the Gododdin capital, with its feasting hall and Christian chapel, has survived on Edinburgh's Castle Rock. But across the isthmus, at Castle Rock, Dumbarton, evidence has been found for another contemporary British capital. Dumbarton comes from the Gaelic for "fort (*dun*) of the Britons," but the original name, as we are told by the early English historian, the Venerable Bede, was Alt Clut, "which signifies Clyde Rock in their language." The site is an almost impregnable volcanic plug at the confluence of the Clyde and the Leven, joined to the mainland only by a narrow isthmus. In order to control this isthmus, in the sixth or seventh century, a fighting platform was constructed of oak beams and drystone rubble, very much on the pattern of the timber-laced, vitrified forts of earlier centuries. Indeed, the defenses of Alt Clut were themselves burned and vitrified as a result of a Viking siege in A.D. 870.

The lords of Alt Clut, like other British and Irish warrior chiefs, imported wine in pottery jars from the Mediterranean. They patronized jewelsmiths, who made Celtic brooches and pins of bronze. These were sometimes gilt as well and were normally embellished with colored enamels or glass inlays. For this purpose, glass might even be imported from factories in Egypt and the Rhineland. High standards of craftsmanship are also evident in the finds from a very small British fort, known as Mote of Mark, overlooking the Solway estuary. In a nonmilitary context the culture of the Britons is best seen at the crannog of Buiston, in Ayrshire. Hereabouts, in the fifth or subsequent centuries, tracts of forest were cleared to make way for grazing and cultivation.

Meanwhile, to the north and west of the Clyde estuary, the small colony of Scots had been consolidating its hold. It seems probable that the shortness of the sea-crossing had encouraged contacts between north-

38

eastern Ireland on the one hand, and the promontory and islands of
Argyll on the other. There is, nevertheless, no direct archaeological
evidence, in the post-Roman centuries, to substantiate the probability.
Historical sources claim, however, that about A.D. 500, three brothers,
sons of Erc of Dalriata in Ireland, invaded Argyll with 150 men and
established the Scottish kingdom of Dalriada. There are mythical
elements about the tale, as about all early historical attempts to explain
the foundation of kingdoms and dynasties. In the seventh century, we find
the three kindreds competing among themselves for dominance in Argyll,
raiding deep into Pictland and fighting off Pictish counterattacks.

The invasion of the sons of Erc was self-evidently a decisive event in
the foundation of the kingdom of the Scots. Their most important
contribution was linguistic, for the Scots introduced Irish or Gaelic speech
to supplant the languages of the Picts and Britons. Although later
centuries were to deride the "Irish" tongue, and Lowland kings sought to
suppress it, the evidence of Gaelic place-names makes it clear that, for a
time, this was the language of the greater part of Scotland. What is the
more remarkable in contrast is that no other traits of Irish culture can be
detected in the archaeological record.

For our knowledge of the culture of the Scots, we turn to excavations
at the two strongholds of Dunollie, overlooking Oban Bay, and Dunadd on
the Crinan isthmus. Both partake of a common Irish Sea culture, which
is shared also with fortified sites in Wales, the territory of the northern
Britons, and Ireland. Dunollie is a fortified headland, and in this it
resembles Dunseverick in Ulster, where the dynasty is reputed to have
originated. But whereas the fortification of headlands is very common at
this time in Scotland, it is extremely rare in Ireland. Dunadd is a type of
fortification totally unknown in Ireland, but found also among the Picts: a
citadel perched on a boss of rock, surrounded by defended terraces. A
footprint, carved in the living rock just below the citadel, is held to mark
the place of inauguration of the Scottish kings. Dunadd also illustrates the
tenuous hold which Erc's dynasty had on Scotland, for in A.D. 736 it was
successfully besieged and captured by the Picts.

The material culture of the Picts is also best known from the
excavation of fortified sites. The historical records link Dunadd with
Dundurn in Perthshire, for both were besieged in A.D. 683 as part of the
swinging fortunes of war between Picts and Scots. Dundurn, indeed,
guarded the economic heartland of the southern Picts, the rich grainlands
of Strathearn and Strathmore, against attack from Dalriada by way of one
of the principal Highland passes. It had a citadel-and-enclosures plan,
comparable with that of Dunadd, but about four times larger. Its principal
interest is that the defensive wall of the original citadel was built of oak
beams and hazel wickerwork, fastened together with iron nails and
filled in with stone rubble. The idea of using nails seems obvious enough,
and in fact is common in western Europe in the pre-Roman Iron Age.
But in Britain it is known only at Dundurn and at Burghead, which, like
Dundurn, is dated to the Pictish period. Other hilltops like Dundurn and
coastal promontories like Burghead were also fortified by the Picts.

There is also evidence that some of the political centers of the Picts
were neither on naturally defensible sites nor protected by major works of
stone and timber. Historical evidence suggests that Scone had already been
a place of importance for the Picts, before Kenneth mac Alpin moved the
seat of his power there. Even more interesting is the case of Forteviot, on
the grain-growing terraces of Strathearn, where the records place one
of the palaces of Kenneth mac Alpin and the Pictish ruler whom he
supplanted. Until recently, the only evidence for this palace was a richly
carved arch, from a monumental building, which had been thrown into a

This house-shaped container, called the Monymusk reliquary, was intended to hold the relics of St. Columba, the great Irish saint and missionary who introduced Christianity into Scotland. Crafted from gilt bronze and silver plaques set with red enamel and blue glass, it reflects the simple form of an early Celtic church. Traditionally the relics of St. Columba were carried from Iona to Dunkeld in this box. William the Lion gave the reliquary to the Benedictine monks of Arbroath, whose abbot carried it to the battle of Bannockburn in 1314. Later the abbot gave the reliquary to the Monymusk family of Aberdeenshire, who acted as its hereditary keepers until 1470, when the Irvines of Drum succeeded as caretakers.

40

nearby stream. Now, however, aerial photography is giving hints of a palace compound and associated burial ground. The most interesting feature is that the surrounding area is densely packed with ritual, ceremonial, and burial monuments extending back to the third millennium B.C. In other words, the Pictish palace was set in a traditional area for ceremony and sanctity. It has long been a commonplace that kingship and ritual were intimately linked in ancient Ireland: it now appears that the same was true of Pictish kingship.

Those Pictish forts which have been excavated produce a repertory of finds not widely dissimilar from the British and Scottish sites already mentioned. The most distinctively Pictish objects are a group of penannular brooches, which served, no doubt, for fastening woolen cloaks. Penannular brooches are universal among the peoples of Britain and Ireland in these centuries, but the Pictish ones are characterized by the elaborate form of their terminals and by being made of silver. That they are of Pictish manufacture is guaranteed by the recovery of the molds in which they were cast.

The fourth population group in Scotland, the Angles, was essentially the northernmost outlier of the Germanic peoples who swept across fifth-century Europe, and who as Angles, Saxons, and Jutes transformed southern Britain into England. Like the Scottish invasion of Dalriada, the Anglian colonization began, according to our historical sources, with the foundation of a dynasty, that of Ida of Bernicia, the northern half of Northumbria. That was in A.D. 547, but there had probably been a peaceful folk infiltration two generations earlier, out of which the dynasty had crystallized. According to English records, Ida began his rule by constructing the promontory fort of Bamburgh, which then became a royal town; but British sources imply that Ida took over, by force or by treaty, a preexisting British fort. It is not inconceivable that he was given this as a base from which to protect the northern Britons against the Picts.

Whether or not the Anglian people, and Ida's dynasty, were originally established peacefully, conflict soon arose. We have already mentioned the British defense under Urien of Rheged and the disastrous expedition of the Gododdin. In the early seventh century, the Angles beat off a Scottish counterattack and advanced into both southwest Scotland and the

This sarcophagus at St. Andrews Cathedral, with sculptured panels from the early ninth century, was used as a shrine for the relics of St. Rule or St. Andrew. In the center panel David defends his sheep from the lion, first by tearing open the jaws of the beast and then on horseback in a hunting scene. In contrast to this classically inspired sculpture, the flanking panels are filled with an animal interlace reminiscent of the ornament on the Hunterston brooch. The St. Andrews sarcophagus demonstrates the skill and versatility of Scottish craftsmen, who were able to produce on this monumental scale the intricate pattern more often found in metalwork.

41

Lothians, where they captured Edinburgh in A.D. 638. This brought them into conflict with the Picts, and a pattern of events very similar to those of the Roman period ensued. Finally, at the battle of Nectanesmere in Angus in A.D. 685, the Anglian attempt to conquer Pictland south of the Mounth foundered in a defeat in which King Ecgfrith himself was slain. But the Angles retained their hold on the Lothians, and it was not until the 950s that Edinburgh passed into Scottish hands. These centuries of Northumbrian dominance must partly explain the lasting anglicization of the Lothians and, ultimately, of Scotland's capital.

Having said that, it must be stressed that anglicization was at the level of the warrior aristocracy, rather than of the peasantry. During the first century or so, the Angles were pagan, and their burial customs involved placing weapons and jewelry in the dead person's grave. In Bernicia, such pagan burials are, indeed, altogether rare; but those which have been found are distinguished by their wealth: rich jewelry in women's graves and costly swords with the warriors. This argues that Ida's followers were few in number, but disproportionately influential because of their aristocratic status. Their impact is best witnessed by the density of English place-names in southeast Scotland.

If the first importance of the post-Roman centuries was that they saw Scotland receiving major ethnic additions, scarcely less important was the establishment of the Christian faith. The Roman-influenced south may have been partly evangelized in the fourth century. This is implied by Christian symbols on the belt-suites from Traprain Law, and it is certain that the men of Gododdin were Christian. But the clearest evidence for Christian beginnings is a group of gravestones from the southwest. These bear crosses, or the Greek letters *Chi-rho* from the first two letters of Christ; they use formulae like *alpha* and *omega*, the first and the last, or "We praise Thee Lord" from the office for the dead; and they specifically mention priests. Some of them are as early as the mid-fifth century, others as late as the seventh. Altogether they represent in concrete terms the historically shadowy mission of St. Ninian, and the establishment of a monastery at Whithorn in Wigtonshire.

Far clearer than Ninian is the figure of St. Columba, who has good

Christian missionaries from Ireland brought with them their writing tools and skills and introduced the art of the book into Scotland. The *Book of Deer* (right), dating from the ninth century, is one of the earliest illuminated manuscripts to survive. The decorative patterns are cosmopolitan: the knot forms and interlaces are found from Coptic Egypt to Celtic Ireland. The book is open to the Gospel of Mark; the figure of the evangelist is highly stylized.

below: St. Fillan was a missionary saint who lived about 750 in his cell by Loch Earn near Strathearn. Inspired by the shepherd's crook, and symbolic of the role of the priest or abbot as leader of his flock, the crozier is the traditional clerical symbol of authority. St. Fillan's bronze crozier head was enriched with silver filigree panels, which were later reused when the crozier was placed in a silver case or shrine. St. Fillan's crozier had a hereditary keeper, the last of which was Alexander Dewar, whose father had emigrated to Canada in 1818. Alexander returned the precious relic to Scotland in 1877.

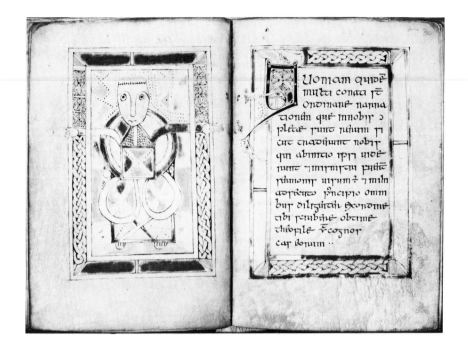

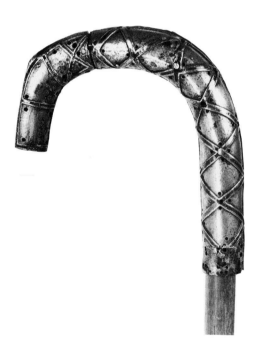

claim to be the major evangelist of Scotland. A member of the Irish aristocracy, he founded the monastery of Iona in A.D. 563, and labored there for some thirty years. Apart from his piety and gift of prophecy, he is best known for his missions to the northern Picts, where in a royal fortress by Loch Ness, he preached to King Brude and his court. The importance of Iona far outlasted Columba's day, and its influence spread beyond the range of his own missions. In the 630s, Northumbrian princes were in exile there, and on their restoration they invited missionaries to consolidate Christianity in Northumbria, which at that time included the whole of southeast Scotland and much of the southwest as well. Although divergent views on the correct celebration of Easter caused some setbacks, missionaries from Iona were ultimately responsible for establishing the faith through northern Britain and parts of eastern England as well.

At Iona, the only remains of Columba's monastery are the supposed foundations of his cell on a rocky knoll, and the bank and ditch which cut the monastery off from the outside world. All else has been swept away by the buildings of the twelfth-century Benedictine abbey. Southwest of Columba's church was Reilig Oran, burial place of Columba's disciple Oran and of many generations of Scottish kings. The absence of early ecclesiastical buildings is not peculiar to Iona. Perhaps because many early churches and oratories were built of wood or of unmortared stone, they have mostly been swept away by medieval building.

In fact, the outstanding monuments of early Christianity in Scotland are not buildings but high crosses and cross slabs. These were set up as memorials to the dead, or as focal points for the celebration of the mass in the days before church buildings were common, or simply as boundary markers for ecclesiastical property. The earliest recorded high cross was a wooden one, erected by the Northumbrian ruler Oswald before the battle of Heavenfield in A.D. 634. By A.D. 700, high crosses of stone were proliferating in Northumbria. They were richly carved with Biblical figures and with interlace ornament which owed something to both Anglo-Saxon and Celtic artistry. An outstanding example of Northumbrian inspiration is the cross at Ruthwell, in Dumfriesshire, which bears, in addition to figural and ornamental carvings, lines from an Anglo-Saxon poem, *The Dream of the Cross.* Northumbrian connections took the idea of the high cross first to Iona, and thence to Ireland for its fullest flowering.

Among the Picts, however, the high cross is rare, and the normal monument is a carefully shaped slab. On one face is a cross in relief, richly embellished with animals and interlace in the Anglian-Irish-Pictish style. The reverse, however, has little of obvious Christian significance. For a start, it will carry so-called Pictish symbols: stylized depictions of animals, objects of everyday use like a mirror and comb, and purely abstract symbols. These had appeared already on pre-Christian monuments, and are thought to be tokens of family and rank derived from Pictish tattoos. The other element on the reverse side of Pictish slabs includes scenes of battle and stag hunts, complete with riders and hounds. It is tempting to think of these as scenes from Pictish life; but the occurrence of eclectic elements such as camels, or Persian angels, warns us that this is probably not so. In any case, it is probable that they represent the battle of good and evil, the hunt of the soul for the good life, and other religious themes.

During the later seventh and throughout the eighth centuries, the church in Scotland, as elsewhere in western Europe, was growing in wealth. Chalices of silver and bejeweled reliquaries of gilt bronze stood on many altars. Many leading monasteries, like Iona itself, were on islands or promontories readily accessible from the sea. The combination of wealth and accessibility made them an obvious target for one of the greatest of seafaring nations, the Vikings, who sailed forth from Denmark and Norway to plunder and to settle. Lindisfarne, the most famous of Northumbrian monasteries, was plundered in A.D. 793, and Iona was attacked two years later. Similar

Found at Ruthwell in Dumfriesshire, this red sandstone cross slab (above) dates from the second half of the seventh century. On this three-and-one-half-foot panel is a depiction of Christ worshiped by desert beasts.

far left: Christian and pagan blend in early Pictish art. On this slab from Papil in the Shetland Islands, the cross is flanked by four hooded crozier- and book-bearing figures which surmount a beast found in manuscript illuminations as the lion of St. Mark the Evangelist.

left: Three Pictish warriors wearing long garments, long curling hair, and pointed beards resemble ancient Greeks as they march with lances and square shields under the totemic images of an eagle and a fantastic beast known as a Pictish elephant. Dating from the eighth century, the stone is from Birsay in the Orkney Islands.

A reconstruction of the Viking settlement at Jarlshof, in the Shetland Islands. Viking farmsteads were built at the beginning of the ninth century and were occupied until the early eleventh. Long bow-shaped houses in which living room, kitchen, and stables were joined follow the traditional building practice of the Norwegian homeland. Typical Scandinavian long houses nestled close to the harbor, easily accessible to their ships. Jarlshof was a permanent Viking settlement; however, fragments of Irish bronze work found in the excavations show that the inhabitants traded with raiders returning from Ireland.

44

This magnificent silver niello Viking sword hilt found on the island of Eigg reminds us that Scotland, despite its remote location, was influenced by many settlers and raiders even before the first millennium after Christ.

raids continued throughout the ninth century and beyond. Because the monasteries were especially vulnerable, and because the only literate people of the day were monks, we have many colorful accounts of Viking piracy and pillage—so colorful, indeed, that some modern scholars have attempted to dismiss them and to whitewash the Vikings.

As settlers the Vikings introduced a fifth and final element into the population of Scotland; as both settlers and raiders they injected a further factor into a political scene which was at once complicated and obscure. Around the middle of the ninth century, the long struggle between Pict and Scot for the dominance of Scotland north of Forth and Clyde was finally settled in favor of the Scots, when Kenneth mac Alpin took over the Pictish kingdom and moved his capital to Scone. In the following century, great areas of peripheral Pictland were stripped away: the Northern Isles to form the Norse Earldom of Orkney; the Western Isles to join with the Isle of Man in the Kingdom of the Isles. In the mid-tenth century, the southern English kingdom of Wessex, fire-tempered by its overthrow of the Danes, advanced through Cumbria to the Clyde Valley and claimed sovereignty over the kingdom of the Scots. In return for acceptance of a token overlordship, Scotland came to include Strathclyde and even Lothian, so that by the mid-eleventh century the Scottish realm, albeit precariously, was acquiring its modern limits.

Meanwhile, in northern and western Scotland, the Norsemen were settling down. Already in the ninth century the graves of women are found alongside those of men, to bear witness to parties of colonizers rather than pirates. The best evidence of the Norse presence is provided by place-names. Some of these are such as seamen might have given; but others refer specifically to farmsteads. These are so dense in the Shetlands and Orkneys that they cannot be plotted on a small-scale map. They continue through the Hebrides, as far south as Islay, at a lower density. Unfortunately, few actual traces of farmsteads have been located. But at Jarlshof, on Shetland, a small single-family farm, established in the ninth century, flourished and expanded in succeeding generations. At Jarlshof, and elsewhere in the Isles, the Norse house is comparable with contemporary dwellings in Iceland, Greenland, and even Vinland (Newfoundland): a long building, with a large central hearth flanked by sleeping benches. In this respect, the Norse Islands, Orkney, and Shetland in particular, belonged to the sub-Arctic world rather than to Atlantic Europe. Ultimately, the Hebrides were reabsorbed into the Gaelic culture of the Scottish Highlands; but the Northern Isles have retained an aloofness to the present day.

3

Medieval Scotland: 1058-1488

Marilyn Stokstad

Literature of the Middle Ages

Harold Orel

MEDIEVAL SCOTLAND:
1058–1488

by Marilyn Stokstad

MACBETH, Shakespeare's great study of power and corruption, has established an almost unshakable image of eleventh-century Scotland as a bloodthirsty, ghost-ridden, brutal, but heroic society. The historic Macbeth was not a criminal weakling but the earl of Moray with a legitimate right to the throne of Scotland; he ruled well for sixteen years. In contrast, Malcolm Canmore (Ceann More or Big Head; 1058–93), when stripped of the glamour given a Shakespearean hero, was, in the words of A. A. M. Duncan, "a brutal opportunist" with no better claim to the throne than his rival. When Malcolm slew Macbeth in 1057 and claimed the throne for himself, he established a dynasty that forged a feudal state along western European lines out of a northern Celtic tribal kingdom. Malcolm III, the ruthless, powerful, and intelligent warrior, only began the transformation; his grandson David I, the skillful, powerful, and intelligent diplomat, achieved the goal.

Change came slowly. In 1058 Malcolm Canmore ruled bands of marauding warriors and a brutish peasantry; by the fifteenth century James I wrote poetry and James II leveled fortresses with cannon fire. Malcolm's subjects lived by barter and booty in earth-and-timber hovels behind palisades; James III minted silver coins that bore as his likeness the first Renaissance portrait in the north, and he looked for support from thriving royal cities. Ruined castles and abbeys mark the passage from the House of Canmore to the House of Stewart, from the heroic age of David I and Robert I (the Bruce) to the century symbolized by the luxurious Rosslyn Chapel of the Sinclairs, and recalled by Sir Walter Scott in *The Lay of the Last Minstrel*.

The conflict between Malcolm Canmore and the aggressive Normans under William the Conqueror determined the direction taken by Scottish culture in the last years of the eleventh century. Malcolm knew England well, for he had lived at the Anglo-Saxon court during Macbeth's reign. After the Norman conquest of England, Malcolm returned the hospitality and gave sanctuary to the Anglo-Saxon royal family, Edgar the Atheling and his sisters Margaret and Christine. In 1071 Malcolm married Margaret and, inspired by her, he invited monks from Canterbury to establish a Benedictine monastery at Dunfermline, one of his principal residences. Nonetheless, Malcolm remained a warrior king. He determinedly tried to extend his kingdom to the south, always looking at the rich lands of England.

Malcolm began his reign as a traditional Scottish ruler with an enthroning at Scone, "Scone of the high shields," "Scone of the melodious shields." This ceremony of enthronement grew out of ancient fertility rites performed by the ruler to insure his power and the prosperity of his people. At Scone, by sitting on a stone from a prehistoric barrow, the king achieved a mystical union with the past and with the earth. The Stone of Scone, or Stone of Destiny, according to one legend, was Jacob's Pillow, and, according to another, St. Columba's Pillow. The king sat on the stone holding a staff of office and/or a sword while his followers draped the royal mantle around his shoulders. To authenticate his right to succession, an orator addressed him with the names of all his ancestors back to Scota, the daughter of the Pharaoh, and from Scota back to Noah. Then his warriors clashed their "melodious" shields to proclaim his power. Scottish and English kings and queens are still enthroned on the Stone of Scone. After Edward I carried the stone off to England in 1296, he commissioned Walter of Durham to make it into a coronation chair. The chair, with the stone in its seat, still stands in St. Edward's Chapel, Westminster Abbey, London.

Malcolm took this essentially Celtic realm and turned it into a feudal state in emulation of the Normans. William the Conqueror and his

Normans, with their mounted knights, their castles, and their efficient administration, had proved too strong for the Scots, just as they had for the Anglo-Saxons. William forced Malcolm, by the Treaty of Abernethy in 1072, to pay homage and send his son Duncan to the Norman court as a hostage in exchange for land in England. Thereafter Scottish kings claimed that they paid homage to the English monarchs for these English lands, not for the kingdom of Scotland. Malcolm cannot have taken the feudal oaths too seriously, for within a few years he led invasions into England again.

The knight and the castle, symbols of the Middle Ages today, revolutionized more than the techniques of warfare; the very structure of society changed from a tribal community to an elaborate hierarchy. Mounted knights needed expensive armor, horses, and long years of training; they became a specialized class supported by the labor of many peasants. In exchange for gifts of land from the ruler, they pledged military support, loyalty, and fair administration of the king's justice in their territory. To hold their new possessions, they needed to fortify their homes. The motte-and-bailey castle became a symbol of domination as well as protection and justice.

Malcolm introduced this type of Anglo-Norman castle into Scotland

The massive Norman piers of Dunfermline Abbey mark a radical departure from the modest Celtic churches of Scotland, and announce the spread of Norman culture to Scotland. This monumental Benedictine abbey church is a permanent memorial to the joint efforts of church and state in unifying the fragmented tribes and religious communities of Scotland. As the final resting place of Robert the Bruce, the abbey church has become a national shrine.

when he adopted Norman military tactics, and in the eleventh and twelfth centuries motte-and-bailey castles appeared throughout the border regions. These early castles were earth-and-timber structures: a mound (motte) surrounded by a ditch and palisade forming the bailey. On top of this steep grass-covered mound, the lord built a timber tower which formed the military strong point and could also be a residence and watchtower. The bailey or courtyard, defended by a ditch, earthen ramparts, and a palisade of upright timbers, might cover several acres and provided space for additional living accommodations for the retainers as well as protection for peasants and their herds. Quickly erected out of materials at hand, the motte-and-bailey castle proved an effective defense against cattle raids and border skirmishes; however, its vulnerability to fire and thus inability to withstand long sieges meant that eventually the king and the great magnates needed to build in stone. Nevertheless, stone castles were so costly that, unlike their richer neighbors, Scots continued to build earth-and-timber structures throughout the twelfth century.

The size of these castles can be appreciated at Duffus Castle, near Elgin, the original seat of the Norman de Moravias, who became the Morays, or Murrays, and the dukes of Atholl and Sutherland. The great motte is now crowned by a later stone castle, and the lower earthworks encircle an eight-acre castle precinct and the more comfortable and splendid residence built in the fifteenth century. Similarly, at Huntly Castle, the stronghold of the Gay Gordons, the "Cocks o' the North," the early motte as well as the ruins of the Renaissance palace survive. The most visited and least noticed motte is that of Castle Urquhart, where the splendid view of Loch Ness makes it a vantage point for monster-seekers.

Castles and medieval warfare are romantic only in retrospect. Malcolm died fighting at the Castle of Alnwick in Northumbria in 1093. Queen Margaret, on learning of the death of her husband and her eldest son, is reported to have died thanking God for sending such tragedies to strengthen her soul. Her saintliness was recognized by the church, and she was canonized in 1251. The younger children fled to the English court, while rival claimants—Donald, Malcolm's brother, and Duncan, his son by an earlier marriage—struggled for control of the kingdom.

St. Margaret's contribution to Scotland was enduring. Not only did she have a hand in establishing a Benedictine monastery at Dunfermline, but she and Malcolm rebuilt St. Columba's monastery and church on the island of Iona and brought Benedictines to Old Melrose. She was devoted to St. Andrew, the patron saint of Scotland, and she sponsored a pilgrimage to his shrine by establishing a ferry, still known as Queensferry, for pilgrims from the south across the Forth. The original monastic buildings at Dunfermline have been destroyed; however, the foundation walls of the early church lie under the nave of the present Christ Church and suggest that it was a small rectangular building with a tower, a square choir, and rounded apse. Although the chapel has been heavily restored, it does give an impression of the Romanesque style of the eleventh and twelfth centuries. The concern of the church with Christian worship and the immortal soul, and with education, the arts and architecture, improved agricultural techniques, and a stable life leading to a higher standard of living, meant that the church could be a model for secular society and the primary cultural agent in the Middle Ages.

After Malcolm Canmore's death, Scotland entered a period of chaos. First Donald and Duncan fought for the kingdom; then in 1097 Edgar (1097–1107), another son of Margaret and Malcolm, invaded Scotland and took the throne; he was succeeded in turn by his brothers Alexander (1107–24) and David (1124–53). Edgar lost the Hebrides, Orkney, the Isle of Man, and all the Western Isles, including Iona, to Magnus Barefoot, king of Norway; on the other hand, relations with England improved. Alexander, after all, was both the brother-in-law and the son-in-law of the English king Henry I.

All of Margaret and Malcolm's children are overshadowed by their youngest brother David. He had grown up in the English court, where his sister Matilda had married King Henry I. David was called the "brother of the queen," not the brother of the king of Scotland, suggesting that the status of Scotland was not particularly high in the eyes of the court. David was a shrewd courtier. His brother Edgar had made him earl of Strathclyde; thus he had personal holdings in southern Scotland; in effect, he ruled a kingdom richer than his brother Alexander ruled when he became king. Then to his lands in southern Scotland he added territories in England through his marriage to Matilda of Huntingdon, the grandniece of William the Conqueror and the wealthiest woman in England. Through Matilda, David became earl of Huntingdon.

When at last he inherited the kingdom of Scotland in 1124, David established his Anglo-Norman friends there as great feudal barons: Robert de Bruce in the Vale of Annan, Hugh de Moreville in Lauder and the Tweed Valley, and Walter fitzAlan in the southwest. Walter fitzAlan became the royal steward, an office from which the family took its name, Stewart. While Normans settled southern Scotland, Flemings went to Clydesdale and Moray. Norse-Celtic lords ruled the western Highlands; northern Scotland remained the land of the earls, the mormaers.

Regardless of its complexities in practice, the feudal system introduced by the king and his barons into Scotland was essentially a simple exchange of land, with the peasants working it for military service. The feudal system originated to provide a measure of security in troubled times; a specialized class of warriors protected the farmers and artisans in exchange for food, clothing, and labor. In theory, all the land in a kingdom belonged to the king. He had the responsibility for providing protection and justice throughout his kingdom. He could grant small estates to knights, who formed a royal army, and he also granted large tracts of land (fiefs) to powerful friends who swore to provide him with military service, hospitality, and some payments in kind, and who also acted as his advisers and governed in his name. The great magnates in turn granted smaller fiefs from their territories to lesser men who had the same relationship to them as they did to the king. This horizontal stratification of society into ranks stood in marked contrast to the traditional social organization of the Scots, where loyalty to an extended family was the overriding duty, defense and justice depended on the head of the family, and pride in the clan extended beyond an individual's material possessions. This clan system survived in northern and western Scotland in defiance of both feudalism and later attempts to form a nation state. The power of the clans was broken only in the eighteenth century.

The feudal system as it developed had distinct disadvantages even where it appeared to flourish. The relationship of the Scottish and English kings dramatizes the results of this complex set of interrelationships based on personal oaths, military strength, and personality. David's marriage to the heiress of Huntingdonshire and Northamptonshire was a brilliant personal financial move, but it made him a vassal of the English king. When he paid homage to Henry I for his English lands, the English king naturally tried to insist that the Scottish king was his "man" doing homage for Scotland as well. Furthermore, when a country was considered to be the personal possession of an individual, the land with its people and their possessions became pawns in the game of personal aggrandizement. David's grandson, William the Lion, literally lost and then bought back Scotland from English kings.

50

Son and successor of Malcolm Canmore and St. Margaret, David was an energetic and able ruler. In the secular sphere he vigorously pursued the feudalization of his kingdom. A devout son of the church, he founded five bishoprics and many monasteries. He also established the first Scottish mint, at Berwick, where this coin bearing his portrait was struck.

In spite of all handicaps Alexander and David created an efficient government for Scotland. Using the Norman model, they introduced written communications and recorded feudal dues in charters authenticated with the royal seal. A staff of royal officers assisted in the administration of the kingdom. First a body of scribes to prepare the charters sufficed, but soon other officers were created. Unlike the English kings, who were constantly abroad fighting or administering their possessions in France, the Scottish king was usually in residence; thus he acted as his own chief justice, although he might send a justiciar around the kingdom to hear cases and dispense justice. For advice and assistance he called a royal council of his friends and relatives, including churchmen and the nobility. At the local level the sheriff became a special royal servant who looked after the king's lands, served the king's justice, and commanded the common army.

David attended to the church as well as to secular government in his realm by organizing the parishes, establishing or reestablishing bishoprics, and providing grants of land for the support of monasteries. As later sovereigns were to note, however, the church was eternal, and lands given to it neither reverted to the crown nor could be shifted around through dowries, wardships, or inheritances. Revenue from church lands was lost forever to the king and the nobles; but the spiritual rewards offered by the church to its patrons were not to be despised—the kingdom of heaven, or hellfire and damnation.

While still earl of Strathclyde, David established the See of Glasgow (about 1115), and by the time he died he had established or revived the bishoprics of Galloway, Moray, Dunkeld, Ross, Caithness, Aberdeen, Dunblane, and Brechin. The bishops, of course, actually received their authority from the pope, not the king. Western Christendom was a united international body; however, for administrative purposes it was divided into archdioceses ruled by archbishops. The pope, under the influence of English prelates, refused to make one of the Scottish bishops an archbishop, and the Scottish bishops, much to their distress and the displeasure of the Scottish king, were placed under the archbishop of York. The ensuing power struggle turned to war. At the Battle of the Standard in 1138, the English king Stephen defeated David and upheld the primacy of the archbishop of York. Nevertheless, by the end of the century, the pope at last recognized the independence of the Scottish church and gave it a special relationship to the papacy. The church owed obedience only to the pope, and the Scottish king carried the golden papal rose as part of his regalia.

An indirect result of the conflict over church authority was the rise in importance of the cult of St. Andrew in Scotland. Andrew was the brother of Simon Peter and one of the first disciples called by Christ from among the fishermen of the Sea of Galilee, but he remains a mysterious figure about whom almost nothing is known. St. Andrew had neither a historical nor a legendary connection with Scotland. His cult had been introduced into Scotland in the eighth century from Hexham, near Durham; supported by St. Margaret, pilgrimages to St. Andrew's church had increased in importance in the eleventh century. When the archbishop of York, whose patron saint was Peter, claimed supremacy over the Scottish church, the fact that Scotland had a powerful patron in St. Andrew took on added significance. The first glimmering sense of nationhood lay, at least in part, in the popular devotion to St. Andrew.

The monastic orders played an especially important role in Scotland; monasteries were centers of learning and economic productivity as well as spiritual support. The Benedictine rule formed the basis for the monastic movement in western Europe but this rule had been subject to many interpretations since the days of St. Benedict in the sixth century. On the Continent the Cluniac reform had reached the height of its power and wealth during David's reign; however, Cluny made little impact on Scotland. Perhaps Scotland was not yet ready to support education and the arts at the level demanded by the Cluniacs. Instead, the more austere Cistercians and Tironensians thrived in Scotland. The Cistercians came to England in 1132 and, at David's invitation, colonized Scotland from Rievaulx in Yorkshire, coming first to New Melrose in 1136 and then to Newbattle in 1140, Dundrennon in 1142, and Kinloss in 1150.

The Tironensians had been founded in 1109 as a reaction against Cluniac Benedictinism by Bernard of Poitiers at Tiron. David may have learned about them while he was living in England, for Henry I was a patron of the new order. As soon as he became earl of Strathclyde, David wrote to Bernard to send him monks, and his first monastic foundation in Scotland was the monastery of Selkirk on the river Tweed. David actually visited Tiron about 1116–17 and took more monks back to Scotland with him. The order grew rapidly. Monasteries were founded at Kelso beside the royal town of Roxburgh in 1128, and then at Arbroath and elsewhere. Tiron maintained a special relationship with its Scottish daughter houses: in France, the second and third abbots of Tiron came from Scotland, and in Scotland Tironensians became the bishops of Glasgow and St. Andrews. The stature of Scottish Tironensian houses is indicated by the choice of Kelso rather than Dunfermline as the burial place of David's son and heir, Earl Henry, when Henry predeceased his father. King William the Lion, Earl Henry's son, was also buried in a Tironensian monastic church.

The Cistercians and Tironensians advocated a return to what they conceived as the simplicity of the original rule of St. Benedict. They reintroduced required manual labor, and they aimed for complete self-sufficiency in their monasteries. The Cistercians preferred rugged, isolated sites, where they built their churches and cloisters in the most austere manner possible. In the twelfth century their farms, worked by lay brothers, were models for the peasantry, and their flocks of sheep became the foundation of the Scottish wool industry. The Tironensians emphasized handicrafts rather than agriculture and had many artists and artisans in the order. The splendid architecture of their churches reflects this interest in the arts.

Cistercians, Tironensians, Premonstratensians, Benedictines, and Cluniacs were primarily rural dwellers dedicated to the service of God within the confines of their cloisters and churches. In contrast, the Augustinian canons, who also lived in communities under a strict rule based on the precepts of St. Augustine, preached and ministered to the public. Between 1119 and 1120 Alexander brought the Augustinian canons to Scone and to St. Andrews. David continued this patronage. He founded an abbey at Holyrood near his castle in Edinburgh, and others at Jedburgh and at Stirling. The Augustinians also had a reformed offshoot, the Arrouaisian order. Almost every new order or reform, every intellectual current, appears early in Scotland, reminding us of the international character of the church and the effective communications network it provided.

As we look at religious architecture in Scotland, we find that the monasteries with their churches, cloisters, and subsidiary buildings are masterpieces of stone masonry, engineering, and efficient planning; but since the country was poor and the reformed orders dominated the church, most buildings do not have the rich figurative sculpture found on Romanesque buildings in France or Spain. Scottish architecture is simple, strong, and direct. The massive walls, small openings, and heavy arches of *right:* David I, as part of his program of religious renewal, invited the Cistercian monks of Rievaulx in Yorkshire to establish a monastery at Melrose. The church was partially destroyed in the fourteenth century, and had to be rebuilt after Richard II burned it in 1385. The ruins, in Late Gothic style, which include the wonderful pig playing a bagpipe, date after the fire of 1385.

below left: The grandeur of the interior of Kelso Abbey can still be seen in the massive piers that support walls enriched with arches and arcades.

below right: Founded by King David in 1128 as a Tironensian monastery, Kelso Abbey, with the soaring verticality of its towered facade and the barbaric richness of the gabled portal, suggests the pride of Norman patrons and builders even in the far north.

Colonized by monks from Kelso in 1178 and dedicated to St. Thomas à Becket, Arbroath Abbey became the burial place for its founder, William the Lion, and served as the site of the assembly of nobles who made and sealed the Declaration of Arbroath in 1320. Arbroath was built in a transitional period, and illustrates both the Romanesque and Gothic styles. Seen from the air, the extent of the monastic complex becomes apparent.

the Romanesque style seem eminently suitable for the realm of Malcolm and David.

The church now standing at Dunfermline, a daughter house of the Benedictines of Canterbury, was begun over and around St. Margaret's Church in the reign of David I, about 1128, and was dedicated in 1150. The great cylindrical piers of the nave are engraved with geometric patterns and support round arches with complex moldings; the nave has a three-part elevation with simple triforium and clerestory and was covered with a wooden roof. Only royal patronage could assure the completion of such a large church in twelfth-century Scotland; Dunfermline at first replaced Iona as the pantheon of the Scottish royal house.

One of the great Romanesque facades can be studied at the Tironensian church at Kelso, where the monastic church, although in ruins, still has the north transept facade. In the church, massive piers carry heavy arches and support walls enriched with intersecting blind arches and open arcades. The building must have been one of the most impressive achievements of early medieval Scottish masons.

From Kelso monks went on to colonize William the Lion's foundation in honor of St. Thomas à Becket at Arbroath in 1178, and the church buildings must have been well along by 1214, when William was buried in front of the high altar. Today the massive ruins of the church stand as expressive evidence of the strength and beauty of Tironensian Romanesque building. At the west the portal is deeply recessed and enriched with sculptured moldings. The Galilee porch supports a tribune which opens both inward to the nave and out to the west. At one time, above this

tribune, there was another arcade, and finally a round window. The west front is flanked by towers also opening into the nave and forming a western transept. The south transept at Arbroath is one of the most beautiful transitional Gothic monuments. The monastery was essentially complete by about 1230. At the end of the thirteenth century a large gatehouse was added to the south tower, where it still extends over one of the principal streets of the town. This fortified gatehouse, protected by a portcullis, admitted the stranger into a monastic precinct originally surrounded by a stone wall. Monasteries as well as houses had to be fortified in medieval Scotland.

The Early Gothic style, seen on a grand scale in the Arbroath transept, can be studied at its most elegant in the ruins of the Benedictine priory at Coldingham. In an elevation composed in two stories of equal height, a refined and elegant arcade of simply molded, pointed arches is supported on slender columns with austere foliate capitals. Oval and quatrefoil recesses in the spandrels further enliven the lower wall. The upper arcade frames the clerestory windows, with a large lancet over the window alternating with two lower lancets. The arches spring from clustered shafts and foliate capitals. The higher arches are stilted on a second range of colonnettes.

More famous now than Coldingham (through its association with Sir Walter Scott) is the Premonstratensian house of Dryburgh, founded by Hugh de Morville in 1150 and colonized from Alnwick. Again the architecture is pure Early Gothic with its lancet forms and ornamental moldings, with the four-petal flowers known as dogtooth molding.

The cloisters surviving at Dryborough, Melrose, and Dundrennan illustrate the efficient planning to accommodate both physical and spiritual needs that must have made monastic life in the Middle Ages superior to secular existence. The monastic plan is a masterpiece of convenience and efficiency. The church was of traditional basilican form, with transept and eastern chapels designed for the use of the monks in the choir rather than for hordes of pilgrims or a secular congregation. Where there were lay brothers, they worshiped in the nave and were separated from the monks in the choir by a screen. Next to the church, and usually on the

Dundrennan Abbey, like Melrose and Dryborough, illustrates the efficient planning needed to accommodate the physical needs of a large community. The cloister garth seen here, with the church in the distance, and the chapter house at the right, was once the center of domestic and scholarly activities in the monastery.

south side in order to catch the warmth of the sun, lay the cloister, the center of monastic life. From the east range one entered the chapter house (so-called because a chapter of St. Benedict's rule was read there each day)—the communal and business center of the monastery. Here too was the parlor, the only place where conversation was allowed. (The monks preserved the rule of silence by communicating in sign language.) Over the east range was the dormitory of the monks, connected to the transept of the church by a stair down which the monks proceeded for night services, and behind the dormitory was the reredorter, or latrine. The buildings were always sited by a stream so that running water could not only provide power for abbey mills and water for the gardens, but could also flush the latrine. On the south side of the cloister stood the refectory, or communal dining hall. Since the monasteries were dedicated to learning, or at least literacy, and in some houses the production of books was an important task, the monastic library and scriptorium usually could be found in the south range of buildings. At the height of the monastic period several hundred people might be living in a monastery. The monastery was, in fact, a self-sufficient city of God.

David's very generous support of the church through extensive grants of land was perfectly appropriate for the age; nevertheless, since in this way the church became a great landholder owing allegiance to Rome, it wielded great political and financial power. As an independent international body it could challenge the king, and since it levied taxes in money as well as in kind in a country where coinage was scarce, the shipping of precious metals abroad could seriously weaken the economy. David needed that money. Like other medieval men he was dedicated to the church, but he also had a taste for worldly luxury that only trade abroad could satisfy. To further trade and industry, he established towns under his royal protection; between 1124 and 1130 he founded Edinburgh, Dunfermline, Perth, and Stirling, as well as the powerful border fortresses of Berwick and Roxburgh. David also became the first Scottish monarch to issue his own coins.

Towns did not spring up overnight with the wave of a royal staff and a royal seal. In the days of Malcolm and St. Margaret, peasants lived in tiny villages and were part-time craftsmen. A few peddlers traveled around the countryside. Gradually larger villages and then towns with full-time craftsmen and merchants grew up beside the protective walls of castles or monasteries. Edinburgh, for example, began as a fortress on Castle Rock. As the cluster of houses outside the walls grew into a town along the ridge of the hill, David made it a royal burgh. He also gave Holyrood Abbey the right to establish a burgh west of its church. By the end of the twelfth century the two towns had grown into one continuous town. The essential element in a town was the market. Thus, towns arose at transportation centers where a market could be established. Within the town, craftsmen as well as traders banded together in guilds for mutual aid and collective security. In short, towns existed for the creation and distribution of goods; they became centers of wealth and power.

The economic basis of the country, however, remained the land worked by peasants. In spite of taxes and marriage and death duties, peasants seem to have been better off in Scotland than in England or France, and at least by the thirteenth century service was not excessively heavy—three days of plowing a year and three days with two men working at harvest, plus some payment in kind (and later in money) for each unit of land. Improved technology increased productivity, and by the end of the thirteenth century many comfortable households and small landholders seem to have been established in the countryside.

Nevertheless, the standard of living was far below that which we

On the preceding page is Urquhart Castle, built on an hourglass promontory jutting out into Loch Ness. The natural defensive contours of the site have encouraged Urquhart's use as a fortress since the Iron Age. Rebuilt in Norman times, the castle later acquired a fine tower, now the best preserved part of the ruined structure.

At right is the broch of Gurness, overlooking Eynhallow Sound on the northeast coast of Orkney Island.

On the west coast of Orkney Island stand the remnants of the Neolithic village at Skara Brae (below). In the winter of 1850 a violent storm washed away sand dunes to reveal this remarkable ruin. A similar disaster must have ended life here, for the houses (occupied between 2500 and 2000 b.c.) were filled with sand, their contents untouched. The village consists of houses connected by covered galleries or alleys. The rooms are rectangular in plan, with four-foot walls of flagstones built without mortar, but filled and plastered with clay. Because there were no trees in Orkney, the residents were forced to use flagstones for furniture as well as walls, and as a result these homes of prehistoric herdsmen are remarkably preserved. The villagers raised cattle and sheep, but did little fishing and raised no crops.

58

Below, at the right, are the king, queen, and bishop of a walrus ivory chess set from the Isle of Lewis in the Outer Hebrides. Chess was originally a war game, devised in India and developed in the Near East as an exercise in strategy, but by the twelfth century it had become so popular among the aristocracy in western Europe that it was considered to be one of the essential knightly skills, and it was also played by women and monks. The Lewis chessmen are unique, realistic representations within the abstract canons of their age—the king enthroned, crowned, and holding his sword, the queen with her gesture of consternation, and the bishop with his miter and crozier. The decorative details of the pieces resemble twelfth-century Norwegian wood carving and British sculpture done under Norse influence; it is likely that they were carved by someone who knew Scandinavian art.

Above is the spectacular ruin of St. Andrews Cathedral and priory, established between 1127 and 1144 but built on the site of a Celtic settlement that may date from the sixth century. Later used by the Picts, who dedicated it to their patron saint, St. Andrews remains one of the most revered cities in Scotland and is also, of course, the site of its oldest university.

Melrose (below), a Cistercian monastery founded in the twelfth century, was pillaged twice by the English in the fourteenth century, rebuilt in the fifteenth, and survives as the finest example of Scottish architecture from the later medieval period.

Near Melrose, on the Tweed River southeast of Edinburgh, is Dryburgh Abbey (right), a monastic complex also dating from the twelfth century. It contains the tombs of Sir Walter Scott and Earl Haig in the section known as St. Mary's Aisle.

62

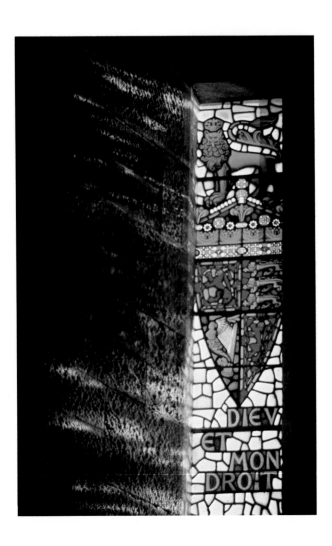

The coin above bears a realistic three-quarter portrait of James III, and thus may be the first numismatic portrait in true Renaissance style outside Italy. Minted about 1485, it is a groat, whose value when it first appeared about a hundred years earlier was a little more than a penny. James III so devalued coinage that in his day the groat was worth about fourpence.

At left is Jedburgh Abbey, one of the grandest in Scotland, founded by David I in the early twelfth century and raised to the status of abbey in 1147. Located on Jed Water in Roxburghshire, the town itself dates from the ninth century and was a favorite royal residence. As one of the chief border towns, Jedburgh became a prized outpost in the border wars between Scotland and England.

Below, at the left, is the modern monument in stained glass to William Wallace, one of the great national heroes of Scotland. It commemorates his decisive victory over the English army at the Forth in 1297.

At right are two views of Eilean Donan castle, located on a rocky promontory at the intersection of three sea lochs: Loch Long, Loch Duich, and Loch Alsh. Originally the site of the hermitage of St. Donan, built in the ruins of a Pictish fort, the castle withstood the incursions of Norse and Danish marauders and was rebuilt as a fortress in the early thirteenth century by Alexander II. Eilean Donan was held for the king by the MacRaes as constables. Destroyed by English gunboats in the eighteenth century, the fortress was restored to its original medieval form in this century and serves again as a clan headquarters.

On the following page is the modern remnant of Edinburgh Castle, the fortress on the slope since Pictish times. Chartered in 1329 by Robert the Bruce, the stronghold supplanted Perth as the capital of Scotland in the fifteenth century.

fica est sup ripam flumims tyebe. in loco qui

The charter of Kelso Abbey bears portraits of its founder David I and his heir and grandson Malcolm. David I transformed Scotland by his strong rule and Norman innovations. Educated in England, he established English feudalism and law in the towns. The many monasteries, schools, and parish churches that he erected greatly strengthened the Scottish church. Owing to the premature death of his son, he left his crown to his grandson, the young child, Malcolm the Maiden, who died too early to make a lasting mark on the country.

imagine today. Peasant houses had walls of wattle and daub, or rough fieldstones and thatched roofs held in place by ropes of twisted heather weighted with rocks. Earth-packed floors and smoky, peat-burning hearths guaranteed that most people lived without the luxury of cleanliness, but this was true of the nobles as well as the peasants. Oatmeal, dried herring, and some cheese were the staples of the diet. As much as a third of the grain may have been brewed into ale.

Often we see history as a long succession of kings, their marriages, their progeny, their battles, while the life of the people goes unnoticed. Even so, some justification for a concentration on the monarch exists. When the kingdom is the personal realm of the monarch, the details of his life can be seen as identical with the history of his people. Marriages cemented political alliances, and dowries were a major source of wealth. Royal progeny insured not only the continuation of the bloodline, but also, in a real sense, the continuation of the nation. The close relations with neighbors established by Scotland all brought Scotland into western Europe, just as did the introduction of monastic orders and the establishment of towns.

David I died in Carlisle in 1153. His son, Henry, had predeceased him, and he was succeeded by his grandsons: Malcolm IV (1153–65) and then William I (1165–1214). Malcolm succeeded at the age of eleven. A boy king, known as Malcolm the Maiden, he was no match for either Henry II of England or his own vassals. He resigned his grandfather's claims to northern England and, as required, paid homage to Henry for the earldom of Huntingdon. In Scotland the earls extended their power until they ruled as independent chieftains. Typical of the earls was the fearsome Somerled, lord of Argyll, the Gaelic-Norse ancestor of the clan Donald, who conquered the west from the king of Norway. Somerled harried the west. His death in an attack on Glasgow in 1164 was attributed to the intervention of St. Kentigern, the city's patron saint.

By the time William the Lion came to the throne, Galloway had become a kingdom within the kingdom and infamous as a refuge for criminals. The fifty-four mottes which still survive in the west stand as

A medieval map of the Central Lowlands, drawn by John Hardying in about 1460, shows the Firth of Tay in the north, Dunbarton and Glasgow in the west, and St. Andrews (Andrewstown) and Edinburgh in the east.

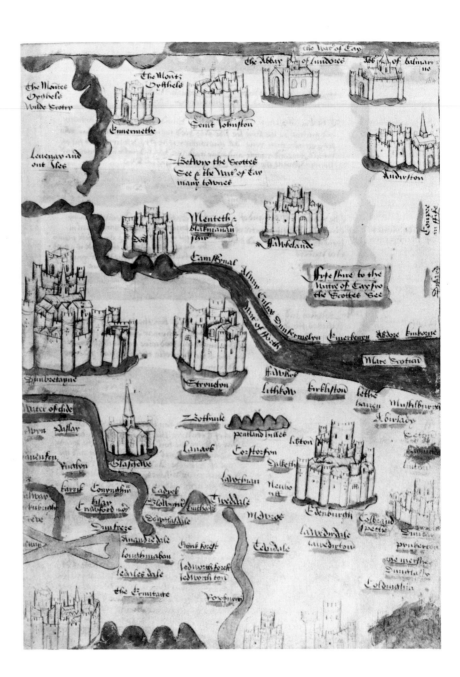

evidence of the futile attempts to control the land and insure personal safety. To make matters worse, the kings of Norway began again to harry the islands; they attacked from every side, and took the Shetlands. Scottish lords remained divided in their loyalties.

In spite of all disruptions, William the Lion made a determined and ultimately successful effort to regain and consolidate his kingdom. In 1165 he formed an alliance with France, the Auld Alliance, that was to involve Scotland in continental politics and wars for centuries to come. Then he attacked England, for he hoped to recover the lands lost by Malcolm. William was defeated, captured, and sent to Normandy; there, in 1174, Henry II forced him to sign the Treaty of Falaise, to acknowledge the English king as his feudal lord, and to do homage for Scotland and Galloway in York Cathedral. William, however, was both stubborn and long-lived. Fourteen years after the humiliation of Falaise he found Henry's son, Richard the Lion-Hearted, willing to bargain. Richard was a great warrior but a poor politician. He wanted to go on a crusade to the Holy

Land, and he needed money for the venture; he cancelled the Treaty of Falaise for ten thousand marks. In effect, Richard sold Scotland back to William in 1189. In a dramatic change of fortune, Richard was captured and held for ransom himself on the way home from the crusade; William the Lion, hoping for more concessions, contributed two thousand marks toward the ransom. When the Lion-Hearted returned to his country to be crowned king of England for the second time, the Lion of Scotland had the honor of carrying the sword of state.

William the Lion had succeeded in laying the foundations for a strong and prosperous state, and his successors reaped the benefits of his efforts. Later generations looked back on the thirteenth century as a Golden Age. Alexander II (1214–49) and Alexander III (1249–86) maintained good relations with England and settled their territorial problems with Norway. The Scottish and English royal houses intermarried, and the possibility of a union of the two kingdoms through inheritance remained a hope. As a consequence, the Scots could turn their attention to the Norwegians. They fought over islands and western lands until Scottish money-diplomacy and nature, in the form of terrible storms which wrecked the Norwegian fleet, brought a settlement. By the Treaty of Perth in 1266 the king of Norway ceded all territory except Orkney and the Shetlands to Alexander III for four thousand marks in cash and one hundred marks a year "forever." Peace in the north was confirmed by royal marriages. Alexander married Margaret, the sister of Edward I, and their daughter Margaret married Erik II, the king of Norway.

The Scottish poet Andrew of Wyntoun described the reign of Alexander III as one of "ale and brede, off wyne and wax, off gamyn and gle..." in his lament for the passing of the Golden Age. Improved agricultural methods and technology brought increased prosperity to Scotland. Towns flourished and life improved for nobles and commoners alike. A glimpse of town life is afforded us by the legend of one of Scotland's few saints, William, the baker of Perth. Bakers, like millers, were not held in high esteem, for they were notoriously corrupt, adulterating their flour and cheating in their measures, "ane [measure] to tak with and ane uther to deliver with." Nevertheless William became a model Christian citizen known for his generosity in giving one loaf in ten to the poor. In spite of his tithing he prospered, and, being a saintly man, he determined to make a pilgrimage to the shrine of St. Thomas in Canterbury. On the way he was murdered and robbed at the very door of the church of the patron of Scotland, St. Andrew's of Rochester. The monks buried him there, and soon miracles began to occur. St. William of Rochester was canonized in 1256, another of the many Scots whose contribution, recognition, and tomb lie abroad.

The growing prosperity of Scots made possible fine masonry architecture on a grand scale. Their religious devotion insured that the resources would be lavished first on the church and only later on secular buildings. Only a few churches have survived the ravages of war, the Protestant Reformation, and later remodeling and modernization. Elgin Cathedral, "the lamp of the north," stands in ruins, but Glasgow Cathedral, the home of the relics of St. Kentigern, though stripped of its western towers, is an outstanding example of the Gothic style.

The bloody history of Scotland suggests that castles are more likely to be found than cathedrals or parish churches. Particularly beautiful examples of masonry castles are at Dinleton, Bothwell, and Caerlaverock, where large round towers were joined by curtain walls and crowned with machicolations. The keep, a tower more heavily fortified than the rest, took the place of the motte in the thirteenth century. French influence is apparent, not surprisingly since Alexander II married Marie de Coucy, the

Glasgow Cathedral was begun during the reign of Bishop William de Bondington and the east end was finished by 1277; but the building of the nave, interrupted by the Wars for Independence, was completed only in the fourteenth century.

St. Kentigern was founded in Glasgow in the late sixth century. In the twelfth century David I reorganized the church and rebuilt the cathedral, and the early church was rebuilt again at the end of the century. It is this Romanesque church that the present Gothic structure replaced with a structure modeled on the buildings of England. The final addition to the church fabric was made in the fifteenth century, when a two-story transept was projected by Archbishop Robert Blackadder, probably as a suitable building to house the shrine of St. Kentigern. Only the lower story had been finished when the Reformation put an end to such ambitious building projects.

above right: Detail of an engraving from *Theatrum Scotiae* by John Sleyer, 1693.

68

daughter of the Sire de Coucy, whose castle in northern France is judged to be the masterpiece of Gothic castle building in that country. Scottish architecture kept abreast of continental developments, and through the Auld Alliance was profoundly influenced by French techniques and styles.

Military strategy gradually changed during the thirteenth century from the use of the castle as a defensive stronghold built to withstand a long siege to a more aggressive stance, with an emphasis on a flexible offense. Thus the keep became less important as the builders concentrated on the curtain wall, which enclosed a large area; from this area troops could sally forth in surprise attack. Any opening in the wall was, of course, a weak point for attack, and gradually gatehouses replaced the keep as the principal element in the castle.

By the fourteenth century the gatehouse castle devised by the masons and strategists of Edward I of England was adopted in Scotland as well as Wales and England. The gatehouse became a completely self-contained structure under the command of the marshal or lord of the castle himself. The gatehouse was a residence and a stronghold within a stronghold, just as the keep had been. The castles were garrisoned in time of war, but otherwise only a castle guard was maintained, and the buildings were used at intervals as the lord moved around his demesne, living off the rents paid in kind.

As the century progressed, the great landholders, and especially the king, preferred to collect their rents in money instead of exchanging land for produce and military service. With money they could buy luxuries in towns and abroad and could hire professional soldiers as they needed them. Since mercenaries fought for pay and not out of loyalty to a feudal lord or a clan, the lord required quarters that could protect him from his own troops as well as his enemies. Furthermore, in order to be secure, he had to control the gate to the castle precincts himself. The gatehouse-keep answered these requirements admirably.

Castle building in Scotland became the primary architectural activity in the later Middle Ages. The building of private castles reflects the power of the nobles and the clans, the troubled conditions of the country, the weakness of the central authority outside the population centers, and later the importance of the castle as the symbol of authority and wealth. The fortified country residence became a distinctive Scottish architectural type. In architecture, the Middle Ages survived to the Age of Enlightenment and beyond.

The peace and prosperity which the Scots looked forward to under their dynamic ruler came to a tragic end in 1286 when Alexander III, traveling from Edinburgh to visit his wife Yolande de Creux, fell from his horse and died. Wrote Andrew of Wyntoun, "Quhen Alysandyr oure Kyng was ded...Oure gold wes changyd to lede." Alexander's only heir was the three-year-old princess, Margaret, the Maid of Norway. Scottish guardians ruled for the maid for the next four years, but Scotland needed an adult king to control the nobles and confront the English. Edward I of England had a son of marriageable age. If Margaret were to wed Prince Edward of England, they could rule their kingdoms as independent monarchs, but eventually their children would inherit both realms and unite the two kingdoms. This splendid plan failed tragically, for the little Maid of Norway died in the Orkneys before she reached her kingdom. Her death ended the rule of the House of Canmore.

The thirteenth century ended with thirteen (fourteen if we include the English king) claimants to the throne of Scotland. As civil war among contenders threatened, William Fraser, bishop of St. Andrews, and the magnates of Scotland called in Edward of England to decide the issue. In 1291, the English king, with twenty-four Englishmen and eighty Scots,

This painting, with its heroic vision of William Wallace, is typical of the nineteenth-century view of history. One of the heroes of the Wars for Independence, Wallace was among the first to take up arms against England in 1297. For more than a year he was the focal point of the Scottish resistance, and successfully gathered an army which he led against the forces of Edward I. After his defeat near Falkirk, he led a wandering and obscure existence in England and on the Continent, was betrayed in Scotland, and was later executed in London. His ardent patriotism and his challenge to the English crown are embodied in the opening lines of the song "Scots, wha hae," the Scottish national anthem.

chose John Balliol, a descendant of Earl David through the oldest daughter and Robert Bruce. Balliol swore allegiance to Edward and was enthroned as king at Scone on St. Andrew's Day (November 30), 1292.

Before Edward could rejoice over this diplomatic stroke, he was threatened by both the French and the Welsh. Even Balliol refused to raise a force in support of Edward's French wars, and when Balliol rebelled, Edward marched on Scotland to take over the border castles. Scottish nobles faced a difficult situation. As members of the old Norman nobility, many of them held estates in England as well as Scotland and were bound through their feudal oaths to both kings. Edward demanded homage from his vassals in Scotland. Among those Scots attending him were the Bruces, the earl of Carrick, and his son Robert. Balliol seized the lands belonging to these men, and he gave the Bruce lands to John the Red Comyn, the king's brother-in-law, thus setting the stage for later confrontation between the Bruce and the Red Comyn—the earl of Carrick's son Robert and the Comyn's son John. Edward easily took Berwick, massacred its citizens, and then defeated the Scots near Dunbar in 1296. He deposed Balliol, who returned to Bailleul, his estate in France, and died there in 1313. Edward forced the Scottish landholders to do homage and sign the "Ragman's Roll," recognizing him as king. Then, as a last insult, he carried off the Stone of Destiny from Scone and the Black Cross of St. Margaret from Edinburgh.

To lose the Stone of Scone and, furthermore, to be subject to military service for the English in France and Flanders was too much for the Scots. The country was already in an uproar when William Wallace, the young son of a Clydesdale knight, killed the English sheriff of Lanark in May, 1297. Wallace rallied the people against the hated conquerors, and the Scottish Wars for Independence began. Wallace found much of his support among the "middle people," the city dwellers and small land-holders. He fought in the name of King John Balliol and thus lost the support of the Bruce factions; however, Andrew de Moray joined him and together they massacred the English at Stirling. Soon they held all of Scotland except the castles of Edinburgh, Dunbar, Roxburgh, and Berwick. De Moray died shortly after the battle of Stirling Bridge, and Wallace carried on alone as the "Guardian of the Realm of Scotland." His glorious career was almost over before it began, for Edward made a truce in France and marched again to Scotland with English knights and Welsh archers. He massacred Wallace's troops at Falkirk in 1298, but he was unable to consolidate his hold on the country beyond Lothian and the borders. By 1304, however, the English had defeated the Scots again and again; they captured Wallace at last and sentenced him to be hanged, drawn, and quartered in 1305. Wallace, loyal to King John to the end, was executed as a traitor to King Edward. His head was displayed on London Bridge until the flesh rotted away.

In spite of growing nationalism inspired by Wallace, the magnates still thought in terms of feudal loyalties, oaths, and homage paid to an individual, and they remained loyal to the English king. The enmity of rival families further divided the country and decreased the effectiveness of Scottish resistance to the English. Only the extraordinary circumstances that developed in the early years of the fourteenth century eventually led the nobility to think of themselves as Scots rather than as individual feudal vassals. In 1306 Scotland again had a king. Robert Bruce and his men killed John the Red Comyn in Greyfriars' kirk, Dumfries. The cause of their quarrel is unknown, but quarrel they did.

Bruce had no choice but to move rapidly and forcefully, for he had committed the most terrible sacrilege: murder within a church. At once he pushed the Bruce claim to the throne first asserted by his grandfather. He

Struck during the reign of Robert the Bruce, this coin provides us with a rough contemporary likeness of the most famous of Scottish kings and heroes.

This is the Great Seal of Robert the Bruce, a regal image of the warrior king, victor of Bannockburn.

rode to Scone, where he was enthroned as king by Isabella, countess of Buchan, sister of the earl of Fife acting in her brother's place. Only the abbots of Scone and Inchaffray and the earls of Atholl and Monteith supported him. The bishop of St. Andrews was forced to say mass for him later. Robert Wishart absolved him of his crime, but Pope Clement V excommunicated him for sacrilege. King Robert I remained only "the Bruce" in the eyes of the pope.

The new king found himself almost without a kingdom. The English defeated Robert and his allies again and again. Although Robert escaped, the English imprisoned the bishops of St. Andrews and Glasgow, Robert's wife, and the countess of Buchan, and executed his brother Nigel and the earl of Atholl. In 1307 two more of Robert's brothers were captured and executed; Robert himself could only hide. In July, however, Edward I, determined with his last breath to crush the Scots, died on the march north at the head of his army. Edward ordered that his bones be carried onward in a leather bag so that even in death he could still lead his men to victory. His son, Edward II, lacked the will to carry out his father's orders, gave the bones to the archbishop of York, and after an ignominious defeat returned to England, leaving the Bruce, supported by Sir James Douglas, to strengthen his hold on Scotland. Bruce killed or drove into exile the Comyn faction. By 1309 he held most of Scotland north of the Forth. In 1313 he took Perth and the castles of Dumfries, Roxburgh, and Edinburgh.

Finally, of the important fortresses, only Stirling remained in English hands. In one of those peculiarly chivalric agreements found in the fourteenth century, the commander of the castle, De Mowbray, agreed to surrender it to the Scots if the English did not raise the siege by Midsummer Day, June 24, 1314. Edward II, inefficient as ever, nearly missed the deadline. He reached Stirling on Midsummer Eve with an army of twenty thousand, including three thousand heavy cavalry, and outnumbering the Scots three to one. The overeager English knights charged at once, but were turned back; and the Bruce killed the famous knight De Bohun in single combat. The combatants settled down for the brief midsummer night. The English forces had moved forward into an easily defensible position for the night. They were surrounded by swamp and water—the Bannockburn and the Forth—and they expected to move out of the marshes to a better position in order to deploy archers and mounted knights effectively. But the Bruce attacked before they were ready. With almost no space in which to maneuver, with cavalry crowding foot soldiers and both of them in the way of their own archers, hemmed in by the Bannockburn and the marshes, pressed by the Scots who fought in the old-fashioned, but under the circumstances effective, close-rank formation, the English fell back in confusion. Retreat turned into rout; Edward II fled; and Stirling Castle fell to Robert the Bruce.

Robert adopted a policy of reconciliation. He restored the lands of those who rallied to his cause and even of those who returned to Scotland later. Only the Balliols and Comyns and the earl of Atholl, who deserted at Bannockburn, remained forfeited. Still, Robert needed papal recognition of his right to rule. In 1320 the Scottish clergy and barons wrote to the pope a defense of the king and their rights as free Scots, known as the Declaration of Arbroath. The document, probably written by Bernard, abbot of Arbroath and chancellor of Scotland, stated in no uncertain terms the position of the Scots: "We fight not for glory, or riches, or honors, but only for the liberty which no true man would yield save with his life." "For so long as but one hundred of us shall remain alive we shall never consent to bow beneath the yoke of English domination." Nevertheless, the pope still refused to lift the ban of excommunication, and the English king refused to make peace.

From a fifteenth-century manuscript called the *Scotichronicon*, the drawing at left by John Fordun shows the great battle in which the independence of Scotland was confirmed. The artist has compressed the entire surrounding landscape from the overlooking height of Stirling Castle down to the bottom of the ravine carved by the Bannockburn. The battlefield dominates the center, and in it Bruce uses his battle-ax to slay the English knight Sir Henry de Bohun.

Then, in 1327, the English queen Isabella and her lover Mortimor deposed Edward II. Robert moved at once, defeated the English, and concluded a peace treaty at Holyrood in which the English recognized him as king of Scotland and gave up all claims to the country. The English Parliament confirmed the treaty at Northampton in 1328. To insure the peace, Bruce's son David married Joan, the English princess, the sister of King Edward III; the Stone of Scone was not mentioned in the treaty, and the English did not return it.

Finally, Pope John XXII removed the ban of excommunication, recognizing Robert as king of Scotland, and in June, 1329, issued a bull authorizing the kings of Scotland to be crowned and anointed as rulers of an independent kingdom. Tragically, Robert the Bruce died of paralytic leprosy before the news of this final international recognition reached him. Even his last request would not be fulfilled; his greatest friend, Sir James Douglas, whom he had asked to carry his heart on the crusade to Jerusalem, died on the way while fighting the Moors in Spain. The crest of the Douglases is the winged and crowned heart of the Bruce.

Scotland was now an independent kingdom, but its king, David II (1329–71), the first king to be crowned and anointed, in 1331, was a mere child. Thomas Randolf, the earl of Moray, proved to be an excellent regent, but he died in 1332. In that year, John Balliol's son, Edward, took advantage of the situation and landed in Scotland with the survivors of the Comyn faction. He defeated the Scots and slew the new regent, the earl of Mar. Edward Balliol was crowned at Scone, but he acknowledged the suzerainty of Edward III. The English king received southern

In the Wars for Independence that followed the challenge of William Wallace and the defeat of the English at Bannockburn, the pope sought to mediate between the two countries and cushion English defeat, but the Scots, having tasted independence, were not to be swayed. In 1320 a Parliament assembled at Arbroath. The representatives of the nation declared their undying loyalty to the Bruce so long as he continued the struggle against England. The overwhelming endorsement of this declaration is evidenced by the number of individual seals.

SO·MONY·GVID·AS···VE·DOVGLAS·BEINE····
OF·ANE·SVRNA···········IN·SCOTLAND·SEINE
RAB

I·WIL·YE·CHARGE·EFTER·YAT·I·DEPART·
TO·HOLY·GRAVE·AND·THAIR·BVRY·MY·HART·

Shortly before his death, King Robert the Bruce gave Sir James Douglas a sword and instructions to carry his heart on a crusade and bury it in the Holy Land. But Douglas died fighting the Moors in Spain in 1330, while on his way to the Holy Land. According to legend, he threw the casket with the Bruce's heart forward, crying "Forward, brave heart." Above, engraved on the sword blade is the Douglas motto, "Forward," and the crest of the Douglas family in the crowned, winged heart of the Bruce.

David II inherited the kingdom as a child of five, but for safety's sake he was raised and educated in France. Scots and French formed an enduring alliance. In 1346 David attacked England in support of his French allies and was captured by the English at Neville's Cross. He lived in England—more a guest of Edward III than a prisoner—until 1357. In this initial from a manuscript of the period, the two kings are identified by coats of arms in the shields above their heads.

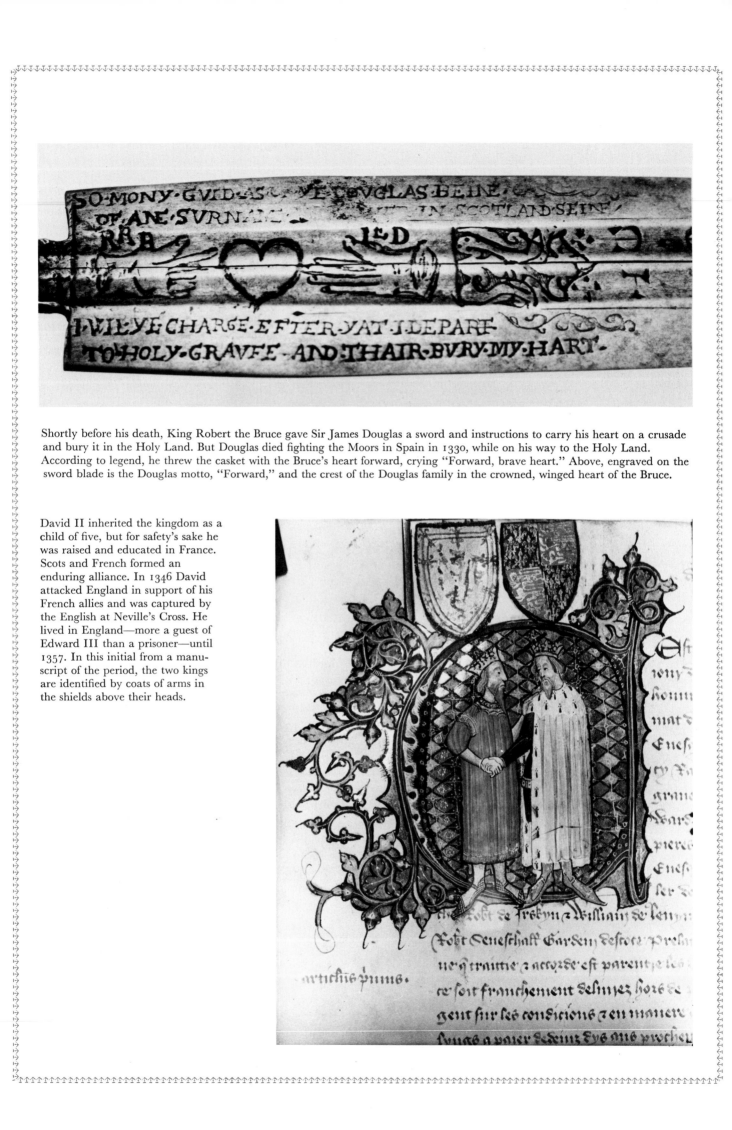

Scotland, which was again open to English immigration, and he built and garrisoned huge castles at a cost which nearly bankrupted the realms. King David and Queen Joan escaped to France in 1334; civil war destroyed their realm as Scots changed sides back and forth with the fortunes of the great magnates.

Slowly the Scots, led effectively by Moray, drove the English back. By 1340–41 the lands north of the Forth were secure, and David returned from his refuge in France. David, only twenty-two, was not a skilled warrior, but he responded to a call for assistance from his ally, the king of France, and invaded England with a huge army. In 1346 he was defeated and captured at Neville's Cross, near Durham. Robert Stewart escaped to become regent. This young man was the grandson of Robert the Bruce and the nephew of the king. (Robert's daughter Marjorie had married Walter fitzAlan, high steward of Scotland. The family took the name Stewart or, later, Stuart.) For the next eleven years David lived as a captive in England, while Robert Stewart administered Scotland. The life of a royal hostage was easy and even relatively pleasant; Scotland suffered more than David, first from the Black Death and then from civil wars.

The great magnates—the Douglases and the Stewarts—increased their power and independence. The strength of these magnates depended on war, for wealth lay in booty, loot, and ransom. Scots fought each other at home and left their country to serve as mercenaries in armies abroad; so impoverished had the country become that loot and wages made warfare a most profitable career. Might and greed replaced loyalty and justice. War wasted the countryside and ruined the economy. Scots needed all their resources for survival in the rugged north; they could ill afford the costs of war and certainly not the cost of a royal ransom; nevertheless, in 1357 David bought his freedom for one hundred thousand marks, to be paid in ten yearly installments. He returned to a land lying in waste, subjects living in misery, and a treasury bankrupt by war and his ransom. He had begun reforms and had worked especially hard to strengthen Parliament when he died, childless, in 1371.

The kingdom needed dynamic leadership that the first Stewart kings could not provide. Robert Stewart (1371–90), after years as regent and subject, inherited the kingdom in 1371 at the advanced age of fifty-four, an old man by the standards of the time and by then too ill to rule effectively. In 1384 he turned over the actual government to his eldest son John, who had been kicked by a horse and crippled; and John thus had difficulty also in leading the strenuous life expected of a medieval ruler. Without the control a king could exert, border warfare remained endemic. The skirmishing finally culminated in the battle of Otterburn, or Chevy Chase, where the earl of Douglas died.

When John succeeded as Robert III (1390–1406) in 1390 (the name John was considered unlucky), he too turned to a younger man for assistance, his brother, Robert, earl of Fife, whom he made duke of Albany. Exemplifying the horror of the times, their younger brother Alexander, the infamous and brutal "Wolf of Badenoch," harried the north and burned the cathedral and city of Elgin among other churches and towns, until his unlamented death about 1404. Robert III's son Robert, duke of Rothesay, "disappeared" after having been arrested by

This is the Douglas standard carried in the battle of Otterburn in 1388 (otherwise known as the battle of Chevy Chase), one of the many border wars between the Douglases and the Percy family of Northumberland. The Douglases won, although the earl lost his life. The pennant has the cross of St. Andrew, the lion of Scotland, and the motto in old French "Jamais areyre" (Never behind), for the Douglases claimed the honor of leading the Scottish army into battle.

75

Albany and imprisoned at Falkland. Robert then attempted to send his remaining heir, the young James, to safety in France, where his cousin along with Archibald, fourth earl of Douglas, fought for Joan of Arc and the French king. James was captured by the English and held hostage by Henry IV. Robert died of shock and despair at the news, and, with James in captivity, the duke of Albany and his son ruled Scotland for eighteen more years.

Under the regency of Albany, Scotland barely functioned as a nation. Albany enjoyed the fruits of his regency and made no attempt to ransom James. Parliament could not meet since only a king called a parliament. The Scottish magnates ruled as virtually independent princes: the Douglases in the south, the MacDonalds in the northwest, and the Mackays and the Frasers in the northeast. They kept the country in turmoil, settled disputes by judicial combat, and fought to extend their territories.

In 1411, Scots of a different color under Bishop Henry Wardlaw, dedicated to learning, not war, founded a university at St. Andrews. A papal bull gave the university the right to teach theology, law, arts, and medicine; the students and faculty of St. Andrews shifted allegiance from Pope Benedict in 1414 to Pope Martin V and convinced the Scottish church to desert the schismatic pope also. The crescent moon on the coat of arms of the university is all that remains to remind the Scots of their Spanish founder, Pedro de Luna. Scottish students had gone to the University of Paris, though Donald of the Isles attended Oxford; but by the end of the fifteenth century St. Andrews, Glasgow (1451), and Aberdeen (1495) could challenge Oxford and Cambridge.

While he lived in England from 1406 to 1424, James I (1424–37) became a well-educated young man; he had ample opportunity to study the English form of government. He went to France with Henry V and, in 1424, after Henry's premature death (1422), he negotiated his own ransom. As part of the agreement he married Lady Joan Beaufort, and part of his ransom was returned as her dowry.

James I returned to Scotland determined to govern well. His remark on his return is always quoted: "If God grant me life, though it be but the life of a dog, there shall be no place in my realm where the key shall not keep the castle and the bracken-bush the cow." In order to establish this authority, James exercised his power brutally. He executed the regent Albany and all his family; he called together fifty Highland chiefs, arrested them all, and executed three. As civil war began to break out, James proved to be a skillful or lucky general and won most of the battles until he subdued the Highlands. In the Lowlands he exiled or imprisoned powerful lords; he soon restored the authority of the monarch. As part of his policy James ignored the council of magnates and turned to a Parliament based on the English model to raise money and to make laws. Parliament began to meet on a regular basis. It included representatives from the towns as well as the nobility and clergy. From Parliament James chose reliable men to settle disputes and set up a new system of regular courts of law. Thus encouraged by the king, the burghs became stronger and gained special privileges in exchange for financial and political support. Merchants and artisans formed a strong new class protected by their guilds and by royal charters.

Needless to say, James made many powerful enemies—his uncle Atholl, his cousin Robert Stewart, and, among the deadliest, the Grahams. Furthermore, he squandered money on Linlithgow Palace, on fine clothes and luxuries, and on Flemish "bombards" (cannon). He was a strong king who attempted to restore order to the kingdom; but his mighty subjects saw him as a spendthrift and a tyrant. In 1437 Sir Robert Graham,

Jacob von gots
genaden küing
von schottland

Sometimes called "fiery face," James II was a well-liked ruler and an able administrator. During his reign important legislation was passed reforming the coinage, providing for the poor, improving the judicial structure, and protecting the tenure of land. He was an able general and delighted in new techniques and weaponry. His pioneer use of cannons in an engagement against the English caused his untimely death when one of the weapons misfired. This portrait of James II is from a German diary.

77

abetted by Atholl, murdered the king at Blackfriars in Perth. Queen Joan escaped with their son to Edinburgh, where he was crowned James II at Holyrood, the first Scottish king not to be enthroned at Scone. The queen's men captured the plotters and executed them by torture in Stirling Castle; nevertheless, Scotland plunged once again into chaos, for only an adult king had enough personal prestige to exercise control over the rival factions.

James II (1437–60) succeeded his father as a boy of six; once again a regent, this time Archibald, fifth earl of Douglas, ruled Scotland, with Bishop John Cameron of Glasgow as chancellor. Douglas died in 1439, and his enemy Sir William Crichton, keeper of Edinburgh Castle, became regent. Crichton hated the Douglases. In 1440 he invited the new earl, a youth of sixteen, and his brother to the castle to dine with the king. The earl and his brother were received hospitably; then legend has it that at dinner a black boar's head was set in front of the earl as a sign of his doom, a story elaborated on by Sir Walter Scott. The Douglases were dragged from the king's presence and executed on Castle Hill in spite of James's protest.

James II as an adult could be just as brutal as his regents had been. On learning of a treaty made by the eighth earl of Douglas with the "Tiger Earl" of Crawford and John of Isles, James invited Douglas to dine at Stirling Castle under a safe conduct. After dinner the king requested

Mons Meg, forged in Belgium about 1450, had a range of nearly two and a half miles and was a formidable piece of weaponry. James II's enthusiasm for new weapons was justified, as they enabled the king to bring the nobility, once safe in their castles, under his control.

that Douglas break his bond, and when Douglas refused, James stabbed him to death. Parliament exonerated the king for the murder on the grounds that Douglas's refusal to break the treaty at the king's request constituted treason punishable by death. Enraged, the earl's brother, the ninth earl, raided Stirling town, with his dead brother's violated safe conduct document tied to the tail of his horse. James sent his army against this Douglas and forced him to submit in 1452. Eventually Douglas fled to England, and James confiscated his vast estates. The acquisition of the Douglas wealth for himself may have been James's goal from the start.

James II had a passion for artillery, and this enthusiasm proved to be his downfall. Cannon like Mons Meg, the largest cannon of the time, enabled the king to destroy castles and bring the nobility under control. James II became an enthusiastic patron of gunnery and learned to use artillery effectively in reducing the castles of his proud nobility. The cost in man power and in money made the cannon a royal weapon, available only to the state.

The introduction of artillery spelled the end of the feudal castle, whose tall towers and high walls were perfect targets for even the most rudimentary cannon. Thus, later military architecture concentrated on defense in depth. Low broad walls that could support heavy cannon were built in interlacing star patterns to allow raking fire while minimizing the target area. The first castle actually designed for the use of cannon was Ravenscraig, built by James II as part of his coastal defenses. Begun in 1460, it was still unfinished when the king died at the siege of Roxburgh in the accidental explosion of one of his own guns.

Again regents ruled Scotland for a boy king. James III (1460–88), only nine years old, was crowned at Kelso. The English Edward IV, working through the exiled Douglas and the Lords of the Isles, hoped to dismantle Scotland as a kingdom and to divide it among the great magnates in exchange for their homage. None of the disaffected lords had the prestige, drive, and intelligence to carry through a plan of such magnitude, and the regents proved to be honest and effective administrators; the government survived without the chaos seen during James II's minority. Scotland reached its greatest size as a kingdom when, in 1468, Lord Boyd arranged the marriage of the king with Margaret, daughter of the king of Denmark and Norway. Margaret brought Scotland Orkney and Shetland in pledge as her dowry. When her father, Christian I, failed to pay the dowry, James took the islands.

James III was neither energetic nor politically wise, and he failed to follow up the advantage of a healthy regency. He became suspicious of the nobility and began to build up the power of new families who would be dependent on him. The king became increasingly reclusive; he even became suspicious of his brothers and arrested the popular earl of Mar and the duke of Albany. The earl of Mar died mysteriously in prison, but the duke of Albany escaped to England. There he established himself as pretender to the throne, with the support of the Scottish nobles, who may have feared they would suffer the same fate as the earl of Mar. In 1488, the heir, James, duke of Rothesay, fled from Stirling Castle to join the group in England, and the nobles rallied around the future James IV. They defeated James III at the battle of Sauchieburn, near Stirling, in 1488. After the battle, James, who had fallen from his horse and lay injured, was murdered.

James III was no heroic monarch; he loved money and the things money could buy. He tolerated political chaos, injustice, and economic decline. Nevertheless, his patronage of the arts and learning remains a redeeming feature of his unfortunate reign. He debased the currency until, in 1483, 1,680 pennies, rather than the true weight of 240, were minted from a pound of silver. These cheapened coins are some of the most beautiful ever minted in Scotland. James's numismatic portrait in three-quarter view is the first such portrait in the north. He and his queen also appear in the altar painted by Hugo van der Goes (d. 1482). James was a patron of the universities and the church. During his reign St. Andrews finally became the seat of the archbishop of Scotland (1472), although, to the displeasure of some, he made his friend, William Scheves, archbishop. James III's patronage of the arts was continued by his son James IV, who has received or usurped credit due his father as the first Renaissance sovereign of Scotland.

Scottish builders made a unique contribution to the history of architecture in their design of fortified manor houses. In the later Middle Ages and Renaissance periods, everyone from nobles to small landholders felt the need for private defenses. Lairds adopted a tower form for their homes that resembled the Norman keeps of two hundred years earlier. The Scottish tower house had the kitchen and service areas stacked one above the other. The storage rooms and service areas were at the ground level, the great hall above, and private rooms still higher. The massive walls were broken by a few small windows and, after the introduction of firearms, by loopholes. The doorway was often high above ground and reached by a ladder. The tall houses commanded the countryside. Inconvenient as they might be for daily living, they provided a measure of security. The tower houses were set in a walled courtyard, called a barmkin, much smaller than a castle ward.

Nothing could be more inconvenient than a house consisting of rooms placed one above the other reached by ladders. Needless to say, the Scots soon began to improve on these buildings. They inserted stairs, passages, and even small rooms in the upper parts of the thick walls. In the fifteenth century masons experimented with additional amenities and added a wing, known as a jam, containing stairs and some additional rooms to the main tower. The entrance to the towers was placed in the reentrant angle of this L plan so that the projecting wings provided a defense and the door could

Hugo van der Goes, the fifteenth-century Flemish master, painted these panels for the Church of the Holy Trinity in Edinburgh. Sir Edward Bonkil, first provost of the church founded by Mary of Gueldres, the mother of James III, commissioned the paintings, and is shown kneeling in front of a golden organ. On the face of the panels, shown here, James III and his son, the future James IV, are under the protection of St. Andrew, while Queen Margaret of Denmark, James III's wife, kneels with St. George.

safely be placed at ground level. Just as in the keep or gatehouse, the principal fortification is at the top of the wall, where crenelated parapets, machicolations, and angle turrets command the ground at the base of the tower.

Of the most famous Scottish castles—Edinburgh and Stirling—very little remains from the Middle Ages. Edinburgh Castle, aside from St. Margaret's Chapel, was destroyed by Randolph, earl of Moray, in 1314, acting on the Bruce's policy of destroying castles so that the English could not use them should they retake the site. The earliest building surviving on Castle Hill other than the chapel is David's Tower, begun in 1367.

Stirling Castle is sited, like Edinburgh Castle, on a towering castle rock. All traces of the fortress that loomed over the battle of Bannockburn have disappeared, and today the earliest parts date only from the fifteenth century. James III rebuilt the castle with gatehouse and Great Hall. The Great Hall was a typical medieval hall: a great rectangular building

covered by a hammerbeam roof. At one end was a raised dais for the
royal family, warmed by a huge fireplace and lit by oriel windows. From
the hall the king could reach private rooms by means of a passage and
bridge to the palace. The fine masonry of the exterior walls was enlivened
with figure sculpture and carried a wall walk with crenelated parapet.
Crow-stepped gables and carved royal badges along the ridge of the roof,
together with the conical-roofed round tower housing the spiral stairs,
gave the hall a dramatic silhouette. The adjoining palace is now a masterpiece of Renaissance architecture built for James V.

When we turn to later religious architecture, St. Giles in Edinburgh
and Melrose Abbey come first to mind. St. Giles Cathedral, the "Townes
Kirke" of Edinburgh, was built over a period extending from the middle of
the thirteenth century to 1911. The bishop of St. Andrews dedicated a
new church in 1243, but in 1385 Richard II destroyed the church, and
shortly thereafter a new church "thatched with stone" was begun. The
present Moray aisle and the Albany aisle date from the end of the
fourteenth and the beginning of the fifteenth centuries.

Another building campaign began after Preston of Gorton returned to
Scotland with a relic of the patron—the arm bone of St. Giles. The bone
was encased in a reliquary of gold and silver made in the form of an
arm and hand with a diamond ring on the finger. To house this relic, the
city council of Edinburgh added an aisle on the north side of the choir.
During the reign of James III further building was supported by taxes on
shipping in Edinburgh harbor and contributions from the guilds. At the
end of the fifteenth century the Crown Tower was added. The open pin-
nacled form, a characteristic feature of Scottish Late Gothic design, is
the most dramatic element of the church as seen from afar. After years of
reconstruction to meet sixteenth- and seventeenth-century needs, St.
Giles's was restored and completed in 1911.

At Melrose the original monastic buildings were destroyed and rebuilt
many times, for Melrose is a border abbey. The English burned and looted
the monastery in 1322 and 1385; the ruins we admire today are those
from the last rebuilding in a Flamboyant Gothic style. The church was
ribbed-vaulted throughout, and splendid flying buttresses supported the
vault—the finest and only genuine medieval flying buttresses in Scotland.
The window openings are filled with the flamelike forms of tracery that
justify the name "Flamboyant" for the style in France, and have been
called "Decorated" in England. The sculpture is both saintly and comical
—from saints and angels to pigs playing bagpipes.

Parish churches rather than monasteries became the characteristic
form in the later Middle Ages as the church conscientiously extended
pastoral care to the entire community. The many parish churches and
family chapels dating from the fifteenth century are impressive evidence of
the piety and the building skills of the Scots. Such a chapel is Rosslyn, in
the village of Roslin, the chapel and pantheon of the Sinclairs. At Rosslyn
Chapel many threads in Scottish medieval culture are woven together—
Celtic, Norse, and Norman, native and foreign, king and baron, castle
and kirk.

The original St. Clairs were Normans who came to England with
William the Conqueror, but sought their fortunes in Scotland, where the
first William St. Clair was the cupbearer to St. Margaret. Throughout
the centuries the Sinclairs were important magnates; they became barons
of Rosslyn and princes of the Orkneys. Their village, Roslin, gained burgh
status in 1456. In 1446 William St. Clair founded a chapel.

So grand was the scheme and so rich the sculptural program that Sir
William died leaving the building unfinished. His son added the ribbed
barrel vault to the choir, but did not continue the building even though all

At Rosslyn Chapel, the so-called apprentice pillar (below) is a cluster of engaged colonnettes wrapped by spirals of foliage. It takes its name from an old tale which relates that in a fit of jealousy the chapel's master mason murdered the apprentice who carved the pillar.

Rosslyn Chapel in Midlothian was established by William St. Clair, earl of Orkney, in 1450. Only the choir, of unprecedented richness, was built. The rest was never completed because the vision outran the purse of its founder's heirs. Rosslyn Chapel now serves only as a truncated token of what might have been the richest example of the Flamboyant Gothic style in Scotland.

82

the foundations had been laid. The chapel today is but an architectural fragment. The architectural structure is based on Cistercian architecture: a barrel vault with transverse ribs supported by transverse barrel vaults over the aisles. The length of the chapel is now slightly under seventy feet, and the vault rises to a height of forty-four feet. In 1592 the altars were destroyed, and in the seventeenth century Cromwell and General Monck used the chapel as a stable, but when Dorothy Wordsworth visited it in 1803 she called it "exquisitely beautiful." Sir Walter Scott chose "that chapel proud, Where Roslin's chiefs uncoffin'd lie" as the site of *The Lay of the Last Minstrel* (1805), and soon Rosslyn became the site of literary pilgrimages. The family restored the chapel in 1861–62 and added the baptistery in 1880–81.

As one approaches Rosslyn, the massive buttresses enriched with pinnacles and decorative flying buttresses create a conflicting sense of architectural mass and ornamental detail. Inside the chapel, ornament overwhelms the architecture. The overflowing richness of sculptural ornament combined with stark mass of stone masonry is reminiscent of the Isabellan Gothic style in Spain, and one wonders how many foreign workmen might have participated in the construction of Rosslyn. Even the vaults are ornamented. The carving is some of the richest work in Scotland —stylized foliage, Biblical narratives, didactic themes (the Acts of Mercy, the Seven Deadly Sins, the Fall of Man, the Dance of Death), fables, and fantasies. The Dance of Death at Rosslyn may be the earliest representation of the theme in sculpture. The most famous detail in the building is the so-called apprentice pillar, where a spiral foliate molding wraps around a fluted pier and dragons on the base suggest the Norse theme of a serpent gnawing at the roots of the sacred ash tree, Yggdrasil. The very richness of overcharged decoration reminds one of the Celtic love of dense, intricate ornament on books, jewelry, and high crosses.

In Scotland during the Middle Ages the best architectural expertise was devoted to castles and abbeys—the reflection of a military society and of religious piety. They survive because stone has little intrinsic value. Disused buildings may become stone quarries: castles must be destroyed in times of war by the enemy and may be left to molder in times of peace; abbeys stand empty when monks are expelled. Still, the shell will last, and it is the castles and abbeys, later the cathedrals, parish churches, and palaces, that record the Scottish creative genius.

SCOTTISH LITERATURE begins in genuine darkness: we know little or nothing of what might have been genuinely Scottish in form or feeling before the tenth century. For one thing, the number of languages was surprisingly high for a limited population: three separate Celtic languages in three independent kingdoms, Norse in a colony established and maintained by Vikings, and English as spoken in Northumbria by the Southron. A few Celtic (or Gaelic) manuscripts survive from the Dark Ages, but not until the Middle Scots period does a professionalism begin to shape literary documents. Yet the swiftness with which talented writers emerge in the fifteenth century—the Golden Age of Scottish poetry, as it has long been known—suggests that domestic quarrels, primitive roads, poverty-stricken environments, and the lack of an evolving literary tradition were less important than a swiftly emerging sense of national identity. England during this century produced fewer writers of quality than Scotland. It is certainly striking that the Scots chose poetry over prose as a medium of literary expression, and Middle Scots rather than Latin in order to secure a wider audience.

Thomas of Erceldoune, also known as Thomas the Rhymer (1220?–1297?), may be considered the father of Scottish poetry. He comes first in time as a known historical figure, hailing from Berwickshire. Thomas—according to a metrical romance written about him over a century after his death—associated with supernatural beings and lived with a fairy mistress for three years. She gave him the gift of prophecy so that he might predict the death of Alexander III, among other events that were to take place after his own death. Though the predictions of wars and rumors of wars between Scotland and England in Thomas of Erceldoune's work are sufficiently cryptic that one may read into them pretty much what one thinks appropriate, the political aim behind the writing of the poem found at least partial sanction in, and was strengthened by, the reputation of Thomas.

Early Scottish poetry is passionate in its sense of contemporary history. John Barbour (c. 1320–1395) wrote his most important work, a *chanson de geste*, about a Scottish hero who had only recently died: *The Actes and Life of the Most Victorious Conqueror, Robert Bruce, King of Scotland* (completed in 1376). It rapidly became a national epic and to this day remains notable for its good humor, matter-of-factness, and stirring evocation of the battle of Bannockburn (1314). It traces the war for independence from the death of Alexander III in 1286 to the burial of the heart of Bruce in 1332. It is, moreover, a stirring apostrophe to freedom:

> A! fredome is a noble thing. . . .
> Fredome all solace to man givis:
> He livis at ease that freely livis. . . .

The *Bruce* was, many centuries later, to inspire Scott. It is a poem about heroes. Although Barbour's hero-model was Alexander the Great, the poem is not myth masquerading as history. Firsthand accounts serve as substratum for Barbour's review of the hard fighting at Bannock-burn. Moreover, the octosyllabic couplet turns out to be, in his hands, an admirable medium for chivalric narrative.

The other great medieval epic of Scotland, Blind Harry's *Wallace*, may or may not have been written by a blind poet. Its meter (heroic couplets, with ten syllables to a line sometimes laboriously counted out) proved no hindrance to slashing action and plain speech. Indeed, the poem offers us more information about its hero than any other source, though some events are recounted which could not possibly have taken place. The description of the crossing to France in book nine is one of the great set pieces of early Scottish literature. The eleven thousand lines of *Wallace* demonstrate familiarity with topography, works of French and English literature (including Chaucer), and a burgeoning sense of Scottish nationalism. In the early-eighteenth-century version that modernized Harry's language, Burns found—if not for the first time, then perhaps with greater pleasure than he had ever found before—"a Scottish prejudice" which, he predicted, would boil within him "till the flood-gates of life shut in eternal rest."

There is no need to review the workmanlike but uninspired *Orygynale Chronykil of Scotland* by Andrew of Wyntoun (1350?–1424), but Wyntoun deserves mention for being, like Barbour and Harry, a versifier of Scottish history, and for surveying the ninety years that had elapsed since the death of Bruce. Canon of St. Andrews and prior of St. Serfe, Wyntoun was a scholar with a taste for good stories. The most interesting moment in his history of Scotland concerns Macbeth's encounter with "three wemen," and their blood-chilling prophecy. Wyntoun admired Macbeth as a holy man, during whose reign the affairs of Scotland prospered, and as a king whose justice was "right lawful."

Four more writers have unreasonably been grouped together as Scottish Chaucerians: King James I, Robert Henryson, William Dunbar, and Gavin Douglas. Unreasonably, because such a term limits one's understanding of their originality; also, because it applies most directly to the author of *The Kingis Quair* (probably James) and much less strikingly to the others, though it is indisputable that they all knew Chaucer's writings.

King James I was less than twelve years old when, in 1406, the ship in which he was traveling to France was captured by the English, at that time at war with the Scots. Perhaps his eighteen years as a captive were not regretted, for he acquired an excellent education in letters and in the art of fighting. He had the honor to accompany Henry V on two expeditions against the French. Not until 1424, when a large ransom was paid for his return, did he go back to Scotland. With him came his English bride, the daughter of the earl of Somerset. An important part of his kingly duties, undertaken with grim pleasure, was the crushing of the House of Albany.

James was an able but stern sovereign, who centralized government by taking away ancient prerogatives from his unruly nobles. The earl of Atholl finally was successful in getting Sir Robert Graham and Sir Robert Stewart to murder him at Perth in 1437.

James's authorship of *The Kingis Quair* and many other works attributed to him has been disputed; but he was known during his lifetime as an intelligent reader, patron of the arts, and author. *The Kingis Quair*, which celebrates James's love for Lady Joan Beaufort while he was in captivity (a romance that led, at long last, to marriage), is plausibly the composition of a talented lover; no thought is recorded that could not legitimately have been James's. *The Kingis Quair* is the finest Scottish poetry written up to its time, composed in a mixture of both Scottish dialect and English that might well have come naturally to a Scot who had been living south of the border for many years. Because of its author's prestige, it popularized the rhyme royal stanza, the seven-line unit that Chaucer had employed so effectively in *Troilus and Criseyde* during the preceding century. The king, instructed to write his story, moves, in his romantic rapture, from Venus to Minerva to Fortune; the 197 stanzas conclude on a strong note of thankful happiness. This is not artful poetry, and certainly not up to Chaucer's level; but it is consistently readable and a convincing blend of biographical material and courtly conventions in poetry.

An even greater poet, Robert Henryson (1430?–1506), may have been a schoolmaster at Dunfermline Abbey. We know that he was admitted as a member of the University of Glasgow (1462), but it is only conjectural that he lectured in law at the university, served as a notary, or died of flux (diarrhea). His name may even have been Robert Henderson. Still, we have his works, including *The Testament of Cresseid* (mistakenly attributed to Chaucer for a full century), his *Moral Fabillis* (by no means limited to Aesop's originals), *Orpheus and Eurydice* ("Quhair art thou gane, my lufe Euridices"), *The Bludy Serk* (i.e., Shirt), and *Robene and Makyne*. Henryson's sense of fun reminds us of Chaucer's delight in nontragic turns of the wheel of fortune. His animals reason like men and women who are shaking themselves free from the bondage of particular historical circumstances, and his adaptation of stories in the Reynard cycle is very witty.

Since he wrote in Middle Scots, Henryson has had an increasingly circumscribed readership outside of Scotland with the passage of time; but the poet's contemplation of the probable fate of Chaucer's beloved Criseyde retains its grim power. Henryson's poem is set in winter and tells us of a promiscuous woman who cannot escape her destiny. Cresseid, in this sequel to Chaucer's great romance, falls victim to leprosy, goes quietly and anonymously to a "Hospitall at the tounis end," and says farewell to her father: "... for all mirth in this eird /Is fra me gane, sic is my wickit weird [fate]." Later, when she goes out to the street, begging with the other lepers, Troilus rides by. She, being blind, cannot recognize him. He, not recognizing her either, is momentarily disturbed by her appearance and throws a purse to her. Soon afterwards she dies. Troilus, learning of her identity, weeps for her and orders an inscription carved on her tombstone:

85

> Lo, fair Ladyis, Cresseid, of Troyis toun,
> Sumtyme countit the flour of Womanheid,
> Under this stane, lait Lipper, lyis deid.

Henryson's "moral" is here not the same kind of moral as was appended to his fables; it is not a schoolmaster's admonition that the wages of adultery are inevitable physical decay and shameful death. Troilus's lamentation, "I can no moir; / Scho was untrew, and woe is me thairfore," rings true at a deep level. *The Testament of Cresseid* is an unexpectedly brilliant addition to, and clarification of, Chaucer's human relationships in *Troilus and Criseyde*.

William Dunbar (1460?–1520?) is, to many readers, an even livelier figure than Henryson. His poetry, which is metrically resourceful and astonishingly varied in its moods and themes, may be the most consistently interesting body of work turned out during the entire century. Dunbar apparently earned degrees at the University of St. Andrews, walked through Scotland and much of Europe as a Franciscan friar, served as poet laureate to James I, went on various diplomatic missions, and may have died at the battle of Flodden. Perhaps his most famous lyric, *Lament for the Makars* [poets], ends each stanza with the melancholy refrain, "*Timor mortis conturbat me*" (The fear of death distresses me). Though cast in formal Latin, the phrase has lyrical power of great personal intensity:

> He takis the campioun in the stour,
> The capitane closit in the tour,
> The lady in bour full of bewte;
> *Timor mortis conturbat me.*

The *Lament* commemorates several poets contemporary with Dunbar as well as Chaucer, who is named as the greatest of Dunbar's predecessors.

In the words of H. S. Bennett, "Once [Dunbar's] work has been read it is impossible to think of Scottish poetry as 'provincial' or 'Chaucerian': it stands on its own merits." Dunbar's canon contains allegories and a great many satires; he attacked the law courts, the dirt of Edinburgh, rival poets, pretentious priests, and "wantoun wiffis." Dunbar's scurrility may not have offended his targets as much as we in a later age may imagine; "flyting," or a certain kind of stylized invective, was, after all, a standard category of poetry; and we know that Dunbar's poetic rival Walter Kennedy, whom he slated mercilessly in the *Flyting of Dunbar and Kennedie*, is remembered with grave affection in the *Lament for the Makars*. Dunbar has been compared to Skelton, Chaucer, and Villon, but he remains his own man despite his obvious affinities with bohemian poets. He uses countless poetical forms and transforms all of them into personal statements. He is not a storyteller of sustained power, and perhaps he is not, ultimately, likable; but he possesses one of the great literary imaginations of the Middle Ages and a wondrous faculty for making old themes new.

Closer to a Neoclassical ideal is the poet Gavin Douglas (1474?–1522). He was a son of the fifth earl of Angus. An important part of Gavin Douglas's life was spent as provost of the collegiate church of St. Giles, Edinburgh, and as bishop of Dunkeld. Though remembered for *The Palice of Honour*, a dream-poem much in the style of *The Goldyn Targe*, Douglas is most important for his introduction to Scottish literature of Virgil's *Aeneid* (it was the first full translation in English literature). He supplied not only a translation of the twelve books (and of the thirteenth by Mapheus Vegius), but added a number of prologues and original verses.

Douglas's new translation is appealing, alive poetry. Its iambic pentameter moves vigorously past all rough moments with an energy, a sheer delight in its own powers, that was later to impress Ezra Pound as being not only the best translation of Virgil, but a translation that was *better* than Virgil. Douglas's version is in some respects a philological curiosity, with lexical items and dialectal expressions borrowed from at least five languages. Virgil emerges (in Douglas's treatment) as something of a wizard, a prophet to be feared as well as respected. Yet for its time the poem was more modern than backward-looking; it praised the vernacular as a medium of expression, indicated more clearly than ever before the reasons why Virgil's poetical greatness demanded respect, and its willingness to embroider and enrich the text looked forward to comparable "improvements" of classical originals by Renaissance poets.

4

Renaissance and Reformation: 1488-1603

Gordon Donaldson

RENAISSANCE AND
REFORMATION: 1488–1603

by Gordon Donaldson

IT HAS BEEN SAID that when James IV was defeated and killed in battle with the English at Flodden in 1513, Scotland "lost a civilization and gained a song." The twenty-five years of James's reign had been a period of great promise and of some not inconsiderable achievements, and it is easy to see how sharply his career differed from those of other Scottish monarchs of the fifteenth and sixteenth centuries. When he came to the throne, in 1488, he was already in his sixteenth year, which meant that this time there was no period of minority to dislocate the machinery of government, as there was under James's three predecessors and three successors. James personally held the reins of power almost from his accession until his death at the age of forty. It was the longest period of personal rule by an able king between the reigns of Alexander III and James VI.

In those days much depended on the king's personal presence, for there was as yet no apparatus of government which would operate effectively without the strong hand of an active monarch. Repeated experience had shown that when the king was infirm or a minor, the direction of affairs was apt to fall into the hands of some noble family or baronial faction, which lacked the prestige of royalty and which could maintain its position only by rewarding allies or buying off rivals, to the detriment of the resources and authority of the crown. Each minority meant a temporary setback for royal power.

Even when a king was ruling in person, there were severe limits on his effective exercise of authority. He lacked adequate and reliable finance, because regular taxation was unknown until the seventeenth century. He lacked official agents to operate on his behalf throughout the country. He lacked a standing military force of any kind and, while he could call on all men between sixteen and sixty to serve in "the host" for up to forty days at a time, the response to his summons depended much on the appeal which the purpose of the muster made to the popular imagination or opinion.

Powerful nobles could not only defy the crown but even repudiate its authority, as the earl of Douglas had done in 1455 when he referred contemptuously to James II as "him that calls himself king of Scots." And in the west lay the Highlands and islands, where the king's writ hardly ran and where the Lords of the Isles presided over a society which has been represented as a kind of fossilized survival of the social structure which had existed in Ireland about seven centuries earlier. During wars with England, each country habitually lent support to malcontents in the other. The most formidable threat to the Scottish crown in this way had been in 1472, when Edward IV of England made a treaty with Douglas and the Lords of the Isles for the partition of Scotland among them.

Yet experience had also shown that the crown had considerable reserves of power which could be used effectively by a vigorous and astute king. The crown, as the ultimate owner or superior of all land, was an indispensable agent in the whole conveyancing system and had ways and means of acquiring landed property: in particular, on suppressing a treacherous noble, or even after trumping up charges against him, the king could annex his estates by forfeiture. The crown was the fount of law, which meant that it could exercise jurisdiction or confer jurisdiction on others. A good king was expected to provide justice, and the intention of ensuring "firm and sure peace" throughout the land was constantly proclaimed, even if the ideal was not realized. It was characteristic that already under James I provision was made for an "advocate for the poor," so that those unable to afford the cost of litigation should not suffer, and there was much well-intentioned legislation designed to safeguard the rights of tenants and ensure a measure of social justice.

A great Renaissance king, James IV possessed learning and culture as well as leadership qualities exceptional in his family. His most notable accomplishments were his successful efforts to reduce the independence of the Highlands and the islands and strengthen the rule of law throughout his realm. He died at Flodden in 1513 in an ill-conceived action against his brother-in-law, the English king Henry VIII.

90

Above is the tomb slab of Murchard of Colonsay, chief of clan Macfie, who died in 1539 and was buried on the island of Oransay. The tombstone of this Hebridean chieftain depicts the main pursuits of the island lords—the hunt, the sea, and the battle. The coat of arms of these adherents of the MacDonalds is the sword above a galley. Here the Highland claymore is beautifully depicted with its characteristic cross guard with four ring quillons.

The two-handed sword known as the claymore or great sword was used by the Highlanders of Scotland. It exemplifies the arrogance and recklessness of Gaelic warriors, who disdained the protection of a shield in order to wield this awesome weapon.

The crown possessed patronage in the widest sense of that term, with the right to confer titles and appoint to offices of influence and profit. The right of, in effect, nominating candidates to high offices in the church had been conceded by the pope to James III in 1487, and James IV was the first king to enjoy the vast extension of patronage which this put at his disposal. All in all, the crown was, in one way or another, the dispenser of things that ambitious men wanted—land, pensions, jurisdiction, titles, offices—and the wise use of this power could reward fidelity and provide incentives to service, so creating or maintaining a loyal following.

Despite interruptions, the fifteenth century had seen a conspicuous increase in the landed holdings of the crown, in an age when land was still the principal source of wealth. James I and James II each annexed important earldoms; James III annexed the earldom of Orkney and lordship of Shetland and brought the Scottish kingdom to its fullest geographical extent. Kings were sometimes criticized for being covetous, but their acquisitiveness was politic. Apart from anything else, if the king could "live of his own" from crown lands he would not have to incur unpopularity by imposing exactions on his people.

What is true of land is also true of jurisdiction: it could be given away. Yet the king could also expand royal justice, and the fifteenth century had seen a significant strengthening of the royal courts of law. For civil justice, there had long been parliamentary committees which from their nature were only occasional, but from James I's reign there had been experiments designed to provide permanent "sessions" of judges, at first chosen from the three estates but latterly based on the council. Before the end of James IV's reign, something like the Court of Session, a central court for civil cases, had taken shape. For criminal justice, an active king could organize—and even conduct—"ayres," or itinerant sittings, which supplemented the courts held at Edinburgh by the justice general and his deputies. Little attempt had been made to extend royal justice into the Highlands and islands after the 1290s until James IV proposed to set up new sheriffs and justices for that area. This was less successful, for the west was still far from being integrated into the realm. The usual royal policy continued to be one which was apt to prove self-destructive, namely, empowering one chief to act against another or empowering great families on the Highland fringe, especially Campbells and Gordons, to put down disorders in the Highlands.

The Stewart line had begun as a baronial family elevated to the throne through the chance of a fortunate marriage and without the resources and prestige which would have set them conspicuously above the great magnates. But in the century between the first Stewart and James IV, the royal house had gained immeasurably. In less concrete terms, the Scottish monarchy had been sustained by belief in a long line of kings stretching back to mythical times, and this belief grew stronger through the continuity of succession, generation by generation, in a royal line which was often tenuous but which did not fail. In centuries when, in England, the throne was contested by Plantagenet, Lancastrian, Yorkist, and Tudor, in Scotland the crown passed undeviatingly from father to child, ultimately through ten generations. Hereditary succession proved so indefeasible that in 1542 the infant Mary, a girl only a week old, was to succeed her father without question.

Nothing had shown more emphatically the reserves of power which the crown enjoyed than the ability of James I, James II, and James III to take resolute and ruthless action against noble families who had entrenched themselves in power—Albanies, Douglases, Livingstons, and Boyds. All in all, the weakness of the Scottish monarchy has been exaggerated. Or, to be more precise, while the crown was weak, there

This sixteenth-century stone carving from Merchants House in Glasgow depicts a trio of merchants, the men who controlled the economic and urban centers of the country as the lairds controlled the land. Their prosperous air and self-satisfied countenances reflect the secular authority of the laity, who saw themselves as God's elect and who attained an equal authority in the governance of the Church of Scotland.

92

was no doubt about the strength of a king in person if he had energy and mature years on his side.

The position which James IV inherited, and the favorable situation in which he ruled, owed something to economic as well as political conditions. While hostilities were frequent on the English frontier, there had of late been no serious English invasions to devastate the country, for England had been occupied with the Hundred Years' War with France and then with the Wars of the Roses, which ended in 1485. The result had been a measure of prosperity in the second half of the fifteenth century such as Scotland had not enjoyed for two hundred years. The southern parts of the country, naturally the most fertile and productive, were able to recover from the effects of war and to play their rightful part in the national economy. It was no accident that under James II, Edinburgh had finally begun to have the semblance of a capital and that James III acknowledged its position as the chief town of his kingdom.

The period saw the foundation of a number of new burghs of barony, in which crafts could be exercised and internal trade conducted but which were not supposed to share in foreign trade. The growing wealth was reflected in lavish expenditure on buildings, especially collegiate churches.

Spacious churches in towns were equally eloquent of the growing wealth of the burgesses. Secular buildings erected by the king's subjects were still austere, at least externally, but some of those stern towers, like Crichton and Borthwick, had highly ornamental work indoors, particularly around the fireplaces. Royal building went on reign by reign at Linlithgow and probably also at Stirling, while at Holyrood James IV finally abandoned the practice of depending on the hospitality of the monks and built his own tower.

In addition to the growing power of the crown, the extension of law and order, and the conspicuous developments in architecture, there was another change, namely, a great flowering of literature. Scottish poetry had begun with the work of John Barbour. In the next two generations there were other enterprises which stimulated the patriotic pride of the Scots in their past: the rhyming vernacular *Chronykil of Scotland* by Andrew of Wyntoun and the great Latin *Scotichronicon*, begun by John of Fordun and continued by Walter Bower.

James I was himself a poet, who commemorated in *The Kingis Quair* his love for Joan Beaufort, the English lady whom he married. Financial records show that James III and James IV patronized poets to the extent of granting them pensions, and among James IV's subjects were three of Scotland's greatest poets—Robert Henryson, William Dunbar, and Gavi Douglas. Henryson, best known for *The Testament of Cresseid* and *Moral Fabillis*, was a schoolmaster in Dunfermline, but William Dunbar, who celebrated James IV's marriage in *The Thrissill and the Rois*, was associated with the court, and Gavin Douglas, who translated Virgil's *Aeneid* into Scots, was a son of the earl of Angus and became bishop of Dunkeld.

Literature and learning enjoyed official encouragement and patronage. The printing press was introduced in 1508. Three universities were founded in a century—St. Andrews (1411), Glasgow (1451), and Aberdeen (1495) —and two of their surviving buildings, St. Salvator's College at St. Andrews and King's College at Aberdeen, reflect the taste and wealth of the time. In 1496 there was the first Education Act: landed men (who, almost by definition, had powers of jurisdiction) were ordered to send their sons to school until they had "perfect Latin" and then to "schools of art and jure" to acquire knowledge of the laws.

James IV had personal qualities which enabled him to make the most of the favorable opportunities he enjoyed. He had a fine presence, was courageous to the point of recklessness, was credited with a knowledge of many languages, and possessed an inquiring turn of mind which led him to patronize scientists and inventors and to experiment personally in surgery and dentistry. It had always been true that, in the absence of effective agents throughout the country, a king could do much by simply moving around the land with his court to show his face to his subjects and bring home to all the lieges the reality of kingship. James IV's restlessness took him from Whithorn in the south to Tain in the north, from Aberdeen in the east to Coll and Tiree in the west. As he went, he made a display and attracted attention with a train of "loud minstrels," distributing alms to the unfortunate and demonstrating his accessibility.

In previous reigns the nobles had been divided, though at the worst the king had always had the support of some nobles and he had been able to create new peerages for his supporters. James IV, however, seems to have had the confidence of his nobles as few of his predecessors had, and this unified the country. Every great Scottish magnate had a following, composed of his feudal vassals, dependents who had contracted to serve him, tenants accustomed to hereditary service to his house, and a vast number of blood relations and bearers of his surname who were not necessarily related to him by blood, and a horde of servitors, who were sometimes little better than hired thugs. In such a social structure, discord among the magnates could divide the whole nation; but when there was unity at the top, as there was under James IV, it provided cohesion throughout the entire nation.

Under James the crown revenues reached a figure almost double what they had been under his father and more than double what they were to be in the minority of his son. A large proportion of the income was expended on armaments. He carried on his father's interest in naval as

The lyric tradition in Scottish music and literature from Ossian to Burns was essentially vocal, with only the most modest instrumental reinforcement. A small portable harp was a common choice of Celtic bards of all ages. The Lamont harp, one of two surviving clarsachs or Highland harps, and dating from about 1500, was preserved by Robersons of Lude, Perthshire. As George Buchanan wrote in the *History of Scotland* (1582), "Their songs are not inelegant, and in general, celebrate the praises of brave men."

James IV tried to make Scotland
a maritime power. His flagship, the
Great Michael, was built in 1511 at
Newhaven, Midlothian.

well as military equipment, partly with a view to controlling the western
Highlands and islands, where operations by sea were indispensable. His
best-known ship, the *Great Michael*, was reputed to be the largest ship of
the day, and James, ever eager for practical experiment, had trial shots
fired which made no impression on her massive timbers. In artillery as
well as in ships the king was something of a connoisseur. He formed an
artillery train of guns known by such quaint names as great curtals,
culverins, sakars, and serpentines which greatly impressed the English, into
whose hands they ultimately fell.

James's armaments suggest that he had no disinclination for foreign
adventure, but although he conducted an expedition against England in
1497, the perpetuation of the old hostility was not his objective. On the
contrary, his marriage to Margaret Tudor, daughter of Henry VII, was
accompanied by a "treaty of perpetual peace." The ultimate result of the
marriage was that a hundred years later the great-grandson of James and
Margaret became king of England as James I. But the immediate results
were less happy, for in ten years England and Scotland were at war again.

Yet war, when it came, was not of James's making; on the contrary,
James could hope to reconcile his new obligation to England with his
country's traditional alliance with France only as long as there was peace
between England and France. Besides, James believed that the powers of
Christendom, instead of fighting among themselves, should combine
against the Turks, who were now threatening central Europe, and he
probably imagined himself leading his fleet in a united expedition against
the infidel. His contemporaries, however, were less idealistic, and Pope
Julius II, instead of uniting the west against the Turks, preferred to form
a "holy league" against France, Scotland's ancient ally. When England
was drawn into this league, James foresaw difficulties and bitterly re-
proached the pope for dividing instead of uniting Christendom.

Then in 1513, when the English actually invaded France and an appeal came for help, James felt he could not stand aside. Thanks to his personal popularity, the efficiency of his government, and the prosperity of his realm, he was able to rally the nation, and he led across the border over twenty thousand men, probably the largest force that had ever left Scotland. His strategy and tactics were not ill-conceived, but once the engagement at Flodden began, he rushed impetuously into the front of the battle, instead of directing operations. His men, fighting in phalanx array with long spears, were almost irresistible as long as they kept on the move, but when they were brought to a standstill, as they were at the foot of Branxton Hill, they were at the mercy of the English, whose long-shafted, hooked-blade bills could cut through their spear shafts and turn away their swords. The victors expressed admiration for the stubbornness of the Scots and the courage of the king, but the truth was that at Flodden there perished not only King James and the flower of his nobility but also a century of progress in Scotland. James's son and heir was only seventeen months old.

The long minority of James V (1513–28), if looked at superficially, seems to repeat an earlier pattern. Except when the king's French-born cousin, John, duke of Albany, acted as regent (1515–17 and 1521–24), leading nobles competed for control of the administration and in the end power fell into the hands of one family, the Douglas earls of Angus, just as under James II it had fallen to the Livingstons and under James III to the Boyds. The Queen Mother, Margaret Tudor, sister of Henry VIII, was an erratic and disturbing influence. Crown finances fell into complete disarray, and the progress hitherto made in the administration of justice was arrested. Yet beneath the surface there were novelties which were to shape the future of Scotland for more than a generation.

The families and factions which competed for power came increasingly to be divided not merely on personal or dynastic grounds but on political issues, the main one being the question of Scotland's international alignment. Some Scots began to feel that the French alliance had been a rather one-sided affair, and that in particular the Scots had entered on the campaign which led to Flodden not in a quarrel of their own making but for the sake of France. They concluded that continued hostility to England and the continued use of their country as a tool of France was likely to lead only to further defeats. From this point on there was a marked reluctance on the part of the Scottish nobles to cross that fatal frontier again and risk a repetition of the disaster of 1513.

Precisely at what point we can say plainly that there was a pro-English or Anglophile party representing something more than the recurring habit of disaffected nobles to intrigue with the English crown might be difficult to determine, but it is clear that there was now, for the first time since Bannockburn, a party which, if not exactly pro-English, thought that Scottish foreign policy should be reconsidered. The duke of Albany, as long as he acted as regent, energetically upheld the French alliance and had plenty of support, but the family which gained control in the last two years of the minority, the Angus Douglases, was committed to an understanding with England.

When James V personally assumed power in 1528 he reacted against the policies of the earl of Angus, his stepfather (because he had married—and subsequently divorced—Margaret Tudor), who had kept the young king in captivity for a couple of years. There can be little doubt that James's personal preference was for the French alliance. He did indeed pursue a tortuous policy, and several years elapsed before it was quite certain which side he would take, but on the whole it seems likely that his many negotiations with the emperor Charles V and with his uncle Henry

VIII were designed mainly as bargaining counters to raise his price in the French market and in the end to prevail on Francis I to permit James to marry his daughter Madeleine, whose hand had been pledged to him in terms of the Treaty of Rouen, concluded by Albany in 1517. When Madeleine died shortly after reaching Scotland, James almost immediately contracted a second French marriage, with Mary of Guise. Scotland was thus again firmly aligned with France.

But the nation over which James ruled was divided. For one thing, pro-English opinion in the kingdom was strengthened with the onset of the Reformation. The church in Scotland had undergone many changes over the medieval centuries, and there were still some clear signs of continuing vitality. There were also some newer and more active institutions. In the late fifteenth and early sixteenth centuries, there were some new friaries which retained their vitality. There were new collegiate churches which were designed to provide worship with a greater splendor than was possible in the normal parish church and to facilitate the saying of a multiplicity of masses for the living and the dead. The main weakness was the neglect of the parishes, which had been starved of resources in the interests of monasteries, cathedrals, and other institutions.

Possibly the feature which occasioned most criticism was the enormous wealth of the church. The emphasis of much of the agitation, both in James V's reign and later, was on the corruption of the church, the immorality and ignorance of the clergy, its lack of discipline, and its oppression of the poor.

Lutheran teaching reached Scotland in the 1520s, and it is quite evident that reforming doctrines were soon being widely disseminated. There were instances of damage to church buildings and their fittings and of refusal to pay ecclesiastical dues. There was a wide circulation of songs and verses, including scurrilous attacks on the clergy, but also some moving expressions of evangelical faith.

Thus, when Henry VIII threw off papal authority, his action was regarded by a considerable number of Scots as an example to be followed. Henry, indeed, tried directly to persuade James to follow him in casting off the papacy and dissolving the monasteries. But James had different ideas. Thanks to the concessions made earlier by the papacy, he had the power to nominate whom he pleased—including his own brood of illegitimate sons—to wealthy abbeys, and once England repudiated Roman authority, the pope, terrified lest Scotland should take the same line, suddenly became, as the Scots said, "more gracious and benevolent" to James than to any of his forebears.

James, in short, was able to get all he wanted out of the church under the existing system, and he saw no need for doctrinal or administrative changes. His policy was in effect orthodoxy at a price. Part of the price paid by the church was, curiously enough, the making over of funds which were used to endow the central court for civil justice, the Court of Session, as a "College of Justice" with salaried judges. James's decision to adhere to Rome and to prosecute Lutherans meant that men of reforming views became even more than before attached to the cause of friendship with England, since England could now offer them a refuge from the hostility of their own government.

It was not only James's ecclesiastical policy which caused division in the nation. He can probably be credited with a genuine concern for the extension of order throughout the country, and his reign saw the revival of the office of advocate for the poor. But the punishments he meted out were not merely stern but vindictive and perhaps sadistic. Not only troublesome borderers, but also many magnates whose offenses are far from obvious, were in prison at one time or another. The king's continued resentment

On the preceding page: Crathes, near the town of Banchory in the vicinity of Aberdeen, is one of the greatest Scottish tower houses. Built in the sixteenth century, the tall castle structure was annexed by a Queen Anne house addition in the eighteenth century.

Seated on a promontory on the shore of the Linlithgow Loch, Linlithgow Palace (at left and above) has been a royal residence since 1124. The present palace, begun by James I and completed by James VI, was the birthplace of Mary Queen of Scots.

Mary Queen of Scots became the epitome of the tragic heroine, beloved and extolled by historical novelists and artists. Robert Herdman painted her in 1867, exquisitely beautiful even as she prepares to lay her head on the block and even more resigned to her fate than the surrounding mourners and reluctant executioners.

Perth, on the river Tay (right), grew as a trading center dominated by the new merchant artisan class. Chartered in 1210 by William the Lion, the city grew as a commune governed by its leading citizens, who supported the king rather than a local magnate. Perth was the capital of Scotland until the mid-fifteenth century.

Traquair, in the border country, is celebrated as the oldest inhabited house in Scotland. Originally a freestanding tower dating to the fifteenth century, the present structure gradually evolved over the next two hundred years. Befitting the owning family's link with the royal house of Stuart, the house sheltered Mary Queen of Scots on her journey to England and imprisonment, and Bonnie Prince Charlie during the rising of '45.

At the commercial center of the royal burgh of Culross, overlooking the Firth of Forth near Dunferline, stood the Mercat Cross. The original cross was set up in 1588, when James VI granted a charter to the burgh (the present cross was erected in 1902 to commemorate the coronation of Edward VII and Queen Alexandra).

Glencoe is the finest, and probably the most famous, glen in Scotland. (Glen is the Gaelic word for valley.) Located in the north of Argyll on the west coast, it begins as a steep-sided narrow valley and descends into a broad gentle depression, terminating at Loch Leven. Painted here by Scotland's leading nineteenth-century landscape artist, Horatio McCulloch, Glencoe was the site of the massacre of the Macdonald clan by Campbells in 1692.

On the following page is Maxwellton House. At first a fortified stronghold, befitting its proximity to the border, this fine manor house shows the changing tastes and needs of its owners over a period extending more than five hundred years. It is best known as the birthplace of Annie Laurie, who left her family home to enjoy a long married life despite the laments of her disappointed suitor, William Douglas of England, who wrote the first version of the famous song.

IACOBVS.QVINTVS.SCOTTORVM.REX

ANNO.ÆTATIS.SVE.

z 8

MARIA.LOTHORINGIA.ILLIVS.IN.SECVNDIS.NVP

TIIS VXOR. ANNO ÆTATIS SVE . Z 4 :

Caught in a struggle for power between Henry VIII and his own Scottish nobles, James V found support for his government in France, the home of his queen, Mary of Guise. The excessive license and favor he permitted the church in its prosecution of Protestant dissenters reinforced the growing animosity his subjects felt toward both the church and his French advisers. Plagued by ill health and shaken by the opposition of his nobles, he died soon after the defeat of his troops at their hands at Solway Moss in 1542.

105

against the earl of Angus, who remained in exile in England after his fall in 1528, led to something little short of a feud against the whole Douglas kin.

One of the less disinterested motives behind the king's severity may well have been financial. When he had taken over the government he had found an almost bankrupt treasury, and he gained a reputation for what contemporaries called covetousness. He used every means at his disposal to increase his income, and was believed to seek causes or pretexts for acquiring the property of his wealthier subjects. He certainly accumulated a great hoard of wealth—partly arising from the dowries he obtained with his French brides—but he indulged as well in conspicuous expenditure which must be seen against the background of a resurgence of cultural interests.

One of James's subjects was John Major, a scholar who was as familiar with Cambridge and Paris as with St. Andrews and who wrote a *History of Greater Britain* which was a plea for Anglo-Scottish friendship. James patronized the poet Sir David Lindsay, whose *Satire of the Three Estates* was a spirited denunciation of abuses in church and state, and the historian Hector Boece, whose account of Scotland's past was lively and vivid, though highly imaginative. James emerged also as the greatest builder of his line, whose ambitious work at Falkland, Holyrood, Stirling, and Linlithgow represented a sophistication imitative of contemporary French châteaus. On the other hand, some thought the country could not afford the standard of luxury which James's court maintained, and his expensive buildings can have done nothing to endear him to those who had to pay for them.

It was, therefore, a deeply divided nation that James tried to lead on a campaign against England in 1542. This time the effort was not merely designed to serve France but was intended to have something of the character of a crusade, in the interests of the papacy, against the schismatic Henry VIII. Success could hardly have been hoped for, because in addition to a generation-old distaste for an invasion of England, there was the sympathy which some Scots felt for antipapal policy and the general loss of confidence in a king who had made himself "ill-beloved of

This splendid oak carving from a ceiling in Stirling Castle, erected on the orders of, and to the taste of, James V, may show the king himself.

his subjects." The consequence was a disastrous defeat at Solway Moss in November, 1542, when it seemed that some Scottish nobles preferred to surrender to the English rather than fight for a king in whom they had lost confidence.

James V, who, in addition to political troubles, had experienced personal loss in the death of his two infant sons within days of each other, suffered a collapse which may have been emotional and nervous, rather than physical, and died in the month after Solway Moss, "a worn-out, desperate man, at the age of thirty years." He was succeeded by his week-old daughter, Mary. During her long minority France and England each sought, by war and diplomacy, to turn Scotland into a satellite, and the people of Scotland themselves were more than ever divided between the friends of England and the Reformation and the friends of France and Rome.

During eighteen years (1543–61) the situation changed with almost kaleidoscopic unpredictability, but the main turning points were in 1543, 1547–48, and 1559–60. In 1543 control of affairs was assumed by a party which included that old friend of England, Angus, now returned from his exile, and a number of lords who had been captured at Solway Moss and had come back to Scotland after entering into engagements with Henry VIII. The party was, if not quite Protestant, at any rate prepared to encourage reforming preachers and to come to terms with England.

The infant queen Mary was pledged by treaty as the prospective bride of Prince Edward, son of Henry, the future Edward VI. But before the year was out the Scottish regent, the earl of Arran, threw off the influence of the pro-English party, came to terms with the Roman Catholic interest under Cardinal Beaton, and in a remarkable volte-face repudiated the treaty with England. England's answers were to intensify Protestant propaganda in Scotland, to tamper, through bribery, with the allegiance of Scottish nobles, and to devastate Scotland in a series of invasions known as the Rough Wooing.

Falkland Palace, begun by James IV but essentially a building from the reign of James V, was the epitome of the Scottish Renaissance palace. As a favorite royal residence and hunting lodge, Falkland became for a time the center of art and culture in the north. Only parts of the palace are preserved: the south wing whose column-decorated buttresses and wreathed portraits reflect the French influence dominant at the court; the ruined east wing; and the fortified gatehouse.

In 1547, after heavily defeating the Scots at Pinkie, English forces settled down to occupy a large area of southeastern Scotland. A divided and somewhat irresolute Scotland was incapable of ejecting those occupying forces by its own resources and had to call in the aid of France. France gave the necessary help, but only on condition that the young queen, who had been designated in 1543 as the bride of the heir to the English throne, was sent to France in 1548 to become the betrothed of the dauphin, the heir to the French throne.

In 1554 the native-born regent, Arran, was replaced by the French Queen Mother, Mary of Guise, and from this point Scotland came more and more under French domination. In 1558 Queen Mary married the dauphin, who the following year became king of France as Francis II. Scotland was now more closely connected with France than she had ever been with England. The prospect for Scotland appeared to be government by descendants of Francis and Mary and ultimately absorption into the domain of the most Christian king of France. Such prospects were far from pleasing to many Scots, and even those who were favorable to the French alliance and were conservative in church affairs were antagonized when they saw a standing army of French soldiers garrisoning Scottish fortresses, Frenchmen thrust into high office in Scotland, and the obvious design to use Scotland once more as a mere tool of France.

The undisguised attempts to make Scotland a base for aggression against England, to cause a Scottish army to cross the border again, and to levy taxation for fortifications all aroused bitter resentment. National sentiment, which in 1548 had sought help from France to drive out the English, had now become anti-French and was prepared to accept English help to drive out the French. Such national resentment went hand in hand with Protestantism, which was growing all the time, just as support of France had gone hand in hand with Roman Catholicism.

There was, however, no prospect of help from England, at least on religious grounds, as long as that country was ruled by the Roman Catholic Mary Tudor. But in November, 1558, Mary was succeeded by Elizabeth, who almost at once showed that she was going to give at least some countenance to the Protestant cause. Six months after Elizabeth's accession, a rebellion broke out in Scotland: among the motives it is hard to disentangle the religious fervor from the national sentiment against the army of the French regent, in whose hands lay the defense of the existing regime. The best known of the reforming preachers was John Knox, who had himself been for a time a prisoner in the French galleys and who had found a home for some years in the England of Edward VI. During Mary Tudor's reign, Knox had ministered to a congregation of English exiles in Geneva and had become an admirer of the Swiss reformer, Calvin. It

Struck in 1540, this coin bears a portrait of James V.

On this coin minted in 1555 is the royal portrait by which Mary was known to her subjects before her return to Scotland in 1561.

was a sermon by him which sparked the rebellion in May, 1559; he advocated an Anglo-Scottish alliance, based on "the preaching of Christ crucified," against France and the papacy. The insurgents had a difficult task, and their success was not ensured until England sent help, in the early months of 1560, to turn the tide. Mary of Guise died early in June, and in July a treaty between England and France was concluded whereby the forces of both countries were to withdraw from Scotland. At this point, when an English force entered Scotland to be welcomed as a deliverer, the Auld Alliance between Scotland and France came to an end, to be superseded by a new alliance between Scotland and England.

above: John Knox was the architect of the Scottish Reformation, a convert to Protestantism, and a victim of Catholic oppression in Scotland. Knox first fled to the protection of the young English king Edward VI, whom he served as a royal chaplain, then spent five years in exile in Geneva during the reign of Mary Tudor, and there became imbued with the strict tenets of Calvinism. On his return to Scotland he became the champion of the new Protestant faith and one of the most formidable of the new queen's opponents.

Nineteenth-century painter David Wilkie depicts the preaching of John Knox before the Lords of Congregation on June 10, 1559. The Lords of Congregation were the sponsors and signatories of the First Covenant, drawn up in 1557 by the earls of Argyll and Morton. The Protestant lords promised to establish a national church free from Rome, and in 1559 Knox returned to Scotland to preach against the papacy. Wilkie imagined the scene when Knox chose as his text Christ driving the money changers from the temple, and equated the bishops, seen at the left, with this corruption. The young woman seated in the center of the picture is Mary's half-sister; Mary at this time was in France, married to the dauphin.

The sixteenth-century Scottish reformer George Wishart horrifies the crowd as he preaches against the veneration of the Virgin Mary, whose image he holds. The artist, William Fettes Douglas, has studied visual and literary sources in an attempt to re-create the appearance of the throng of listeners. Standing guard with a sword at the right is John Knox who, as a youth, became a follower of Wishart and acted as his bodyguard. Wishart was arrested, tried, and burnt at the stake in 1546.

The withdrawal of the English and French forces in effect left the Scots free to settle their own affairs, and this they did by legislation which abolished papal authority, forbade the celebration of mass, and adopted a reformed confession of faith. The absent queen declined to ratify this legislation, and the future was uncertain because it was thought that she might not now return to a country which had repudiated France and what France stood for. A kind of provisional government, mainly of Protestant lords, controlled affairs, and there was some talk of finding another sovereign to take Mary's place. But in December, 1560, Francis II died, and Mary, with a poor future in France, decided to return to Scotland, where she arrived in August, 1561.

Mary, who had been out of Scotland for thirteen years and was barely nineteen, faced a difficult situation involving her attitude to the now triumphant Scottish reformers, her relations with Elizabeth of England, and the question of her marriage. The policies she adopted showed considerable skill, and even if they owed a great deal to her advisers, particularly her half-brother, the earl of Moray, and her secretary, Maitland of Lethington, it was creditable to her intelligence that she accepted the counsel of such wise statesmen.

Although herself a practicing Roman Catholic, Mary conceded to the reformed church both official recognition and a measure of financial support. But she could not be head on earth of the Church of Scotland, as Henry VIII had been of the Church of England, nor could she even

above: Celebrated as the most beautiful woman of her time, Mary brought the glamour and brilliance of French court life and costume to Scotland. In this necklace of twenty-seven gold beads, the large filigree beads were designed to contain perfume. Such finery enlivened the court, but scandalized puritanical subjects.

above left: The handsome Henry Stewart, Lord Darnley, future husband of Mary Queen of Scots, was a direct descendant of Margaret Tudor, Henry VIII's oldest sister. He was "the first prince of the blood in England" and second cousin to Mary. Henry and his young brother, Charles, stand in the Hall of Holyrood House, one of the new Renaissance palaces of Scotland.

above right: Mary Queen of Scots and Darnley are shown during the period of their brief marriage.

be supreme governor of the realm in ecclesiastical causes, as Elizabeth was in England. Consequently, the Scottish reformed church had to develop an organization independent of the crown. Administration was mainly in the hands of superintendents or reformed bishops, and supreme authority lay with a General Assembly, which was virtually equivalent to a Protestant Parliament. In it the three estates of clergy, barons, and burgesses were represented.

In its internal organization and in its worship the reformed church was strongly anticlerical and laid great emphasis on the participation of the general body of the laity both in worship and in discipline, especially in the local kirk sessions. All but the most bigoted were satisfied with Mary's compromise, and it was to her advantage that she had great gifts of personal charm which won the affection of her intimates and the loyalty of the mass of her subjects.

Difficulties arose for Mary not directly because of her relations with the reformed church in Scotland, but because of her relations with Elizabeth. Mary claimed that she had a better right to the English throne than Elizabeth, who had been born to Anne Boleyn while Henry VIII's first wife, Catherine of Aragon, was still alive and who was, therefore, in Roman Catholic eyes illegitimate. Mary might have been prepared, as she was advised, to acknowledge Elizabeth as queen during her lifetime on the understanding that Mary should be recognized as Elizabeth's heir. Mary's religious policy in Scotland, while it made her acceptable to Roman Catholics in England, did not eliminate the possibility that she might accept Anglicanism as a step to the English succession.

Much in the forefront was the question of the marriage of this eligible widow. There was talk at first of Mary's marriage to the earl of Arran, which would have committed her irrevocably to the intransigent Protestants. Then there were prolonged negotiations for a match with Don Carlos, the son and heir of Philip II of Spain, which would have committed her to the militants of the Counter-Reformation. For political reasons there was much to commend a husband selected by Elizabeth, who might be presumed to have an interest in the probable progenitor of her own successors.

The policy of moderation in religion, combined with an accommodation with England, shipwrecked on the irresolution of the English queen. Elizabeth, who refused to take seriously the possibility of her own demise, declined to consider any arrangements for recognition of a successor and was entirely negative in her attitude toward any matrimonial plans for Mary. Finally, when it was evident that Mary had nothing to gain by trying to conciliate Elizabeth, she married her cousin, Henry Stewart, Lord Darnley, who stood next to her in the line of succession to England and, although not personally a practicing Roman Catholic, was to some extent acceptable to English Roman Catholics as a possible heir to Elizabeth.

Mary's decision to marry Darnley seems indeed to have owed more to personal affection than to policy, but it had political repercussions. The marriage was by Roman Catholic rites, and a papal dispensation was obtained to legalize this marriage between first cousins. Some Protestant lords, including Moray, raised a rather aimless rebellion, which Mary easily suppressed, but she seems now to have reflected that she had nothing to gain by persisting in trying to conciliate the Protestants, and she began to pursue a policy more favorable to Rome.

The reason why the Darnley marriage proved disastrous was again largely personal. Darnley was greedy for political power, but quite unworthy to be entrusted with it. The schemes of nobles who felt they were excluded from political influence, and Darnley's resentment at not being allowed to share authority with his wife found a focus in hostility to David Riccio, an Italian secretary whom Mary employed and whom Darnley professed to suspect of undue familiarity with the queen. After Darnley's participation in the brutal murder of Riccio, almost in the queen's presence when she was six months pregnant, the relations of the queen and her husband were probably never again sincerely cordial. Their son, the future James VI and I, was born on June 19, 1566, but it was soon evident to all that the marriage had broken down and that Mary was increasingly attached to James Hepburn, earl of Bothwell.

Darnley was murdered in February, 1567. The whole truth about the event has never been, and probably never will be, discovered. Every

This painting by William Allan is a romanticized version of the brutal affair in which the queen's Italian secretary was surprised with the queen in her chamber and murdered before the eyes of his hapless mistress. Aside from being the object of her husband's jealousy, David Riccio's Latin manners and southern gentility were repellent to the rougher northerners.

This contemporary drawing of Kirk o'Field shows Darnley's murder in 1567. In the upper right Darnley and his page lie half-naked from the force of the explosion; below, even the roof of the church has been blown off. The funeral procession can be seen at the lower left and the burial at the right. Darnley was found to have been strangled; the explosion was a crude attempt to hide the crime. The seven-month-old James VI sits in his cradle above, at the left.

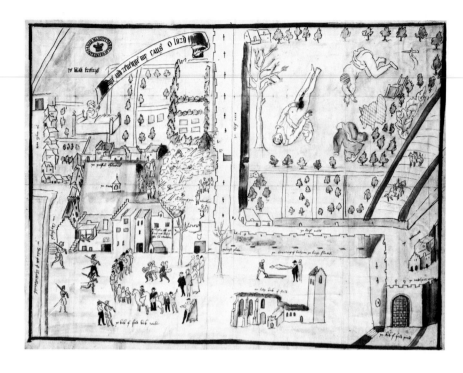

accusing finger pointed at Bothwell, and when Mary married him with what seems almost indecent haste, it was thought that she shared in his guilt. Mary was deposed in July, 1567, essentially because she was suspected of adultery and murder.

It was an infant only a year old who was crowned to take his mother's place, and Scotland therefore had to suffer another uncommonly long minority, troubled in an even more complex manner than those of Mary and James V. Mary's abdication had been extorted by a party of nobles whose professed intention was to "liberate" her from Bothwell, but some of whom soon showed that they had no intention of ever allowing her to rule again. Therefore not all those who initially took action against her were in favor of her subsequent imprisonment in Lochleven and the coronation of her son. When she escaped from Lochleven in May, 1568, she was almost at once defeated and had to flee to England, where she looked for aid and found captivity. But there was a strong Marian party which maintained resistance for five years against the young king's regents and surrendered only when English help was obtained to batter down the walls of their last stronghold, Edinburgh Castle.

Then followed several years of firm and effective rule by James Douglas, earl of Morton, the fourth of James VI's regents. But during Morton's regency the first signs appeared of new problems which were to play a part throughout not only the whole of James's reign but those of his son and grandsons, during more than a century. These were ecclesiastical problems, derived partly from the peculiar circumstances in which the Scottish Reformation had been carried through. The reformed church had been set up not on royal initiative but in defiance of the crown and as an outcome of two revolutions—one in 1560 against Mary of Guise and the second, in 1567, against her daughter. Something of a habit of disobedience had therefore been sown from the start, and it was reinforced in the 1570s by Andrew Melville, who was the real founder of Scottish Presbyterianism.

When Mary had been replaced by a king who was brought up as a Protestant and the country ruled by Protestant regents, the question arose whether the church should now be governed by crown and Parliament, which were now by definition "godly," or whether the General Assembly

above: According to the inscription on the tablet to the right, this painting by Lieven de Vogeleer was commissioned by Darnley's parents, the earl and countess of Lennox, so that "the king of Scots . . . may have a memorial from them, in order that he shut not out of his memory the recent atrocious murder by the king of his father." The infant James VI kneels in front of his father's tomb. Behind the boy king kneel his grandparents and uncle. Clearly the painting is more than a cry of mourning from the bereaved parents; it is a call for revenge and an attempt to indict Mary as well.

Forced by some of the Scottish nobles to abdicate her throne, Mary took refuge in England, where she endured seventeen years of confinement by order of her cousin, Elizabeth I of England. An expert needle-woman, she occupied herself in fashioning elaborate allegorical embroideries, like this one bearing a pruning knife with the motto "Virtue flourishes with wounding." Mary signed the piece with her cipher, at the left: MA for Maria, and the Greek letter Phi for Francis, her first husband.

Deprived of parental affection and guidance, and having lived as the pawn of factions contesting control of the state, James VI and I developed an instinct for survival and an ability to mask his thoughts and emotions. His need for perpetual vigilance is mirrored in, if not symbolized by, the hawk, in this panel painting by Arnold Bronckorst.

should continue. Problems also arose concerning church organization and endowment. The difficulty was to reconcile the administrative needs of the reformed church with the continued existence of the old ecclesiastical structure, which had remained intact and whose revenues were now at the disposal of the crown.

The solution adopted in 1572 was that ministers of the reformed church should be appointed by the crown and should exercise the powers formerly vested in the superintendents, under the supervision of the general assembly or at any rate responsible to it. Melville challenged this solution. He proclaimed the parity of ministers and advocated the abolition of individual overseers like bishops or superintendents and the substitution for them of committees of ministers called presbyteries. And he urged that the church should be governed by a General Assembly consisting solely of ministers and elders—elders who were no longer laymen but were in effect ordained for life as a branch of the ministry.

Melville taught that church and state were "two kingdoms," and that the sovereign of the state had no more authority in the church than any other member had, but also claimed that ministers, as the spokesmen of God, could "teach the magistrate his duty" and dictate government policy. He was ultimately to put forward his claims in their most startling form in an interview with the king in which he plucked him by the sleeve and called him "God's silly vassal." As Andrew Melville prevailed on the majority of the General Assembly to adopt his views, a head-on collision between the assembly and the crown became inevitable.

When the regent Morton finally fell from power in 1580, the king was still only fourteen, no further regent was appointed, and a contest for the control of affairs took place. It must be remembered that during the period of almost seventy years since Flodden there had been three minorities, so that in that span of time there had been no more than about twenty years of rule by a monarch of mature years. The great families had become accustomed to competing among themselves for the direction of affairs. At this stage, in 1580, there were two fairly clearly defined factions in the country, whose rival policies covered a wide range of political and ecclesiastical issues. On one side there was what may be called a conservative faction, to some extent the heir of the old Marian party.

Although Mary's adherents were dwindling with the years, her existence, until her death in 1587, was something of a threat to James almost as much as it was to Elizabeth. The conservative faction was sympathetic to Mary to the extent of being prepared to consider her restoration, if only in association with her son; some of its members were favorable to Roman Catholicism, and as a whole it preferred episcopacy to Presbyterianism. The existence of this group constantly aroused hopes among Roman Catholic agents that Scotland could be rallied to the papal cause. They were overly optimistic, but the existence of Scottish Roman Catholicism had significance at a time when attempts were being made to organize crusades against heretical England, crusades for which Scotland might serve as a base. On the other side was an ultra-Protestant faction, anxious that Scotland and England should stand together against the papalist powers of the Continent. This faction gave some countenance to the Presbyterian ministers, who in turn used their pulpits for propaganda in favor of an English alliance and against Mary and anyone else tainted with "papistry."

Between 1580 and 1585 there was a series of palace revolutions, or *coups d'état*, as one party or the other sought the ascendancy, and the young king found himself the puppet of each of them in turn. By 1585, however, James, now eighteen, was himself becoming a factor of some importance and from that point he began to exercise personal influence on policy, though largely guided for some years by his able chancellor, John Maitland of Thirlestane. James had been taught by his childhood experiences to abhor dependence on a faction and to detest violence of any kind; he had seen enough of Presbyterian attempts to meddle in politics to be convinced that his best chance of controlling the church would be by maintaining or restoring bishops; he felt impelled to cultivate Puritans on one hand and Roman Catholics on the other with a view to smoothing the path to the English throne. He obviously could not turn his back on the Protestantism that was officially maintained in England. Yet at the same time he was aware of the strength of Roman Catholicism there and of the possibility that Spain might intervene to overthrow Elizabeth. He, therefore, had hopes that if he maintained amicable relations with Roman Catholics at home and abroad he would commend himself to English Roman Catholics and perhaps even succeed to England under Spanish and papal auspices. Besides, he had a prudent regard for his own safety, and severity to Roman Catholics might encourage the pope to authorize some fanatic to assassinate him.

James, who proclaimed his ambition to be a "universal king" not tied to one party, would gladly have maintained a balance between the two parties in Scotland. But he had neither money nor any means of coercion at his disposal and was therefore driven to subtlety, conciliation, cajolery, and sometimes trickery, all of which he employed with singular success. He was first driven to lean on the Protestant faction until he had gone some way toward securing his prospects in England and suppressing the more militant of his own Roman Catholic subjects.

That the Auld Alliance with France should be replaced by a new one, between a Protestant Scotland and a Protestant England, seemed logical, but the persistence of faction in Scotland and the irresolution of Queen Elizabeth combined to delay the making of a formal bond until 1586. From that point it was ever more likely that James would succeed to England, and no one was surprised when he peacefully ascended the English throne as James I in 1603. The formal league of 1586 was accompanied by an English pension for James and an assurance from Elizabeth that she would not oppose his claims to the English succession unless he provoked her. Such a strong inducement insured James's acquiescence in his mother's execution in 1587 and his neutrality when the Spanish armada sailed against England in the following year. All this was satisfactory to the Scottish Presbyterians, and James made a direct major concession to them in 1592, when parliamentary recognition was granted to the Presbyterian system.

After thus gaining the support of the Protestants, James was able to put increasing pressure on the northern earls who favored the cause of Rome, and he obtained their submission in 1597. It was then possible to turn on the Presbyterians. From 1597 he began to undermine the general assembly and make moves toward the revival of episcopacy. After much tactical maneuvering he succeeded in taming the assembly, which found it could now meet only with royal sanction and under royal control. By 1610 Melville was in exile, and the powers of bishops had been restored. James's answer to Melville's concept of two kingdoms was that there was only one kingdom, comprehending both church and state, over which he ruled as God's vice-regent, with bishops as his agents in the church. It was, however, a genuine compromise, for presbyteries and kirk sessions continued to operate, and the king did not meddle seriously with the forms of worship which had developed since the Reformation. This middle-of-the-road course was widely acceptable.

In the same years when he was bridling the church, James was carrying through measures for more effective secular government. Much

The arrangements for the trial of Mary Queen of Scots at Fotheringhay Castle in 1587 are shown in the anonymous drawing above. Mary (indicated by the letter A) sits at the upper right.

right: A contemporary engraving by John Wierix shows the martyred queen at her death, welcomed into the ranks of female saints and granted the crown of immortality.

*En tibi magnanimæ spirantia Principis ora,
Omnia quam mundi mirantur regna, venustæ
Non decus ob formæ tantum, prolemæ decoram,
Innumeraśæ animi dotes, quas divite dextra
Fudit ei natura potens: sed mascula virtus,
Relligionis amor, fidei constantia mentes
Plus rapit attonitas hominum, quam forma vel oris
Gratia rara fui. Rege hæc genitore creata,
(O pudor, o probrum, nostriæ, infamia sedi)*

*Barbarico ritu, contra ius, fasque, piumque,
Carcere bis denos latuit detenta per annos:
Imperioque trucis fædæque virginis Angliæ,
(Nulla Caledoniis qua bellua tetrior undis
Innatat, aut Lybiæ campos pervurrit arenæ)
Fussa mori tandem, superis concessit in auras,
Mortis at horrendam faciem monumenta loquentur
Omnia scriptorum, Deus ulciscetur, illi
Præpositi populis Reges, quos publica causa
Spretaæ Maiestas et Regia iura mouebunt.*

The execution of Mary Queen of Scots was recorded in a watercolor by a contemporary. The inscription reads: [On the] viii of February Mary Stuart, Queen of Scots, fervent Roman Catholic, was beheaded, having tried to cause much unrest [and] to make herself mistress of England, which was completely proved against her by the Council of the Parliament.

was done to improve criminal justice and to preserve the peace, some financial reorganization was achieved, and the first steps were taken to institute something like regular and adequate taxation. In the borders, the Highlands, and the western and northern Isles, James established royal authority as it had never been established before. His task was made easier by his accession to the English throne, because the borders could be settled only by Anglo-Scottish cooperation, and the West Highlands, which had always been in close communication with England's troublesome subjects in Ireland, could be settled only when the plantation of Ulster by Englishmen and Lowland Scots drove a wedge between the Celts of Ireland and those of western Scotland.

James would never have achieved what he did had he not been a man of remarkable shrewdness and tenacity. There were few executions or forfeitures, and James, who was by temperament as well as policy a peacemaker, preferred to avoid head-on collisions. As Scottish society was still largely dominated by the great barons and their followings, it was evident that if the king could appease the nobles he could largely disregard the ministers. For winning the nobles to his side he had unprecedented opportunities. His wiser predecessors had always used their patronage to gain support, but as the Reformation had put the crown in control of much church property, James had at his disposal patronage on an unprecedented scale.

In effect, he bought the nobles with the lands of the monasteries. Yet James did not depend much on nobles for the conduct of his administration. He declared at one stage that he would no longer use great men to manage his affairs, but only "such as he could correct and were hangable." The "hangable" men on whom he relied—and none of whom he ever hanged—were younger sons of noble houses or men of middle-class origins who became professional administrators of a type seldom known before in Scotland. Such men, selected by James in the 1590s, served him well throughout his reign. James's assertion of divine right for his kingship was a necessary answer, framed by a man who was himself a theologian, to the claims of the Presbyterians that ministers could instruct him in his business. Yet, while he dogmatized about divine right, he had an easy familiarity with nobles and commons alike which gave him opportunities to use his undoubted gifts of cajolery.

James's accession to the English throne brought him enlarged prestige as well as security from such *coups d'état* as had punctuated his earlier years. There had been a riot in Edinburgh in 1596, for which militant ministers were blamed, and there was to be a riot in Edinburgh in 1637, in the reign of James's son. But between the two stretched forty years of a tranquillity such as Scotland had seldom, if ever, known before. The stability resulting from "King James's peace" was conducive to cultural activities. Himself a poet of some competence, James had invited French poets to his court and had gathered round him Scots like Alexander Montgomery, John Stewart of Baldinneis, and William Fowler, who carried on the native tradition but whom the king encouraged to imitate continental models in their verse and imagery. Later in the reign Sir William Alexander and William Drummond of Hawthornden were writing poems of at least very good second-class quality.

Prose works of a scale and character hardly known before appeared— Knox's *History of the Reformation*, the *Histories of Scotland* and other writings of George Buchanan and John Lesley, and two remarkable autobiographies— the *Memoirs* of Sir James Melville of Halhill and the *Autobiography and Diary* of James Melville, brother of the Presbyterian leader. John Napier of Merchiston, the inventor of logarithms, was the first Scot to attain European status in such a field. Two universities were founded—Edinburgh in 1582 and Marischal College, Aberdeen, in 1593—bringing Scotland's total to five. A statute of 1616 was the first to order the maintenance of a school in every parish.

The gaiety and brightness which prevailed are still to be seen in the surviving examples of mural and ceiling painting. Secular architecture took on a new character, largely because with King James's peace the emphasis on defensive work declined. Hitherto the only purely domestic structures of significance had been royal palaces, but now palaces were built by Robert Stewart, earl of Orkney (the king's uncle), at Birsay and by his son, Earl Patrick, at Kirkwall, and others of the king's subjects erected handsome mansions at Pinkie, Seton, Fyvie, and Huntly. The tower-house tradition survived, but with a much more refined and sophisticated quality and a far less military aspect; the finest of many examples is Craigievar. Scottish building, even at its most domestic, retained a character different from that of the Jacobean mansions of England, but in language and literature the trend was toward assimilation to England.

The Scots never had a printed Bible in their own vernacular, but depended on English versions, and the reformed church was a great instrument in habituating the people to standard English, with the result that the Scots tongue practically disappeared as a literary vehicle even before the Union of the Crowns. A common language, like a common Protestantism, did much to bring the two peoples together. There was much well-intentioned economic legislation, some new industries did take

Craigievar is an incomparable, classic mountain château, the very epitome of the Scottish baronial castle. Its owner made his fortune as a merchant in the Danzig trade, and this house, virtually unaltered since its completion in 1626, testifies to his success. The tartan carpet and upholstery, shown here in the great hall, became popularized by Queen Victoria, who decorated her Highland residence at Balmoral in this fashion.

root, and there is also a good deal of evidence of expanding commerce—exports of coal and salt, for example. However, probably less was done to stimulate economic expansion by legislation than by the new condition of order and security. There is ample evidence of the increasing wealth of the merchant classes and the farmer alike.

Economic prosperity helped to make men content with James's government and added to his subjects' respect for him. It was not mere flattery when one of his servants referred to "this delectable time of peace under your majesty's happy reign and most excellent government," and the time was to come when men would look back with regret to "the wisdom of blessed King James."

5

From the Union of the Crowns
to the Union of the Parliaments:
1603-1707

Henry L. Snyder

FROM THE UNION OF THE CROWNS TO THE UNION OF THE PARLIAMENTS:

1603–1707

by Henry L. Snyder

This coin, struck in 1591, bears a contemporary portrait of James VI, and on its obverse are two traditional Scottish emblems, the lion and the thistle.

HISTORIANS are wont to divide the past into convenient periods. One may say that the accession of James VI in 1567, the termination of the regency in 1578, the death of James VI in 1625, or the Bishops' War of 1638 all make equally suitable points from which to narrate the history of Scotland in the seventeenth century. Yet the Union of the Crowns in 1603, with the consequent departure of the king to London, is surely as important for Scotland, who lost its resident sovereign, as for England, who gained him.

The impact upon the social and cultural life was perhaps the most immediate. The court was a major influence in every sphere. This influence, the circle that supported it, was now gone. The kind of centrifugal force it imparted to the society, an important counter to the clan chieftains, was no more. Edinburgh was reduced from being the capital to a provincial center. Yet we should not overstate the loss.

Though James had worked diligently to restore the financial solvency of the crown, his success had been limited. The church lands had been granted out to men loyal to the crown, the lords of erection, to provide a counterpoise to the old nobility. Customs receipts were still modest, other taxes of disappointing return. James was a poor, even impecunious, monarch. To finance his journey to London he had to raise a loan from the city of Edinburgh and was obliged to send ahead to his English council for additional funds when his travel expenses exhausted his purse midway in his progress. No wonder that he chose to remain in the comparative luxury and comfort of his new court rather than return to the uncertain and cramped surroundings of the old.

James no longer had to fear for his personal safety. As late as 1600, in the Gowrie conspiracy, his person was in jeopardy. So long as he remained in Scotland the hazard of a coup or assassination was always a real one. Even the privacy of his own bedchamber was not guaranteed in Scotland. The respect and courtesy he was greeted with on his arrival in England presaged a new and welcome change that the king was not about to relinquish.

Yet if the threat of English arms allied with the lure of English gold gave his voice added authority in his homeland, the main credit for the peaceful era that ushered in the seventeenth century was due in large measure to the astuteness and political guile of the king himself. He had learned how to manipulate the factions so that he emerged the victor. The government itself had been entrusted to bureaucrats loyal to the king. Above all James VI knew his Scots. The strengthened government was a blessing, though using the Privy Council, an executive agent, rather than the Parliament, a representative one, led to despotism rather than democracy.

The relative peace was not necessarily the consequence of prosperity. Scotland was a poor, backward country with limited resources. Although the long reign of James VI saw a great number of new royal burghs created, this was hardly the manifestation of a major shift in population from country to town. Most of the burghs were extremely small, ranging in size from Edinburgh, alone over ten thousand, to a number which had less than one hundred inhabitants. That they increased rapidly in size is undeniable. By the end of the seventeenth century, Edinburgh had some thirty thousand inhabitants, surpassing Norwich and equal to Bristol, the largest city in England after London. The great majority were probably no larger than a thousand and concentrated heavily in the Lowlands and along the northeast coast.

Edinburgh was hardly a place of beauty. Its development along the spine of an ascending ridge did give it an impressive skyline. Now known as the Royal Mile, the long road that connected these two bastions was

As king of England, James I had access to wealth and power that far exceeded the means or dreams of any of his predecessors on the throne of Scotland. For his coronation, a series of pageants, processions, and displays were staged from his entrance into London to the ceremony in Westminster Abbey, providing ample evidence—to both the king and his Scottish entourage—of the affluence of his new subjects. In 1604 Stephen Harrison made this engraving of the Triumphal Arch that ushered the king into London.

The new importance of James in Europe prompted pictorial representations and written accounts of his coronation. This contemporary German engraving is a composite, including the processions of the king and queen to Westminster Abbey, the coronation service, the jubilation of the populace, and the military and naval salutes after the ceremony. James is represented three times: under the canopy, in front of the choir screen, and at the high altar.

Here is a typical Scottish townhouse of the seventeenth century, whose residents would have greeted James, duke of York, on his arrival in Edinburgh to take up his government. One of the best preserved houses of the period, called Gladstones Land, built in 1620 by the merchant Thomas Gladstones, it is now under the protection of the National Trust for Scotland.

itself an impressive sight. Built up during the course of the seventeenth century, it had gained an appearance by the time of the union that it bears to this day.

Because of the precipitous drop from both sides of the ridge, the houses were jammed together and built up to as many as eleven or twelve stories. The lanes, or wynds, which led off the sides were steep and narrow, "troublesome to those who walk in [them] . . . especially if their Lungs are not very good," according to Daniel Defoe. The lungs of visitors and residents alike would also suffer from the fetid atmosphere, a combination of mist, coal smoke, and decaying waste. The lack of adequate sanitation and the crowded conditions gave the city a high mortality rate. Garbage and human waste were tossed indiscriminately out of the windows. The crowds of paupers and dayworkers barely eking out a living threatened the safety of the residents and provided a ready mob to riot and carouse through the town on the least excuse.

Agriculture was inefficient, barely more than subsistence level, which meant that little surplus was available from the farms for the support of the towns or industrial workers. Grain imports from the Baltic were critical, especially in the early part of the century, to sustain the populace. The population was distributed much more evenly between the Lowlands, the borders, and the Highlands than it was to be in later centuries. But even that distribution began to change in the seventeenth century. The reduction of raids and feuds brought about by the king's peace did mean that agriculture and animal husbandry had a better chance to prosper. The movement of cattle from the Lowlands to Highland pastures for the summer or to markets in England from the borders became relatively unimpeded; consequently, herds and flocks grew in size. The growth to some extent was at the expense of farming, crops giving way to pasture, reducing the need for farmhands. This process helped to shift the balance of population to the Lowlands and the towns.

The greatest relief for the increase in population which took place between the mid-sixteenth and mid-seventeenth centuries was emigration. Scot traders and merchants were familiar sights around the Baltic and on the Atlantic littoral of Europe. Many Scots went into foreign military service, notably in the Thirty Years' War, 1618–48. This tradition continued into the later seventeenth century and the eighteenth century.

Scottish regiments were a staple element in the Dutch army for more than a century. After the Revolution of 1688, Scottish Jacobites joined their Irish brethren to man regiments and officer units in the armies of France, Prussia, Russia, and Spain. In several cases the emigration was officially sponsored for colonizing purposes. James VI planted colonies of loyal Scotsmen in Ulster. The colonies waxed and prospered, and continuing waves of new settlers soon made them an element to reckon with in Ireland. One venture farther afield also bears mention. At the beginning of the seventeenth century, North America was the objective. The king granted Sir William Alexander a charter in 1621 to establish a colony in Nova Scotia, selling baronetcies to help finance the project. But the forbidding climate and the lack of money limited its success.

This kingdom that Charles I inherited in 1625 as part of his triple crown had fared well under his father. Though the despotic measures of James were likely to cause trouble for the son, Charles had the choice of assuaging or exacerbating the fears of his subjects. Lacking his father's understanding and flexibility and committed to a rigid, hierarchical scheme in polity, above all in the church, he unwittingly and disastrously chose the latter. To be sure he had been brought to England at the age of three and did not return to his homeland for three decades. But his unfamiliarity was compounded by his lack of sensitivity and compassion, equally evident in his English and Scottish policies. Years of adversity and overclose association and communion with his subjects had taught James how far he could reach. He knew Scotland, its concerns, and its moods at first hand. These essential qualities were all lacking in his son and heir.

The contrast in temperament and shrewdness between father and son was as great as the difference in their physical appearance and deportment. Charles I has achieved immortality through the genius of the court painter, Sir Anthony Van Dyck. A diminutive figure, elegantly clothed and fastidiously groomed, he had a face that revealed his humorless, pedantic, single-minded determination. Yet it also depicted a man who seems eternally depressed, borne down by his cares. This was not the carriage or outlook of his father. The description left by Sir James Weldon is both too famous and too delicious to omit.

> He was of a middle stature, more corpulent through his clothes than in his body, yet fat enough; his clothes ever being made large and easy the doublets quilted for stiletto-proof; his breeches in great plaits, and full stuffed. He was naturally of a timid disposition, which was the greatest reason of his quilted doublets. His eyes large, ever rolling after any stranger came in his presence, inasmuch as many for shame have left the room, being out of countenance. His beard was very thin; his tongue too large for his mouth, which ever made him speak full in the mouth, and made him drink very uncomely, as if eating his drink, which came out into the cup on each side of his mouth. His skin was as soft as taffeta sarcenet, which felt so because he never washed his hands—only rubbed his finger-ends slightly with the wet end of a napkin. His legs were very weak, having had, as was thought, some foul play in his youth, or rather before he was born, that he was not able to stand at seven years of age—that weakness made him ever leaning on other men's shoulders. His walk was ever circular, his fingers ever in that walk fiddling about his codpiece.

Charles's marriage to a French Catholic princess, Henrietta Maria of France, soon after his accession, was regarded as an affront by Presbyterians and Anglicans alike. His attempt to revive his father's Commission for Grievances was met with so much opposition that he was forced to abandon it. But his most challenging effort was the Act of Revocation. It was traditional in Scotland for a king, upon attaining his majority, to resume grants of crown lands made during his minority. But Charles was twenty-four on his accession and had been an active partner with his father in the governance of the realm for some years. Yet his Act of Revocation extended back to 1540 and included church as well as crown lands. By fixing the right of collection with the landowner rather than with the "titulars," those to whom the lands had been granted originally, and by guaranteeing the share of the clergy, Charles effected an important and long-lasting settlement of the tithe question to the direct benefit of both landowner and the church. His manner of carrying out this reform served rather to alienate all three groups, nobility or titulars, landowners, and clergy. By his persevering in what has been termed "the greatest economic revolution recorded in Scottish history," Charles united most of the society against him.

In 1633 Charles made his long-awaited visit to Scotland. He was met with apprehension and anxiety rather than joy, and the fears that preceded his arrival were soon realized. At his coronation ceremony in the chapel of Holyrood House, he ordered English rites used and prescribed white vestments, which smacked of popery to the more puritanical clergy present. But it was the king's orders to the Parliament that gave the true measure of his intent. The agenda was prepared by the Lords of the Articles, chosen after the model introduced by his father. The nobles chose eight bishops, all of whom were the king's men. The eight selected in turn found eight docile nobles from among the sixty or so eligible. The sixteen in turn co-opted eight commissioners of the shires and eight of the burghs. The thirty-two, clearly subservient to the crown, joined by eight officers of state, prepared a series of bills to the king's consequences. Sir James Balfour, a contemporary, deemed it "the ground-stone of all the mischief that followed after, both to this king's Government and family; and whoever were the contrivers of it deserve, they and all their posterity, to be reputed by these three kingdoms infamous and accursed for ever."

Like so much of what Charles did, the manner in which he did it was as much the problem as the act itself. To begin with, he rushed through its enforcement, forcing the issue, rather than working out a settlement gradually. The church lands had been granted out by his father to build up a body of new nobles who would be loyal to the crown and to set against the haughty, autonomous clan chiefs. Charles's action now alienated these lay supporters of the crown, forcing them into an alliance with the clergy. It was Charles's intention to permit the current holders to compound for their properties and retain their titles; of this he gave no intimation to allay their fears.

Few families in Scotland were unaffected. He removed the civil judges, the Lords of the Sessions, from the Privy Council to insure an obedient majority to confirm his orders and then appointed commissioners to supervise the survey and negotiate the agreements. The surrender of teinds, or tithes, was most praiseworthy and farsighted. The ownership of tithes had largely fallen into lay hands. They were often rapaciously collected and then put to sectarian use. He permitted the heritors or life-tenants to buy out their obligation to pay the satisfaction and presented them to the Parliament. The three estates, deliberating and voting together, were not permitted to vote on individual bills but had to consider them *en masse*. Little wonder then that they passed 168 acts in ten days, including the ratification of the Act of Revocation.

Equally critical were acts which confirmed all the legislation of King James concerning the nature of the church, thus reaffirming the episcopal structure the king had imposed. Another bill gave the king the right to determine the apparel of the clerics. When some members protested the ban on debate and prepared a written supplication of their views, the king refused to receive it. A year later he tried Lord Balmerino for treason, merely for having a copy of the supplication in his possession.

The basis if not need for revolt had been given by the king in the Act of Revocation. The immediate grounds for starting a revolt were derived once more from the church. In 1636 the king, on his sole authority, introduced a book of canons in which he was designated as the absolute head of the church. To enforce his orders he created a new Court of High Commission in October, 1634. The climax came in 1637, when he introduced a new service book to replace John Knox's Book of Common Order. Modeled on the Anglican book of common prayer, its use was made mandatory and it was first employed in the service at St. Giles on July 21. The service was disliked on many grounds: it appeared popish; it hailed from England; it was imposed by royal order; and it was believed to be the work of Laud. A riot broke out in the church, and the uproar was replicated throughout the country. Petitions against its further use were denied by the king through the Privy Council and that body was moved to Linlithgow and other sites to avoid pressure from the Edinburgh mob.

In 1635 the great Flemish portraitist Anthony van Dyck was engaged to picture Charles I in his hunting attire.

When it was exhibited in 1830,
George Harvey's painting *The
Covenanters' Preaching* was accompanied by a verse from Graham's
"Sabbath": Dauntlessly/ the
scatter'd few would meet, in some
deep dell,/ By rocks o'er
canopied, to hear the voice,/
Their faithful pastor's voice.

The several estates were united in their opposition. Unable to deal
directly with the distant and perambulating council, the protestors
created four committees, or tables of four, each to represent the classes in
meetings with representatives of the crown. The tables in turn presented
a collective supplication to the council demanding that the bishops, the
dominant element among officeholders on the council, be removed so as not to
prejudice the hearing of the petitions; the supplication also urged the recall of
the new liturgy. The struggle was joined when Charles's proclamation in
response was read at Stirling on February 19, 1638. He simply declared all
the supplications and convocations illegal. The aggrieved laymen now
resorted to arms. They invited the nation to enter into a covenant with them
to demonstrate the breadth of their support. The National League and
Covenant proffered the citizens on February 28 was based, cleverly, on the
Negative Confession of Faith drawn up by order of James VI in 1581
against the Catholics. The bishops fled south to escape justice at the hands
of the mob.

Charles appointed James, marquis of Hamilton, as royal commissioner
to make a settlement with the rebels. He was a poor choice, indecisive
and lacking in candor. As one in the royal line, he had personal aspirations
to the throne. When Charles agreed to a General Assembly of the church,
Hamilton presided at its meeting in Glasgow in November. When those
assembled attacked the bishops and sought to deprive them, the marquis
dissolved the assembly. It continued to meet without him and after

deposing the bishops, remodeled the church, nullifying the Book of Canons, the new liturgy, and the Five Articles of Perth, restoring the church to the Presbyterian model of the early Reformation.

In this assembly the earls of Montrose and Argyll emerged as the leaders of the opposition to the crown. Since the king refused to ratify the acts of this illegal body, the rebels took to arms. Seizing Edinburgh and four other royal strongholds in March, 1639, they defeated a royalist force under the marquis of Huntley in the northeast, turned back an invasion fleet captained by Hamilton, and sent an army south to Berwick under the command of Alexander Leslie. When Charles met Leslie at Berwick in June he had only eight thousand troops to the Covenanters twenty-one thousand, and he sued for a parley. The Pacification of Berwick, which the First Bishops' War ended, was a surrender to all the rebels' demands.

The king called a new assembly in August, which sanctioned the acts of the Glasgow Assembly; the Privy Council was ordered to make subscription to the covenant compulsory throughout the land. The assembly was followed by a Parliament which ratified the work of the previous body. But when the king's commissioner refused to abolish the episcopacy, the Covenanters resorted once more to arms.

In the Second Bishops' War, Charles had failed to obtain resources from the English Parliament. Once again outnumbered and resigned to meeting their demands, he sent commissioners to meet his northern subjects at Ripon in October. This time the Scots would not disband until they had come to an agreement with the English Parliament as well. New elections in 1641 in England had returned the "Long Parliament," which was dominated by the opposition. The king, unable to stem the equally aggressive English commoners, returned to Scotland for aid.

After accepting the acts of the Glasgow Assembly and the even more humiliating demand that his official appointments be made with the advice and approbation of Parliament, he was unable to obtain funds for troops, so great was the suspicion and lack of trust he engendered. A plot to liberate the more moderate leaders whom the Covenanters had imprisoned miscarried, and the king returned to England empty-handed. When he took to the field against English rebels in August, 1642, raising his standard at Nottingham, the Scots now had to choose which side they would support.

The success of the Scottish opposition to the crown had been the result of a union of several parties—the kirk, the nobility, and the gentry or lairds. The objectives of these groups were hardly identical, and even within them there were factions that could easily come to the surface and disrupt the apparent unity of the Covenanters. The religious focus of the opposition was due to the convenience such an issue gave to the king's opponents to mobilize the country and the predominant role played by the kirk. In England the laity had been able to keep the church firmly under control and had determined the nature of the reformation. Scotland was so underdeveloped and backward, the feudal nobility so dominant in the country, that the independent, self-confident laity which characterized England had failed to emerge. Moreover, the country had not developed a strong merchant class or educated professional or officer class to complement them. The clergy had filled the gap and had consequently established their hold on the society. The supine behavior of the Parliament meant that the General Assembly was the closest approximation to an independent, national representative legislature, and it filled that function not only in the seventeenth century but, due to the Union of the Parliaments in 1707, has done so down to the present century.

The Edinburgh riots in 1637 had been organized by two clerics,

Alexander Henderson, from Fife, and David Dickson, from the west, in consultation with Lord Balmerino and Sir Thomas Hope, the king's advocate. The petitions to the council to suspend the prayer book had also been organized by Dickson. The Edinburgh meeting of the estates which followed and the tables which they created to represent them were only possible because of the support already generated by the ministers. The national covenant was the joint endeavor of Henderson and Archibald Johnston of Wariston, "a brilliant and fanatically religious young lawyer."

Despite the initial unity of the estates in opposition to the king, rifts between these groups appeared as early as the Glasgow Assembly of November, 1638. The ministers were disturbed by the substantial intrusion of laymen. Though Henderson was elected as moderator and Wariston as clerk, the body of assessors chosen by Henderson to assist him was dominated by laymen. Though the assembly had a majority of ministers (140 out of 240), it was elders such as the earls of Rothes and Loudoun who took the leading roles, and Lorne, heir to the earl of Argyll, who emerged as the most powerful of the Covenanters. And it was the pusillanimity of the king, his slow reaction to defy the Covenanters, and the weakness of Hamilton which caused so many lairds and nobles to accede to the militants. The growing disenchantment of the earl of Montrose was evident as early as June, 1640, when he objected to the convening of Parliament in the absence of the king or his commissioner.

The committee of estates appointed by the Parliament ignored the proper claim of the earl of Montrose to be charged with the subjection of the anti-Covenanters in Atholl and impowered Argyll to head the expedition and raise men from his own sheriffdom for that purpose. Argyll's expedition to the north and east was successful, but it drew him into further conflict with Montrose. The decision to invade England in August was carried through in a high-handed manner by Argyll, the committee, and the army. The more moderate members were ignored and took refuge in the Cumbernauld Band, a pact of sympathizers led by Montrose which, though subscribing to the covenant, was clearly aimed at Argyll and his supporters. The commissioners who negotiated with representatives of the English Parliament at Ripon in October, 1640, and thereafter at London were all zealous Covenanters. In London they were joined by four clergymen sent to extend the Presbyterian revolution to England and overturn its episcopal system. By the fall of 1641, when the Scots army was paid off and sent home and the commissioners had been dispatched, it became clear that the English parliamentary leaders had rejected the model of the Scottish church in favor of a modified episcopal system more reflective of their own tradition. The emissaries on their return found the unity of the covenant dissipated by the reaction to Argyll's claims for leadership.

By the time the treaty of London was completed, in June, 1641, the breakup of the Covenanters was already advanced. The treaty itself fell short of the original demands but it did not seem politic to continue the negotiations any longer. Significantly, when the treaty was signed in August, after approval by the Scots Parliament, only six of the eleven commissioners were empowered to sign. The loyalty of the other five was already under suspicion. The existence of the Cumbernauld Band had become known in November, 1640, and its dissolution followed. But Montrose and some kindred sympathizers had opened direct negotiations with the king. If the king would guarantee the religion and liberties of Scotland the "plotters" were prepared to defend his cause. They were afraid that the king's concessions had gone too far and that Scotland would be reduced to anarchy, with the commonalty pitted against the aristocracy.

James Graham, fifth earl of Montrose, emerged as the key supporter of Charles I in Scotland in the events leading up to the civil war, in which he emerged as the greatest general after Cromwell. Compromised by the vacillation and unreliability of the king, he escaped to Norway in 1646, only to return in 1650 to avenge Charles's death. He was eventually defeated, brought to Edinburgh, and sentenced to death by Parliament.

129

The Irish rebellion now occupied the attention of all parties both in Scotland and England. The Covenanters favored sending troops to protect the Scots in Ulster, to forestall invasions by the Irish, and as an excuse to maintain their army. The king was desirous of Scottish assistance to reduce his dependence on the English Parliament and lessen the possibility of the return of the Scots army into England. The English Parliament was in agreement because it did not want to finance an army for the king nor did it want to weaken its own position in England by manning an army in Ireland.

The army was in the field by April, 1642. The Scots followed events in England closely, recognizing that the coming conflict between king and Parliament there would inevitably involve them. The General Assembly, which met in the summer, appointed a standing commission to act for them in concert with the Committee of the Estates, now known as the Conservators of Peace, and the Privy Council. By December the council had received appeals from both the Parliament and the king to intervene in the civil war which had broken out in August. The royalist and parliamentary parties in Scotland prepared to act each according to its lights. Montrose offered to raise an army for Charles, but the king preferred to take the advice of Hamilton, a dubious counselor. In August the General Assembly, in concert with the Convention, accepted the offer of an alliance from the English Parliament. The basis was the Solemn

The chiefs of the Highland clans were virtually powers unto themselves until the abolition of their heritable jurisdictions in the eighteenth century. Their adoption of individual liveries and colors, their homage to a personal family and lineage, and carriage and conduct befitting independent princes are reflected in this painting of 1660 by J. Michael Wright.

League and Covenant. Finally, on January 19, 1644, Alexander Leslie, now the earl of Leven, led the Scots host across the Tweed to remain in England for three years. The intervention of the Scots army was decisive. It wrested control of the north away from royalist forces and at the battle of Marston Moor on July 2 gave the victory to Parliament.

Meantime Montrose had received his long-desired commission to organize the royalist forces in Scotland on February 1. He slipped away north to Perth to take command of a small force of Highlanders and Irish sent over by the marquis of Antrim. Their leader was Alastair Macdonald, a gigantic and ferocious Highland chieftain. Though Montrose's forces were small in number (1600 men), they fought successfully against far larger, but ineptly led Covenanters. In one battle after another Montrose defeated troops of the kirk, which culminated in the defeat of Argyll himself at Inverlochy on February 2, 1645. His exploits were capped by the sack of the Covenanters under Baillie at Kilsythin, Stirlingshire, on August 15. Glasgow, then Edinburgh capitulated, and Montrose was so much the conqueror of Scotland that he was emboldened to summon a parliament in the king's name to meet at Glasgow in October. But the ultimate triumph was to elude his grasp. By employing the barbaric Celts to achieve his aims, he had turned the rest of his countrymen against him. When the king's forces in England were vanquished at Naseby in June, the Scots army in the south was no longer required and returned home under Leslie to meet the royalist champion of the north. On September 13, at Philiphaugh, near Selkirk, Montrose's forces were routed by David Leslie. Those of his followers who were taken were put to the sword. No one was spared.

The Covenanters now ruled supreme. The king himself threw the next apple of discord when he rode into the Scottish camp on May 5, 1646, and surrendered to the army of his northern kingdom. He presented them with an impossible situation. If they let him go abroad he would unquestionably return with new support to renew the civil war. As he refused to accept the covenant he could not be taken to Scotland, where his presence would give heart to his supporters.

When he spurned their offer of assistance on their terms they had only one choice. They sold him to the English Parliament for the payment of the arrears due them. But though he was returned in January, 1647, and the Scots troops made their way back across the Tweed in February, negotiations between Charles and the Scots had not yet ended. The nobles, having achieved their aims, were prepared to work for his restoration. Three commissioners concluded an "engagement" with Charles at his prison on the Isle of Wight, putting the Scottish army at his disposal. Hamilton met the estates to gain their assent and found a commanding majority for the agreement, so weak was the love for the covenant among the laity.

The Parliament sent an ultimatum to its English counterpart demanding the liberation of the king and the establishment of Presbyterianism in England. But when Hamilton moved to raise an army, the dominies preached resistance and the ragtail force which resulted was quickly defeated by Cromwell after a few days of fighting in August. Cromwell himself made his way to Edinburgh to parlay with Argyll. The Covenanters and the kirk were once more in power. Events now moved out of Scots control. In December Pride's Purge put an end to the power of the English Parliament and on January 30, 1649, Cromwell and the independents executed Charles I.

The purge under different auspices was paralleled in Scotland. By the Act of Classes passed in January, all those who had supported Montrose or the engagement were barred from office. But though the kirk reigned, the Scots were horrified by news of the king's death. Charles II was immediately proclaimed, though with the prudent stipulation that he would not be permitted to assume authority until he accepted the National League and Covenant. By the summer of 1650 he had landed in Scotland and made his peace with the kirk. But the new king's rule was short-lived. Cromwell was not one to let events dictate his conduct. Responding rapidly to the challenge, he moved into Scotland and after a short campaign defeated the Scots at Dunbar on September 3. Though the war dragged on for another year and General Monck was left to complete it a year to the day later, the defeat of Charles by Cromwell at Worcester gave Cromwell indisputed control over the three kingdoms.

For Scotland the radical phase of the civil war and Commonwealth was yet to come. The naive Presbyterians had thought they could enforce their discipline on the English. Now they found themselves the object of reformers. Although the government of the 1650s was a military dictatorship managed by the major generals of the army, the English were nevertheless determined to impose their social revolution on the Scots. The basic cause was to protect the revolution in England. Scotland and Ireland must be made safe. Cromwell and his soldiers saw their mission in

Head of the most powerful clan in Scotland and a leader of the Covenanters, Archibald Campbell, first marquess of Argyll, made common cause with Cromwell and the Roundheads in England in order to reduce the king's power in Scotland. By shifting his allegiance to Charles II after Charles I's execution, he incurred the enmity of the Commonwealth, and lived under a ban until the Restoration. Evidence of his collaboration with Cromwell led to his execution on the warrant of Charles II in 1661.

another light. They sought to decentralize power and laicize the church. The Parliament would be in the control of the country gentry. The narrow and exclusive kirk was to be curbed. First promulgated in the Protector's Council by the Ordinance of Union in 1654, the reforms were confirmed by the second Parliament of the Protectorate in 1656. The church courts were emasculated, the clergy put under the civil law. Toleration rather than a compulsory subscription to the covenant became the byword.

The reforms were far-reaching. The laws of Scotland were now merged with those of England, the courts remodeled, the system of justices of the peace extended to the whole of the realm. Gone were the hereditary rights and jurisdictions of the chieftains. English justices were sent on circuit in the country to enforce the new order. What started as a puritan revolution to remodel the church in England ended as a social revolution to remodel the society and constitution of Scotland.

Many of the reforms were salutary and enlightened. The use of Latin was abolished in the courts. The control of the kirk over the universities was terminated, the school system enlarged, the curriculum reformed, even a college of physicians established. Ministers were provided for the neglected Highlands. English-style poor law administration and relief were introduced. But the revolution failed in the north as it did in the south. It never enlisted the sympathies of any substantial element of the ruling classes. After Cromwell's death it was General Monck and the Scots army who marched on London, restored order to the disintegrating government of Cromwell's son and heir, returned the purged members to the Parliament, and managed the return of the king. The period of innovation was at an end. The old order was restored.

The breakdown of the Cromwellian union had begun with the dissolution of the last Parliament of the Protectorate and the recall of the Long Parliament in England in 1659. The Scottish deputies petitioned for a new union, but the contest between the Presbyterians and the sectarians, each seeking a privileged position, delayed a decision on the bill until the dissolution of the Long Parliament in October gave it the quietus. The dissolution gave Monck the excuse to summon a meeting of representatives of the burghs and shires to maintain the peace in his absence. These commissioners and the successor convention which met in February, 1660, sought to perpetuate the union. But the restoration of Charles II killed all immediate prospects for this goal. Scotland was to have a Parliament of its own once again, but, like the previous one, a hapless tool in the hands of the king.

With the end of the Commonwealth and Cromwellian union, the customs union was also abolished. The economic prosperity encouraged by the elimination of economic barriers received a sharp setback. But the greatest loss was the stability and liberty created by the stern but tolerant protector.

The return of the king was greeted by most Scots with rejoicing. But the king soon gave the lie to their hopes. The next three decades were to bring a government as oppressive and tyrannical as Scotland was ever to see. The church was once more made the creature of the executive branch of government. A new Privy Council was appointed without reference to the Parliament, the natural councillors of the crown. Those chosen were all submissive to the royal authority.

When the Parliament was finally summoned on the first of January, 1661, it proved as amenable to the royal will as any of its predecessors. An extraordinary 393 acts were passed before it was prorogued on July 12. By then the absolute monarchy of James VI was restored. By a single Rescissory Act, every act of Parliament since 1633 was declared null and void. While it was still sitting, a clear message to all those who opposed the king was registered by the execution of the marquis of Argyll.

The fate of the church could have been guessed. In England the full episcopal structure was restored. The church had sent two emissaries to persuade the king of the efficacy of the kirk in its present form. James Sharp had represented the Resolution party of the church to Cromwell and was regarded as a reasonable and shrewd agent. Robert Leighton was an intellectual, and far less worldly, more sincere. The two returned as prelates, Sharp as archbishop of St. Andrews and primate of Scotland, Leighton as bishop of Dunblane. The duplicity of Sharp after his return soon made him the most hated man in Scotland. His assassination in 1679 was regarded by all but the most hypocritical as a fitting climax to his apostasy.

In December, 1661, four bishops were consecrated; in May another six. In the same month legislation was passed by the Parliament permitting the return of the bishops and restoring them to their former responsibilities and rights. They soon demonstrated their worth. The restoration of the former method of selecting the Lords of the Articles gave control once more to the bishops, and they made good advantage of their opportunity. The king's instruments were now in place. It followed that the parish clergy must be reduced to complaisancy. On October 1, 1662, the council decreed that the ministers must pay homage to their bishops or lay patrons within the month. A new period of Babylonian servitude was at hand.

The English lion holds the Scottish thistle, emblematic of Charles II's restoration and the reconciliation of the two kingdoms.

This detail of an engraving of Dunblane is from *Theatrum Scotiae*, published by John Sleyer in 1693.

In contrast to his father and grandfather, Charles II allowed his English ministers to play a major role in Scottish affairs. Lauderdale emerged as the principal adviser and earned a place in the ruling CABAL, which succeeded as the collective head of the English government after the fall of Clarendon in 1667. (Cabal was a contemporary acronym made up of the initial letters of the names of the chief ministers. The "L" stood for Lauderdale.) His rival, Middleton, was disgraced by his challenge to the entrenched secretary in London.

In Scotland the executive was conducted by the restored Privy Council. Like its predecessor it was dominated by the aristocracy. Once again the lack of trained administrators to man an efficient government was evident. It had the same problem of trying to maintain law and order, especially in the Highlands, without the aid of troops. Tax revenue had dropped with the end of the customs union. Trade was off. But two-thirds of the council's business was taken up with matters affecting the church.

The remodeling of the church was intended to effect subordination to the crown. But the parishioners were recalcitrant. Many refused to disavow their old ministers. Even though they were forbidden their pulpits, the clerics continued to tend to their worshippers under penalty of sedition. Clerics foreign to the regions to which they were assigned met only with hostility and rebuff.

To relieve the council a Court of High Commission was created to deal with the offenders. Not the least who suffered under this persecution were nearly nine hundred supporters of the Commonwealth who had been exempted from the Act of Indemnity in 1662 and had to buy their pardon under penalty of imprisonment. To hasten their compliance, troops were quartered in their houses in 1666. These repressive measures inspired the inevitable rebellion. In November, 1666, a kidnapping of the military commander in the southwest sparked an uprising and a march on Edinburgh. Intercepted by government troops under Sir Thomas Dalziel, the rebels retreated west only to fall victim to Dalziel in battle in the Pentland Hills. Hangings and torture were the lot of the defeated until the intervention of Lauderdale mitigated the ferocity of the crown's commissioners.

With the exile of Middleton to Tangiers, Lauderdale was the unchallenged arbiter of Scotland for a dozen years. He was a man of considerable talent and real intellect though his crude behavior and coarse appearance capped by a shock of red hair belied his executive ability. He attracted able colleagues in the council, and his ministry revealed a flair for efficiency and creativity that was as welcome as it was unexpected. Though elevated customs barriers in France and restored barriers in England demanded greater efforts, trade generally prospered.

Glasgow was the main beneficiary of economic growth, advancing to become the second city in the nation. Leith, the port of Edinburgh, prospered from the Baltic trade for which it was the main entry. The 1670s saw a commercial boom as the neutral British kingdoms garnered trade at the expense of Holland, France, and the Scandinavian powers who were often engaged in hostilities. Shipping above all benefited from the circumstances, the number of carriers doubling during the course of the decade. Trade to the Baltic, to France, and to Holland peaked at levels among the highest of the century.

The legal profession and its discipline also show a marked advance in this period. Its greatest ornament was James Dalrymple, later first viscount Stair, one of the key figures in the creation of Scottish law as a coherent, rational system with a national identity yet firmly grounded on Roman models. His great work, the *Institutes* of 1681, was the fruit of his labors in the Lauderdale era. The age also produced Sir George Mackenzie of Rosehaugh, lord advocate in 1677, who wrote the standard treatise on Scottish criminal law. The Court of Justiciary, founded in 1672, soon established so strong a reputation that it was able to impose its will on men of all stations. The Court of Sessions as the principal civil court became a center and arbiter for the men of property and influence.

And finally the increase in litigation and in resort to law strengthened the legal profession, and it began to wield the kind of influence and power it had exerted in England for the better part of a century. A not unexpected result was the intrusion of this element into the Parliament in larger numbers and the employment of their expertise to provide a stand against the crown. Yet in spite of the ascendancy of the rule of law, so long as the executive power was unchecked by constitutional or legislative safeguards, it could serve as well to obstruct justice as prosecute it and to enforce tyranny rather than defeat it.

Of all the objectional proceedings of the Restoration government, the proscriptive enforcement of the church code was the most defied and least successful. After the Pentland rising of 1667, Lauderdale tried, through letters of indulgence, to entice the rejected ministers and their flocks back into the fold. Most of them stood fast. To add to the perplexities of the government, the episcopal synod of Glasgow was as strong in condemning the indulgence as were those at whom it was aimed. Conventicles—clandestine meetings led by the defrocked pastors— increased rapidly in number. Field preaching resulted when the worshipers were denied the use of the churches. The participants carried arms to defend their right to worship as they pleased.

Lauderdale responded with the Clanking Act of 1671, denying their right to bear arms. But it was to no avail. Ever more severe reprisals by the crown's agent only seemed to increase the fire and determination

above left: James, duke of Monmouth, was the eldest and favorite bastard of Charles II. Basing his right to the throne on the claim that Charles had in fact married his mother, thereby establishing his legitimacy, the young Protestant duke invaded England in 1685, thus contesting the crowns of Scotland and England with his uncle James II. His defeat and subsequent execution brought an end to a rash enterprise.

above right: Stuart ties to Scotland were reinforced in the Restoration period by the marriage of James, duke of Monmouth, to Anne Scott, second countess of Buccleuch in her own right and heiress to one of the greatest Scottish fortunes. In recognition of her precedence, Monmouth was created first duke of Buccleuch.

of the Covenanters. Perhaps encouraged by these signs of resistance, the nobility led by Hamilton spoke out against Lauderdale in the Parliament. A second indulgence promulgated in 1672 provoked still stronger reaction. To stifle the critics and reduce the protesters to submission, the crown applied sanctions first used against the Catholics. In 1674 landlords and masters were made responsible for the religious conformity of their tenants and servants. When this new power failed to fulfill the intent of its promoters, an act of council in 1677 required all landowners to sign a bond for the good behavior of their tenants. When many of the owners refused to acknowledge an order which they lacked the power to carry out, the government responded by introducing troops into the west to forestall a repeat of the Pentland rising. Even the quartering of soldiers on their property failed to produce the conformity required.

This campaign came to its inevitable and tragic conclusion in 1679. Following the murder of Archbishop Sharp, armed recusants defied the government in meetings west of Glasgow. When met by government forces, they routed their opponents and then moved on Glasgow. Failing to reduce the city's defenses, they retired to Hamilton, where they met a royal army commanded by the duke of Monmouth, bastard son of Charles, and a Scottish landowner by virtue of his marriage to the heir of the Buccleuchs. The Whiggamores, or Whigs, as the rebels were named (they gave their name to the political party formed in England at this time), were outnumbered and outsoldiered by the disciplined government forces. Some four hundred were killed, more than a thousand taken prisoner.

Lauderdale's term in office was over. Petitions from Scottish nobles and English commoners finally told. But the cure was worse than the illness. Lauderdale's replacement was the king's brother and heir, James, duke of York.

James was an exile from England because of the agitation over the popish plot and his Roman Catholicism. While he was away, the exclusion controversy raged, an effort by the Whigs, led by the earl of Shaftesbury, to exclude this papist from the English succession. In his government of Scotland, James was to demonstrate all that ruthlessness and obstinacy combined with vigor and determination that were to mark his short and unlamented reign as sovereign.

The Covenanters tipped their hand. By energetic field preaching in violation of the ban and through a series of inflammatory tracts declaring war on all those who conformed to the official church, they deliberately invited reprisal and prepared themselves for martyrdom. The government responded with the Test Act of 1681, which required all officeholders to take an oath to uphold the royal supremacy in church and state and disavow any intent to change the constitution, secular or religious. Another exodus of ministers followed. But the most notable figure to suffer from the act was Archibald, earl of Argyll, son of the civil war leader. By stating in Parliament that he would subscribe to the act only with reservations, he was held guilty of treason and permitted to flee the country. Though James returned to England, the government continued its policy of harassment. The Covenanters were all but exterminated, the group led by the fanatic Richard Cameron achieving undying fame as the Cameronians for their religious zeal and military prowess. The legacy of the duke of York in Scotland was an evil one.

When Charles II died in 1685, James succeeded him as James VII and II, the opposition to exclude him having been destroyed in the reaction which followed the popish plot. His accession was remarkably peaceful and for the nonce uneventful. The Parliaments of both kingdoms were packed with subservient royal supporters. Yet out of these complaisant assemblies and cowed citizens he managed to inspire an opposition which was to drive him from the throne.

137

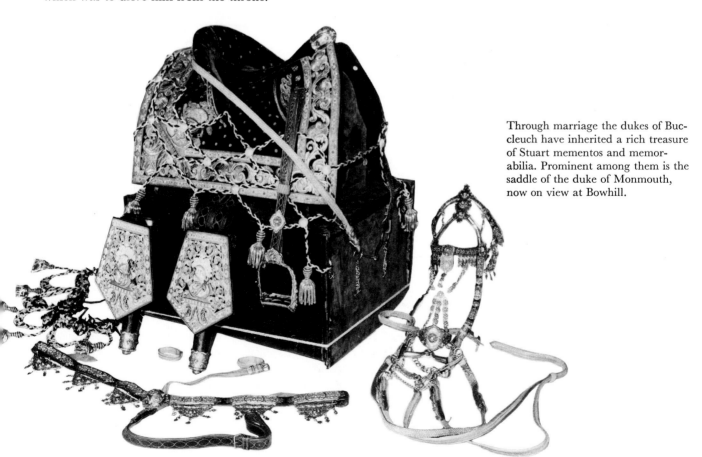

Through marriage the dukes of Buccleuch have inherited a rich treasure of Stuart mementos and memorabilia. Prominent among them is the saddle of the duke of Monmouth, now on view at Bowhill.

THE ROIALL PROGENEI OF OUR MOST SACRED KING IAMES BY THE grace of God King of E.S.F &I &c. Descended from ye victorius King H.7 & Elizabeth his wife wherin ye 2 devided fam̃ils ware vnited together.

The familie of Lancaster.   The familie of Yorke.

above: Obsessively concerned with the nature of his authority as king and a champion of hereditary descent, James II used print and picture to reinforce the legitimacy of his royal inheritance in England.

left: The Order of the Thistle is the highest order of Scottish chivalry. Conceived by James V, it was not formally instituted until 1687, when James VII created it to rouse the spirit of nationality among the Scots. This robe was worn by James, fourth earl of Perth, one of the original knights of the order.

Initially only the remnants of the Covenanters refused to submit. The government took this act of defiance at face value. As a consequence it was known as "the black year, the killing time." Hundreds of recusants who could not prove their loyalty suffered transportation to the American colonies and the amputation of an ear. The estates were summoned by the duke of Queensberry, acting as the king's commissioner. The assembled gave ample proof of their docility and obedience, meeting the king's demands for revenues and passing still more severe laws against the recusants. By the terms of the new legislation, any individual whose presence at a conventicle could be proved was to be punished by death and the confiscation of his property.

While Parliaments sat in both countries, each was witness to an invasion by exiles bent on dethroning James. In Scotland the expeditionary force from Holland was led by the earl of Argyll. Unfortunately for the returning peer, the government was forewarned and had quartered troops in his own country to prevent a sympathetic uprising. Landings in the Orkneys and on Mull resulted in only modest reinforcements. Division in the party which accompanied him and alert dogging by the royalist forces forestalled any effective resistance. Argyll himself became separated from his followers and was apprehended on the road to Glasgow. Taken to Edinburgh, he was immediately executed on the charge of treason.

The king soon gave evidence of his intention to change the constitution of the country. The steady promotion given to Roman Catholics in the government and in the army united Presbyterians of every stripe in the defense of their religion. Conversion became the only way to favor.

139

The government was soon reduced to a clutch of Roman Catholics drawn out of their secluded retirement and sycophantic converts who were despised equally by their new co-religionists as well as their old. When Parliament refused to do James's bidding in repealing the penal laws against the Catholics, it was dismissed and the Privy Council remodeled until it was prepared to carry out the act by executive fiat.

Even the bishops of the established church demurred and were systematically removed. To gain adherents to his cause, the king issued three successive letters of indulgence which allowed dissenters "to serve God after their own way and manner" provided they accepted his authority in the state. This action had the unexpected effect of returning the exiled ministers to their parishes, where they quickly took the lead in organizing resistance to arbitrary government. Their return gave a unity and sense of purpose that was a major factor in the success of the revolution the next year. Only field preaching remained under a ban.

The end to James's reign came suddenly and without Scottish intervention. William of Orange, stadholder of the Netherlands, consort of James's elder daughter Mary, and nephew to James by his mother, was the deliverer. Called to save Holland from the overweening ambitions of Louis XIV and the might of his armies in 1672, William had turned back the French, and then had gone on to build a great European coalition to stem French aggression and restore the balance of power in Europe. As he and his allies entered a new and perhaps decisive stage in this contest in 1688, with the outbreak of the Nine Years' War and Louis's invasion of the Rhineland, William recognized that he needed English gold and ships to sustain his forces. Moreover, the birth of a son to James and his second wife, Mary of Modena, in 1688, meant that William's wife, Mary, hitherto the heir to the English throne and he himself as third in line after his wife's sister Anne, would now be deprived of their inheritance. The infant Prince of Wales would be raised a Roman Catholic, and the Protestant religion of which William was also the European champion was now in mortal danger in the British kingdoms. Embarking from Holland, he ferried his troops across the channel to make a landing in the southwest of England at Torbay. Prior to his embarkation he sent a special message to the people of Scotland offering to free them from the misdeeds of King James and save the Protestant religion. He was accepted as a deliverer in both countries.

The revolution in England was accomplished virtually without bloodshed. The king's troops deserted rather than fight the Protestant hero and the king himself, afraid for his own life and that of his family, fled to France with his queen and the infant prince. William was left as *de facto* ruler, and his position was soon confirmed by an offer of the crown made jointly to himself and Mary. In Ireland the Roman Catholics had already taken control of the organs of government and declared for King James. In Scotland a power vacuum followed the "abdication" of the king. Many prominent Scots rushed off to London to make their peace with William, and at their urging he summoned a meeting of the Scottish estates.

When it met on March 14, 1689, conditions were most unsettled. The duke of Gordon held the castle for James, and Edinburgh and the surrounding countryside housed supporters of both James and William. William followed the practice of Charles II in naming a Privy Council before the meeting of the estates. He kept no portion of the council in England, however, retaining only a secretary. This gave the occupant of that office, Lord Melville, considerable authority.

The Parliament was not to prove so tractable. As his chief minister in Scotland, the king chose Sir John Dalrymple, whom he appointed lord advocate. William's letter to the convention in 1689 was temperate and modest. The success of William's friends in the convention was due in no small matter to the favorable response his invitation received. When William's nominee, James, duke of Hamilton, was chosen as president of the convention, the allegiance of the majority became clear. On April 11, it passed a claim of right defining the constitutional power of the estates and made an offer of the crown to William and Mary. They accepted the offer in London on May 11.

The irregular nature of the convention meant that there was no Committee of the Articles, and the participants enjoyed a freedom of action previously unknown in the history of the estates. When it reconvened as a Parliament in June, 1689, it abolished the committee over the objections of the king. A fierce contest ensued between the obstreperous legislature and the executive. Parliament insisted on naming the Lords of Session. The king refused and ordered the court to sit. Parliament issued a counter order and the court was silent. When the session came to an end, early in August, numerous issues were left unresolved, the courts were closed, a scheme for the church had not been approved, and no taxes had been voted for the support of the army. The heady air of freedom and the lack of restraints had turned the legislative process into one of near anarchy.

For the moment concerns about the Parliament were set aside. A Jacobite insurrection occupied the government's attention. Edinburgh Castle had been surrendered to the forces of the crown on June 13. But a much greater threat loomed in the Highlands. The Jacobite party (after Jacobus, the Latin name of James) in Scotland was far stronger in England than in Scotland. The presence of a greater number of Roman Catholics, the small but politically significant body of Episcopalians for whom there was no place in the remodeled kirk, and Highlanders who resented Lowland politicians and their control of the organs of state; these and other disaffected groups brought ready recruits to Viscount Dundee, who mobilized the north in favor of the exiled monarch.

Sir John Graham of Claverhouse, now Viscount Dundee, the scourge of the Covenanters under Charles II, gathered a Highland army at Dundee. Overburdened by demands for troops and funds in other theaters, William had few resources to spare to put down the rebels. Major-General Hugh Mackay took what could be scraped together and met Dundee near the castle of Blair Atholl in Perthshire on July 27. Meeting on a rocky hillside, the Highlanders had the advantage of the heights and routed Mackay's men in a precipitous descent. Only the halt of the victors to collect the spoils of the battlefield and the cover of night enabled Mackay to withdraw with the survivors. The death of Dundee did give hope for a reversal of fortunes at the next engagement.

The battle of Killiecrankie was to be the only Jacobite success. The agent of their ultimate destruction was the Cameronians, the persecuted victims of the royal brothers. Persuaded to accept service in William's army in order to mete out retribution on their hated oppressors, they enlisted as a regiment under unique conditions of service. They proved a formidable host. On August 21 at Dunkeld they repelled an assault by a Highland force four times their strength. The military threat to the new regime in Scotland was now ended.

The Parliament was convened on April 15, 1690. Melville, direct, able, trusted, was sent up from London to act as commissioner. Forewarned that the government's majority was small, the king and his agents took effective measures to protect their plurality. Discrete bribes helped to ensure a pliant body of supporters. The church was the main topic of debate. Resolutions denouncing royal supremacy and restoring all Presbyterian ministers ejected since 1661 showed the way to a settlement. The ratification of the Westminster Confession as the creed and the triumphant restoration of presbytery as the basis of the government of the church completed the task.

The abolition of lay patronage was a final blow to the Stuart system of church governance and one passed over William's objections. The implementation of these acts was left to the General Assembly, which met in October. Commissioners were appointed to review the sitting ministers. Those sympathetic to episcopacy were summarily dismissed, and a series of ejections, especially in the north, appeared to repeat the age-old pattern. But now the laity were left in peace. Two dissenting bodies survived outside the church—the Episcopalians and the Cameronians. Unity in faith was sacrificed to the stern demands of the strict Presbyterians.

Though liberty had been restored to the realm and royal efforts to impose a hierarchical structure on the church were permanently abandoned, William's rule was not very attractive to his Scottish subjects. The Highlanders renewed the war on behalf of James in 1690 but were soon dispersed by the government. As the western districts seemed to be the main source of possible future discontents, Mackay established a fort at Inverlochy and named it in honor of the king. But the continuing threat of French intervention and continuing operations in Ireland through 1691 were disquieting. The council sought to defuse the discontent in the north by first arranging a truce and then by buying off the chieftains with claims against Argyll. When some clans held back, the threat of extreme

Captain Robert Campbell, fifth laird of Glenlyon, leader of the band of soldiers who massacred the Macdonalds at Glencoe, was easily persuaded to carry out this act of savagery because his own clan pride was involved. The act was all the more outrageous because the perpetrators, by murdering their unsuspecting hosts, violated the unwritten law of Highland hospitality.

measures to enforce obedience and submission had the desired effect.

By the deadline of January 1, 1692, all but one clan had subscribed to the oath of allegiance. Alexander Macdonald, chief of Glencoe, long an opponent of the government, waited until too late and then when he decided to make his submission did not find a proper official to administer the oath until January 6. Dalrymple, with a personal grudge against Macdonald and anxious to set an example for potential malcontents, represented the circumstances in such a way to the king that William gave the order to administer fire and sword to force submission. Dalrymple's agents visited the clan at Glencoe, enjoyed their hospitality, and then fell upon them unawares early in the morning. Thirty-eight were murdered, some eighty escaped only because of the clumsy execution of the massacre. The barbarity of the proceedings and the unethical conduct of the ministers aroused strong protests against the government. Dalrymple was forced to retire from the king's service. The ignominy of the act reached to William. At the very least it left a sense of ill will and distrust that marred the king's relations with his subjects to the end of his reign.

The strongest basis for discontent was the economic reverses which impaired the prosperity of the country in the 1690s. For the 1690s saw a famine which, if not the worst in Scottish history, is the best remembered and also the last. At the beginning of the decade the country was prosperous. The expansion of trade which occurred in the 1670s had been attenuated in the 1680s, but the level was still substantial. Crops were good and food supplies could be supplemented by imports from the Baltic.

The outbreak of war in Europe into which Scotland was drawn by its new king caused the first reversal. Trade to the Continent was interrupted or terminated. This was followed by a series of bad harvests. Added to these calamities were the depredations of French privateers. The shortage of grainstuffs and the consequent high prices hit the poor particularly hard. Their misery was accentuated by the changes in church government, which resulted in a substantial cut in poor funds. The crisis had reached national proportions by 1695, and the bad harvest of that year was repeated in 1696 and 1698. By the turn of the century the crisis was over. The country lost 5 to 15 percent of its population in the last five years of the century due to starvation, typhus, and emigration to Ulster.

The other great calamity of the reign was the collapse of the Darien scheme. Excluded from the trading with the English colonies after the Restoration, Scotland smarted under this prohibition and the profits reaped by mainland Europe in trading with other continents. The steady exodus of immigrants, especially to the Americas, whether by choice or by order, had provided the basis for a lively colonial trade. The more enterprising leaders at home were now determined to follow the example of their southern rivals, and at their urging Parliament created "a company trading to Africa and the Indies" in 1695. Efforts were made to raise capital in England and on the Continent, but the active opposition of English merchants, jealous of any competition, frustrated their efforts. Nothing daunted, the projectors now raised the extraordinary sum of £300,000 wholly from domestic sources. On the advice of the economist William Paterson, the decision was taken in 1696 to establish a colony on the isthmus of Darien (Panama). Here, where the two continents of the Americas and the two great oceans of the world were joined, was the nexus of what could become a great trading empire. An expedition with twelve hundred settlers put out in July, 1698. Less than a year later the colony had to be abandoned, the victim of poor planning, tropical diseases, English hostility, and Spanish arms. A second expedition fared as badly. The country was incensed. The loss of such a great investment could not easily be borne by the poor and backward country. England and William were given the blame.

In the month of March, 1702, when William died, to be succeeded by his sister-in-law Anne, England and a reluctant Scotland were once more committed to another continental war. The War of the Spanish Succession, which lasted until 1713, was the first of the international, trade-inspired conflicts between England and France which were to give England its maritime and economic predominance by the end of the eighteenth century. Heavily committed on the Continent both in man power and money to provide the armies to withstand French aggression, England could not afford to have a hostile power on its northern border. So long as the Union of the Crowns lasted, it seemed possible to coerce Scotland to march to English pipes. But Anne's only surviving son had died in 1700 and with him the hope of a native-born, Protestant heir to succeed her. William had persuaded the English Parliament to settle the crown on the electress Sophia of Hanover and her heirs. He died, however, without securing the succession in Scotland.

The Scots, still smarting from the failure of the Darien scheme and indignant at being harnessed to England's interests and needs, now saw their opportunity. William had recommended a union to his successor, but commissioners appointed by Anne in 1702 to treat of one failed for lack of English interest. A new Parliament was elected in Scotland in 1703, the first since 1689, and it proved an almost insurmountable obstacle to a peaceful solution of the contest between the two countries. Its membership was divided into three parties: a court party; a country party dedicated to Scottish interests and headed by the duke of Hamilton; and a Jacobite party, composed of opponents of the regime and the revolution settlement in church and state. The latter two, united in their animosity toward England (if and when they cooperated), could have sufficient interest to carry the Parliament. This Parliament now put Scotland on a collision course with England. After opening the trade of foreign wines to permit French imports, then affronting the queen by an act barring her successor from declaring war without the consent of Parliament, it proceeded to pass the famous Act of Security. By this measure Scotland would deliberately choose as successor to Anne someone other than that designated by the Parliament of England unless Scotland was granted freedom of government, of religion, and of trade.

Godolphin, the English prime minister, was obliged to advise the queen to sign the measure, because Parliament refused the cess, or principal revenue measure, until it was approved. The situation of England and her allies in Europe was so perilous that the much-needed revenues could not be delayed. The English Parliament responded in kind. It decreed that if the succession in Scotland was not ordered to follow that established in England, Scotsmen would lose all their rights as citizens in England which they had enjoyed since the accession of James I, and the importation of Scottish goods into England would be prohibited, to take effect Christmas Day, 1705.

The challenge delivered by the Scottish Parliament had been returned. The economy, never overstrong, had been weakened by the loss of the European trade due to the war. Scottish exports were by now almost wholly to England so that the proposed ban would cause an economic disaster. Added to the losses suffered in the Darien scheme, the country could simply not stand this further blow to its already shaky economy.

The queen appointed the young duke of Argyll as commissioner and restored the duke of Queensberry and the earl of Seafield to the ministry. Together they were charged with bringing about a union. The

young duke of Argyll was only twenty-five, but he had already won respect for his service in the army in Europe. As the grandson of the civil war general and the son of the leader of the rebellion against James VII, he evoked potent loyalties. His position as head of the clan Campbell gave him a following tantamount to that of an independent prince. The combination of the three ministers proved equal to the task. In spite of strenuous opposition, authority was granted the queen to appoint commissioners to negotiate with England for a union. The defection of the mercurial Hamilton turned the assembly to a majority for the bill.
On the authority of the two Parliaments, the queen appointed thirty-one commissioners for each country. Argyll declined membership and Hamilton was omitted, but otherwise the commissioners included the principal ministers of both countries, augmented by dignitaries known to be favorable to a union. Only the Jacobite George Lockhart, among the Scottish commissioners, was a recognized opponent. The two sets of commissioners met separately in London after a joint session on April 16, 1706.

From the beginning, the English insisted on a parliamentary union which the Scots had to accept unless they decided to give up the negotiations. Once that point had been accepted, the English were more agreeable on others. From the first, the Scots had seen that free trade was the main point to be gained and this too was agreed. The disparate size and wealth of the two countries presented the other major hurdles. Scotland had a population one-fifth that of England, a revenue less than a thirtieth. As a compromise the two parties agreed upon a representation of 45 Scottish commoners to be added to the existing 513 members in the English Parliament. In the Lords, the Scots would be represented by 16 peers elected on the occasion of each new Parliament by their fellow nobles. The English national debt, built up as a result of the two French wars, was a burden the Scots were loath to assume. They were granted an "equivalent" of £400,000 to compensate them for the share of the debt they would assume. In fact, the sum provided was used to pay off the stockholders of the ill-fated Darien scheme. Each country was to retain its own courts and laws. Through separate acts passed subsequently by each legislature, the integrity of the national churches was protected.

The great work was completed on July 23. The denouement was now at hand. The Scottish Parliament met first, on October 3. The excitement was intense, and the Edinburgh mobs a constant threat to the proceedings of the estates. The heat of the debates and the eloquence of the harangues are memorable even from this distant vantage point. Although all the ministers were effective contributors, Sir John Dalrymple, now earl of Stair, was preeminent. Having done penance for his share in the Glencoe tragedy, he now gained immortal fame as the spokesman for the Moderates, who saw the union as inevitable and in the best interest of the country.

The opponents were equally vocal, and two of them also stood out from the rest—Andrew Fletcher of Saltoun and Lord Belhaven. Fletcher has gone down in history as the archetypical patriot and defender of Scottish liberty and independence. After three months of strenuous debate, marred by the death of Stair eight days before its passage, the Act of Union received the royal assent, the tumultuous assemblies, disruptive crowds, anathematizing preachers, and riotous protesters notwithstanding. The passage in the English Parliament was relatively uneventful. On May 1, 1707, the union took effect. Queen Anne declared the sitting English Parliament the first Parliament of Great Britain and summoned the requisite Scottish representatives to take their places. The Union of the Crowns had now been capped by the Union of the Parliaments.

6

"That Part of the United Kingdom Known as Scotland": 1707-1850

William Ferguson

"THAT PART OF THE UNITED KINGDOM KNOWN AS SCOTLAND": 1707–1850

by William Ferguson

146

ON MAY DAY, 1707, England and Scotland, two ancient independent kingdoms that had shared a common monarch since 1603, joined under one imperial crown to form the United Kingdom of Great Britain; but, though under one government and having one Parliament, the United Kingdom was not otherwise homogeneous. Not only did England and Scotland retain their own legal systems and their separate established churches (Presbyterian in Scotland and Episcopal in England) but they also differed in society and in social provisions. Thus, such important matters as education and poor relief were unassimilated, and in general, as the Articles of Union fully recognized, much remained predicated on the past.

Consequently, the changes that occurred in Scotland after the union pose a complex historical problem. For, while some important changes followed from the terms of union and their implementation in succeeding ages, much was attributable to the response of the British Parliament to new problems as they arose, problems which the treaty makers could not possibly have envisaged. In brief, just as the union did not entirely negate the past, neither could it entirely preempt the future. The parameters of change were often drawn by preunion conditions, and postunion developments were also heavily influenced by the *Zeitgeist* of their period. The influence of the Enlightenment is often stressed; but it is apt to be forgotten that the Age of Enlightenment, with its emphasis on improvement, was followed by the even more influential Age of Science.

Change, however to be explained, is the keynote of Scottish history from 1707 to 1850, as it was that of other countries of western Europe. But the Scottish case is a particularly complex one, largely because of the temptation to ascribe all change to the union. Cause and effect are difficult to disentangle, and since the profoundest changes involved a multiplicity of factors and emerged gradually, neat mathematical proof is out of the question. Other complicating factors are that the extensive social and economic changes did not affect every part of the country equally or at the same time, and local conditions were often determinants of change. But the following conclusion can hardly be disputed: the economy improved over the eighteenth century; this, in turn, forced social change; and in the end social change built up pressures for political reform.

In attempting to justify such a conclusion, the argument must begin with the nature of Scottish society in 1707. Its leading features had analogues elsewhere in western Europe, and the differences that made up "Scottishness" were often of degree rather than kind. Population, for example, the basic consideration, shared the uncertainty that was common to the Europe of that period; for the first official census was not taken until 1801 and the earliest unofficial one, Alexander Webster's important pioneer essay in demography, dates from 1755.

The soundest guess would be that in 1707 the total population of Scotland was just over a million, as against a "guesstimate" for England of about five million. Of that million or so in Scotland the great majority depended on agriculture, which was still organized on a traditional and unproductive open-field system known as runrig that kept living standards low and life expectancy short. The land and its use shaped the people, and in both Highlands and Lowlands this rural ambience influenced the customs, the literature, and the religion of the country. Those influences were powerfully reinforced because the population was then more evenly dispersed over the country as a whole than is the case today.

Wide areas of the Highlands that are now depopulated were then inhabited and relatively prosperous. Indeed, no vast economic gulf then divided the Highlands from the Lowlands. The creation of such a gulf in

The Duke of Queensberry presenting
the ACT of UNION to
Queen Anne.

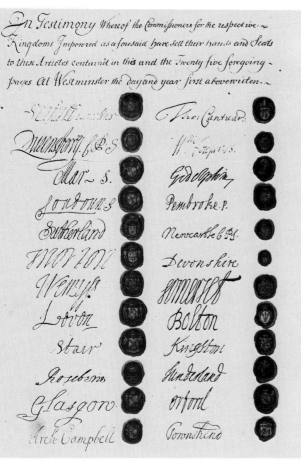

left: The signatures and seals of the sixteen Scottish and sixteen English commissioners appointed to Queen Anne to negotiate the parliamentary union of 1707 are affixed to the original copy of the treaty, Scots at the left, English at the right.

above left: In this contemporary engraving, James Douglas, duke of Queensbury, presents the Treaty of Union to Queen Anne. The treaty marked the abolition of the separate Scottish Parliament and government and closed a turbulent period of six hundred years of Scottish independence dating from the victories of Robert the Bruce.

above: John Campbell, second duke of Argyll and Greenwich, was an eccentric and celebrated nobleman who achieved prominence at the age of twenty-four after inheriting the dukedom, as one of the key statesmen who engineered the Union of 1707. His military prowess in the War of the Spanish Succession and his command of the king's army against the Jacobite rebels in 1715 gave him a lasting reputation and earned him the sobriquet "Red John of the Battles."

reality was to be one of the most prominent achievements of the period now under consideration. Differences between the two major divisions of Scotland were to grow steadily from the mid-eighteenth century on, but in the early part of that century the differences between Highlands and Lowlands were mainly linguistic and cultural.

In the Highlands the Gaelic language, which was closely related to Irish, was spoken, while Scots, which was gradually being assimilated to English, was still the language of all classes in the Lowlands. Highland society was more conservative and clung tenaciously not only to the old Gaelic language but to kinship and time-hallowed customs. However, both Gaelic and the clan system had been under attack, and the Highland area was being steadily penetrated by Lowland influences. This assault produced a nervous reaction among most Gaels and especially those under threat from the expansionist Campbells of Argyll, whose chief, the duke of Argyll, was at once a West Highland potentate and a political magnate of standing in Edinburgh and London. But in 1707, in spite of fears for the future of the Gael, the patriarchal clan system, with its military attributes, still flourished in the Highlands, resisting all efforts at subjugation.

The Lowland countryside at the time of the union showed regional variations of one dominant pattern that was crosshatched by feudal concepts and runrig farming. There were two main classes in this society: at the top was a relatively small number of feudal landowners, lords or lairds, who constituted the ruling class at the local and national levels; and at the bottom there were masses of small tenant farmers, many on joint tenancies, who for the most part suffered from insecurity of tenure.

This was the world that Sir Walter Scott understood and described so well, the world of Cuddie Headrigg, the ploughman in *Old Mortality*, of Davie Deans and the laird of Dumbiedykes in *The Heart of Midlothian*, and of the Baron of Bradwardine in *Waverley*. That world was to vanish in most parts of the Lowlands as a result of the agrarian reforms carried out in the course of the eighteenth century. But in the union period a feudal regime still operated, buttressed for good and for ill, by heritable jurisdictions whose survival was guaranteed by the Treaty of Union. Under this dispensation the countryside was regulated by private courts, which saw to it that the will of the lairds prevailed, that order was maintained, and that the tenants dutifully performed their prescribed labor services.

In some ways the old feudal system in Scotland bore a marked resemblance to the *ancien regime* in France, and it was once fashionable to press the comparison, though a crucial point of difference was too often left out of account. Before 1789 nearly a third of the soil of France was owned by peasants; there was no corresponding peasant proprietorship in Scotland. From that difference much flowed. Scotland was and remained a country dominated by large estates; a country where the proprietors had a wide range of rights carefully protected by law and where tenants were numerous and only slowly and painfully won security of tenure. In 1707 the greater part of the total population lived under this feudal regime at the mercy of the lairds and their baron bailies.

In the early eighteenth century urbanization was not a dominant feature of Scottish life, for, though burghs had long existed, most of them were small and had a distinctly rustic character. Edinburgh was the largest and most important of the sixty-six royal burghs and had about forty thousand people crammed within the narrow confines of the Old Town. Next came Glasgow with about twelve thousand, followed by Aberdeen, Perth, and Dundee, with populations of about four thousand each. The remaining royal burghs were even smaller, some having only a few hundred residents. Though small by modern reckoning, the royal burghs as a group were important. Their royal charters granted extensive

economic and legal privileges to which they fiercely clung. They furnished commercial and marketing facilities and virtually engrossed foreign trade; and they alone of the burghs were represented in Parliament. However, the parliamentary representation of the royal burghs was cut at the union from sixty-six to fifteen, a mathematical feat performed by setting up fourteen districts of burghs, each of which was a constituency, leaving Edinburgh alone with an M.P. to itself.

Most of the royal burghs were medieval in origin. They were numerous in the east of Scotland and only three were located in the Gaelic-speaking area. In addition to the royal burghs, there were numerous burghs of barony which had been created and were controlled by feudal superiors. By the time of the union some burghs of this type were growing in importance, and after the union that process was to continue. Indeed, by the end of the eighteenth century such nonroyal burghs as Greenock, Paisley, or Kilmarnock far outstripped in population and prosperity most of the royal burghs. It was not the least of the problems of late eighteenth and early nineteenth century Scotland that the latter held on to their privileges, and continued, for example, to monopolize burgh representation in Parliament until 1832.

In sum, Scotland in 1707 was what would be described today as an underdeveloped country. Its economy rested on a stagnant agrarian base, initiative was fettered by prescriptive rights and outworn traditions, its trade was declining as mercantilism restricted its old European markets, and its few industries—principally coal, linen, and wool—were rudimentary, undercapitalized, and backward. Indeed, free trade with England and its colonies was one of the lures for which independence was bartered in 1707. But no economic miracle ensued. On the contrary, the immediate economic effects of union on Scotland were depressing. The woolen cloth industry, for example, which had a heavily developed English counterpart, was killed off by 1711. This failure was made all the more bitter by inability to disburse money promised for promotion of the coarse wool trade by Article XV of the Treaty of Union. Not until 1727 was this administrative bottleneck solved by the setting up of the Board of Trustees for Manufactures.

The linen industry, on the other hand, readily responded to the prompting of the Board of Trustees. Essentially a peasant craft, the linen trade was then organized on the "cottage" system, which ensured that profits were shared by the many and not restricted to a few capitalists. In

General Wade, commander-in-chief for Scotland, realized that efficient communications could be the key to the pacification and control of the Highlands. In ten years he built 260 miles of roads and bridges to link Fort William, Fort Augustus, and Fort George, and to open up hitherto inaccessible parts of the country. This bridge at Aberfeldy, Perthshire, built in 1733, is characteristic of the excellent engineering and handsome design used by Wade's builders.

addition to producing for the market, each household spun and wove for its own needs. But the various processes of production had been primitive and the finished cloth of poor quality long enough. The board at once addressed itself to those problems, and the results of its labors were soon evident. In 1710 one and one-half million yards of linen of all sorts were produced; by 1728 the figure had risen to two million, and to twice that amount by 1733. Production continued to rise steadily, and further stimulus came from the Bounty Acts of 1742, which enabled coarse Scotch linens to compete on favorable terms with European linens in the American colonies.

A fine linen industry, too, rose in the west to meet the needs of the American trade, and by 1771 Glasgow was exporting nearly two million yards of linen clothes of all categories. In spite of the marked expansion of the linen industry, however, it remained largely domestic in its organization. Yet, though it remained loosely organized, linen was the staple industry of Scotland over the greater part of the eighteenth century.

In commerce Glasgow was the first burgh to benefit from the union, which is ironical considering that Glasgow had violently objected to the treaty. Glasgow profited from the marked shift in economic gravity from east to west that was accelerated by the union, and Glasgow was able to utilize knowledge of the American trade obtained before 1707 by illicit trading. The early ventures in this trade after 1707, however, were small-scale and hampered by lack of capital, suitable shipping, and lack of an adequate supply of barter goods. But from about 1720 the colonial trade, mainly in tobacco and sugar, steadily expanded. By the 1760s Glasgow had secured a virtual monopoly of the lucrative tobacco trade by outstripping its rivals, Bristol and Liverpool.

Less dramatic at the time, but of more abiding importance, were the improvements that were being made in agriculture. Here the union clearly initiated change by removing all restrictions on the cattle trade with England. In the southern counties, parklands were extended, pastures improved, and turnips and artificial grasses sown for fodder. The new way caused evictions and loss of rights of commonty, giving rise to some disorder, but the importance of the cattle trade as a money earner confirmed the improvers in their work. Interest in agricultural improvement grew, especially after the founding of the Society of Improvers in Agriculture in 1723, and it soon became clear that tillage as well as pasture could profitably be changed.

Improved tillage, however, was incompatible with runrig. The new style of farming could only operate on compact unitary farms. Fewer and more efficient farms and fewer and more professional farmers came to be the rule. But agricultural improvement was a long and drawn-out business which needed a heavy capital outlay for enclosures, draining, extensive use of lime, working out of suitable crop rotations, and the planting of trees. In the end the face of the countryside was changed, and Scottish society underwent the greatest transformation it has ever known.

The new ways, however, were ill adapted to the Highland terrain, and their impact on that area was minimal. But district after district of Lowlands gradually succumbed to the mania for improvement. The inertia of the tenants was overcome by the introduction of long leases which contained a schedule of improvements to be made. Slow though the work was, by the end of the eighteenth century the agricultural revolution was well advanced in the Lowlands. Rents and productivity both rose spectacularly, and though there were fewer farmers, they achieved high standards, and an increasing population could be fed without fear of famine. Not all the displaced tenants, however, were employed as farm laborers or as village craftsmen, and as the old farm towns and rural communities were either destroyed or radically altered, the drift from country to town began.

By the mid-eighteenth century the first stirrings of a new society became noticeable, and as a corollary the union was winning acceptance. All the same, in the first half of the eighteenth century hostility to the union had considerable political effects. That hostility was at its peak in the first decade of the union. Various sectors of Scottish opinion then had their misgivings about the union reinforced. Those who had hoped for an economic miracle were disappointed. Chauvinists fumed at the English law of treason being foisted on Scotland in 1709. The Presbyterians had their fears about the union with prelatical England reawakened by Greenshields's case, which enforced toleration for qualified Episcopalians, in this instance the Reverend James Greenshields, and led to the abominated Patronage Act of 1712 restoring private patronage in the Church of Scotland. The review jurisdiction over the Court of Session assumed by the House of Lords, which lay at the root of Greenshields's case, worried Scots lawyers since it posed an insidious threat to Scots law.

The Scottish peers, who resented having only sixteen representatives in the House of Lords, had their hopes of acquiring hereditary seats via United Kingdom peerages dashed by the decision in Hamilton's case in 1711, in which the duke of Hamilton was allowed entry into the British peerage but was denied a seat in the House of Lords. Thus in the opening years of union the deal seemed to be all loss and no profit. The disenchantment came to a head in 1713, when a motion to repeal the Act of Union, sponsored by its former authors, was only narrowly defeated in Parliament. And, of course, the Jacobites made all they could of those difficulties.

To compound all those difficulties, the administration of Scotland was weakened. This was the worst aspect of the union; indeed, the problem of government has been its Achilles' heel ever since 1707. The cardinal error was made when, one year to the day after the union became operative, the Scottish Privy Council was abolished by act of Parliament. The government saw the folly of such a move but was forced into it by the opposition, which feared that the Privy Council would be used to rig parliamentary elections in the government's favor. That fear was probably justified, for the loss of the Privy Council led to palsied administration and lack of governance.

Only slowly and painfully did a new administrative and political complex emerge which made it possible for central government to achieve a measure of control over developments in Scotland. The key lay in the rise of "management," which was really a means of organizing corruption in the government interest. Here the historic Lord Advocate became a vital cog in the dispensing of patronage; but the system itself evolved slowly. After 1707 the duke of Queensberry had tried to maintain his preunion magnate status by manipulating the feudal franchise and by introducing fagot votes. Both were to become standard ploys, but Queensberry died in 1711 before his interest could be consolidated at Westminster. Anyway, the union militated against his endeavor, and the loss of the Privy Council made it unworkable. The very times were against it. The turmoils of Queen Anne's last years, the bitter clash of Whigs and Tories at Westminster, the problems of the Hanoverian succession and the Jacobite rising of 1715 all made for a very unstable situation. Robert Harley, well aware of the problem of government in Scotland, had hoped to solve it by setting up a commission of chamberlainry and trade in 1711–13. But Harley's plan came to nothing.

Weak government, however, favored the Jacobites. On the other hand, if the Scottish Jacobites had had the benefit of sound leadership

James Francis Edward Stuart was the only surviving son of James II. His father's enemies spread the story that he was a bogus heir, smuggled into the queen's bedroom (while she was supposed to be in childbirth) in a warming pan to ensure the Catholic succession in England. The nursery song, "Rock-a-bye baby in the tree tops," was originally a satirical song impugning his royal birth. On the death of James II in 1701, he was recognized by the king of France as James VIII and III of Scotland and England. After the birth of his son and heir Charles (Bonnie Prince Charlie) in 1720, he was known as the Old Pretender.

A prominent Scottish politician under Queen Anne and Secretary of State for Scotland, John Erskine, sixth earl of Mar, went over to the Jacobite cause in 1715, thus gaining the nickname "Bobbing John" after losing favor at court under George I. His weak ineffectual command of the Jacobite forces helped ensure the failure of the Pretender's cause. He is shown here, in a painting by Godfrey Kneller, with his son Thomas in 1717.

A public execution was a great entertainment in eighteenth-century London. As this 1716 engraving shows, the execution of two Scottish lords who took up arms against George I in 1715 drew a large crowd. The Earl of Derwentwater and Viscount Kenmure were beheaded in the Tower of London in 1716. Other Jacobite leaders escaped or were sent abroad and their estates were forfeited.

they would not have stirred, for by September, 1715, the Pretender's opportunity had clearly been missed. By then the Hanoverian succession was an accomplished fact, and the Chevalier (as James, the Old Pretender, was also called) could expect no help from France. Foolishly, however, the Jacobites allowed themselves to be saddled with the leadership of the earl of Mar. Mar, former unionist and scourge of the Jacobites, found that, as a Tory minister who had promoted the Treaty of Utrecht that ended the War of the Spanish Succession, he could expect no favor from "a wee German lairdie" who regarded the peace as a betrayal of the continental allied. Rebuffed by King George, Mar remembered King James; and, dreaming of a dukedom, he promptly turned Jacobite general, thus immortalizing himself as "Bobbing John."

Soon Mar had mustered a force of twelve thousand men; it was a formidable turnout, containing traditional Jacobite clans as well as a large contingent from the northeast Lowlands. The government forces under the duke of Argyll were of poor quality and outnumbered by three to one, and Mar's campaign, which was launched at Braemar on September 6, 1715, began bravely enough. But, once in possession of Perth, Mar dawdled there, waiting for the Pretender and imaginary French reinforcements. As a result, this rising known by its date as "the '15," and including the lesser risings in southern Scotland and northern England, became a fiasco.

Argyll doomed Mar's rising by keeping a firm grip on Stirling, the key point, and he finally quashed the rebellion on November 13 at Sheriffmuir. Sheriffmuir was a strategic victory for the Hanoverians, and the melting away of Mar's disillusioned army could not be prevented by the belated arrival of the uninspiring Pretender. Instead, on February 4, 1716, "Jamie the Rover" was obliged to return to France whence he had come, becoming the "King over the Water" again that he was to remain until his death on New Year's Day, 1766.

"Bobbing John's" career illustrates much more than the ill-conceived and ill-managed '15. It reveals how the Scottish politicians of the union period were in fact corrupt and self-seeking. At Westminster, their status was diminished, and they were regarded not only as venal Scots on the make but also as "odd-looking dull men." They spoke little in Parliament, and when they did speak their broad Scots convulsed their sophisticated English colleagues. The '15 made their situation worse, for the English were convinced that it was a "Scotch rebellion."

Neither John Wilkes nor Dr. Samuel Johnson invented English detestation of the Scots: they merely made it memorable. As late as 1775 David Garrick refused to appear in tartan as Macbeth, not because such buffoonery offended his sense of history but lest he be hissed off the stage of Drury Lane. In view of all this, it is not surprising that the forty-five Scottish M.P.s in the House of Commons and the sixteen representative peers in the House of Lords were in the van of the long process of anglicization that followed. Education in England would in time make the Scots lairds feel less gauche in London. Intermarriage with the English aristocracy also speeded up the process, and by the end of the eighteenth century many Scottish aristocrats were becoming strangers to Scotland and its ways.

The accession of George I, the maintenance of the union, and the triumph of the Whigs made the anglicization of the upper classes in Scotland inevitable. It also led to less-fevered, stable government in Britain. As a result more concern was shown for the affairs of Scotland, and that concern was not confined to punitive measures against the Jacobites. Though forfeitures and disarming acts were the order of the day for a while, government policy also aimed at creating a more prosperous and more peaceable country. Thus, after Sir Robert Walpole became prime minister in 1721 he strove for the improvement of Scotland in order to strengthen the union and weaken the Jacobites.

His long tenure of power also left its mark on the political system that was evolving in Scotland. By 1721 the Queensberry interest had disintegrated. The Squadrone, another preunion group, survived into the 1740s but was weak and amorphous. Walpole turned to the Argathelians, who, following the duke of Argyll, constituted the dominant political interest in Scotland. Argyll was a difficult colleague, however, and Walpole came to rely more and more on the duke's brother, the earl of Ilay, who, after the Shawfield riots over the malt tax in Glasgow in 1725, became chief manager for Scotland. Ilay diagnosed Scotland's trouble as lack of governance. Here the Scottish secretaryship, which was retained after the union, was a stumbling block mainly because contending groups in Scotland feared that the secretary, if allowed to control administration, might become a virtual satrap.

The best answer seemed to lie in the development of management, and Ilay became the main begetter of that graft-ridden but effective system. So good did he become at management that he survived Walpole's fall in 1742. Ilay's great discovery was that skillful use of patronage could guarantee government the support of most of the forty-five members from Scotland, and his position was fortuitously enhanced in 1746 when the marquis of Tweeddale was dismissed from the office of secretary and the office was not filled. Ilay, by then his brother's successor as duke of Argyll, was left in an unassailable position. A lawyer by training, he had the necessary knowledge and the right temperament for management, and he became indispensable to successive ministries. His death in 1761 left a vacuum that posed difficult questions for his nephew, the earl of Bute, who was George III's favorite, but highly unpopular, minister.

By the 1740s a modest degree of prosperity and high hopes for the future made the union more acceptable, as even the Jacobites were forced to recognize. But their hatred of the union was as great as ever, and their recognition of the fact that it was gaining acceptance does much to account for the rebellion of 1745. Intent on forcing aid from France, which

154

Fealty to the exiled Stuarts may have been more sentimental than real. It was the issue of an independent Scotland rather than an attachment to the Stuarts that inspired expressions of loyalty to the "King over the Water." These Jacobite toasting glasses are mementos of that nostalgic attachment.

was then at war with Britain and had promised to send an expedition to help the Jacobites in Scotland, Charles Edward, the Young Pretender, forced the pace. He set out in secret for Scotland, bringing neither troops nor supplies, and raised his father's standard at Glenfinnan in Inverness-shire on August 19, 1745. His prospects were bleak, but what followed was unexpected and astonishing. The Young Chevalier raised a sizable force in the Highlands and, helped by the folly of the government commander, Sir John Cope, easily took Edinburgh on September 17.

The defeat of Cope at Prestonpans on September 21 by the able Jacobite general, Lord George Murray, left the rebels controlling most of Scotland. Nonetheless, though this stunning victory encouraged more Jacobites to join Charles's army, south of Tay the rebels still found no real support. The Presbyterians bitterly opposed the rebellion, and those who were prospering through trade and industry feared a change of regime. Thus, Glasgow gave the Jacobites' force a surly reception, furnishing neither plaudits nor recruits and only producing supplies grudgingly and at sword point.

The Jacobites' march into England fared no better. The much-talked-of English Jacobites failed to materialize, and at Derby on December 4 ("Black Friday"), Charles was forced by the chiefs to turn back and begin the long retreat into Scotland. The vital help promised by France did not come in sufficient quantity, and, in spite of a spirited victory at Falkirk on January 17, 1746, over Cope's equally incompetent successor, Hawley, the enterprise was doomed. The Jacobites, starved of supplies and

During the reign of George II heavy taxes led to constant conflicts between the royal excise men and local smugglers. This explosive situation came to a head in 1736 when the captain of the Edinburgh guard fired on a crowd gathered at the execution of two popular smugglers. Four bystanders were killed and eleven wounded. Captain Porteous, sentenced to death, was reprieved by Queen Caroline, but the outraged citizens seized Porteous and carried out the sentence. This melodramatic nineteenth-century painting by James Drummond of the crowd in the Grassmarket caught the spirit of a lynching. But Scott, in his novel *The Heart of Midlothian,* described the Porteous affair as an act of justice in which the executioners even paid for the rope they took for the hanging.

The most romantic figure in Scottish history, "Bonnie Prince Charlie" or the Young Pretender proved to be an indecisive leader and a failure as a general. The handsome, promising youth, portrayed by Antonio David in 1732, spent most of his life as a dissolute, irresponsible wastrel.

On July 25, 1745, Prince Charles landed on Eriskay, in the Outer Hebrides, in his ship the *Doutelle*. When the island lords advised him to give up his foolhardy venture, Antoine Walsh brought the prince and his seven followers to the mainland, leaving them on the shore of Loch Nan Uamh in Moidart. This idealized drawing of the prince's farewell to Walsh (above) was given by the prince to Walsh after the failure of the rising and Charles's subsequent escape to France. By August 19, Prince Charles had made his way to Glenfinnan on Loch Shiel (below).

The ill-fed, poorly clad, and poorly led troops of Bonnie Prince Charlie were no match for the disciplined, well-fed forces of the crown. In this contemporary engraving of the battle, fought April 16, 1746, in front of Culloden House (9), the protagonists are clearly identified—the duke of Cumberland (1) at the right and Prince Charles (3) fleeing on horseback at the left.

weakened by dispersion for foraging, were finally crushed by the duke of Cumberland at Culloden, the last battle fought in Britain, on April 16, 1746.

Charles Edward, after five months of evading the redcoats in the Highlands and Western Isles, finally made good his escape to France, to spend the rest of his days (he died in 1788) dissipating by vile living the fairytale legend of Bonnie Prince Charlie. Yet the legend lives on, preserved in song and romance, impervious to proof as to the deplorable character of its hero. History battles unequally with romance, and Charles Edward's one glorious year of crowded life in 1745–46 has certainly outweighed an age without a name.

Romance, however, did not come to the aid of the luckless rank and file of the Jacobite rebels. Cumberland cruelly exploited his victory, ravaging the Highlands indiscriminately. The government also clamped down on the Highlands. Some of the leading rebels were forfeited and executed, and many who escaped were also forfeited. The forfeited estates were latterly annexed to the crown and a commission set up to run them with a view to introducing improvements. Resistance was feeble and easily overcome.

The Highlands were effectively disarmed and pacified by such measures as the abolition of the heritable jurisdictions. In order to break the military organization of the clans, military land tenures were also abolished; and for a time even Highland dress was forbidden. Under those pressures, which were all reinforced by strong garrisons, the traditional Highland society began to disintegrate.

But misconceptions can easily arise. It was not just a step from Culloden to the notorious Highland clearances. Between the two lay over half a century and a world of thought. The essential truth is that the second half of the eighteenth century, once the aftermath of the rebellion was over, was a period of general optimism in the Highlands. Landlords and governments alike believed that peace must beget prosperity. And for a time it so appeared. The cattle trade boomed, due largely to the needs of the army and navy in the Seven Years' War, the War of American Independence, and the French Revolutionary and Napoleonic Wars. Cattle, too, brought in money; and money, it was fondly imagined, would open up other possibilities—such as agricultural improvement, the promotion of fishing, or the setting up of the linen industry. And in the last decade of the eighteenth century many landlords struck it rich when kelp, obtained from burning seaweed and in great demand as a source of alkali, soared in price.

All these ventures were labor-intensive; so Highland landlords of that period bitterly opposed emigration, which nonetheless occurred because of the failure of the tacksman class, important leaseholders under the old system, to secure its footing after 1746. Government likewise frowned on emigration, and in an attempt to keep a large military reserve in the Highlands the forfeited Jacobite estates were restored in 1784. The extraordinary number of regiments raised in the Highlands during the French Revolutionary and Napoleonic Wars more than justified that policy, and none did greater service to George III than the old Jacobite clans.

But, almost unnoticed, a dangerous situation was arising. As a result of the policies adopted by landlords and governments, the population of the Highlands and islands increased dramatically in the late eighteenth century.

In Highlands and Lowlands alike changes in the material culture brought new ideas in their wake. Not everyone, however, welcomed change and many feared for the old values. In 1725 the Reverend Robert Wodrow, pious historian of *The Sufferings of the Church of Scotland*, had predicted that wealth and carnality would banish godliness. Churchmen of the older type were alarmed by new schools of thought stimulated by Cartesianism and Newtonianism. Under those influences the Scottish universities were coming out of their medieval shells, reforming themselves, absorbing and teaching the new philosophies, and, in some quarters at least, showing scant regard for the traditional scholastic Calvinism. Revelling in this new-found freedom was John Simson, professor of Divinity at Glasgow, who was latterly accused of Arianism, which denied the divinity of Christ.

Simson's pupil, Francis Hutcheson, steered clear of heresy by steering clear of theology, and that came to be the Moderate answer to the problem of thought and belief. David Hume, the great sceptic, was less timid, but his intellectual honesty denied him a university chair. At Glasgow, Principal Leechman adopted the latitudinarian standpoint, and Glasgow's days as the citadel of orthodoxy seemed numbered. Mathematics, science, and medicine made great strides, especially at Edinburgh. General literacy was growing due to the extension of the parish schools and the work of the Scottish Society for Propagating Christian Knowledge in the Highlands. The question came to be: Could the new culture be reconciled with the old religious standards?

With intellectual horizons expanding, the Church of Scotland was soon torn between those who, like Wodrow, insisted on seventeenth-century-style piety and those who, in Adam Smith's phrase, regarded enlightened

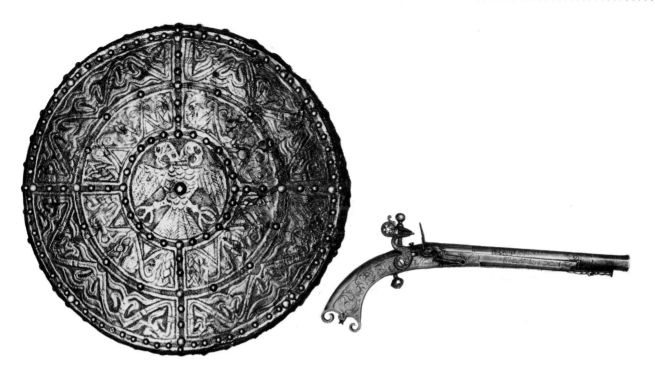

One of the great heroines of Scottish
history, Flora MacDonald saved the
Young Pretender's life after the defeat
at Culloden by dressing him as her maid.
In spite of the enormous reward of
£30,000, no Highlander betrayed the
prince.

A proud relic of the Highland past, this
shield, or targe, is made of wood covered
with leather. Embossed patterns and
nailheads create a rich decorative effect.

In the sixteenth century Highlanders
abandoned the claymore for the more
flexible and efficient broadsword and dirk.
This seventeenth-century dirk is inscribed
"Thy King and Countries cause defend
though on the spot your life should end,"
and "A soft answer tourneth away wrath."

This scroll butt pistol by Alexander
Campbell of Doune is of steel inlaid with
silver, and brilliantly engraved. Doune
firearms were considered the finest in
Scotland.

philosophy as the antidote to the poison of enthusiasm and plumped for polite learning, good relations with the state, and fat livings from the kirk's patrons. Patronage, which never really fitted in well with the Presbyterian system of church government, caused much friction. It provided the occasion for the original secession that was headed by Ebenezer Erskine, minister of Stirling, in 1740. Patronage favored the lairds, and the Moderate ministers who cultivated the patrons, and Erskine, sympathizing with the plebs, demanded a church that ministered to the people.

Presbyterian dissent grew, notably with the rise of the Relief Church after 1761, and from the relief emerged the "voluntary principle" which demanded the complete separation of church and state. The paradox is that while the Church of Scotland was gaining strength by wearing down Episcopalian opposition in the Highlands and northeast Lowlands, it was at the same time being weakened by schism in the areas of its greatest strength. Nor did those schisms rid the establishment of all contentious elements. It was still troubled by strife between the Moderates, who from 1752 dominated the church, and the increasingly resentful Evangelicals, who remained within the fold.

One such Evangelical, John Witherspoon, bitterly satirized the Moderates before emigrating to the American colonies to become principal of Princeton College and to sign the Declaration of Independence. He left many like him in Scotland who abominated enlightened deism with its vague and sententious moralizing and preached the gospel. Their opponents, the Moderates, contributed much to the culture of eighteenth-century Scotland. But they also contributed to the undermining of the national church.

All those various trends (economic, social, and intellectual) were operating by the middle of the eighteenth century, and great changes were either wrought or impending. But Webster's analysis of the population in 1755 still showed a preponderance of rural dwellers out of a total population of 1,265,380, and only a limited growth of towns. Significantly, however, Glasgow's population had risen to 23,546, almost double what it had been in 1707. Edinburgh and Dundee were also growing fast, but increases in the other burghs were more restricted.

After 1770, with the passing of an Entail Act which eased credit for owners of entailed estates, the agricultural revolution gained momentum. By 1815 in all parts of the Lowlands runrig was no more. Fewer people depended on the land, and this fact, together with rising population, created a mobile labor force. True, the American War of Independence checked economic progress by seriously reducing trade; but by 1791 the volume of trade was restored and continued to expand.

This remarkable feat of economic resiliency was due largely to the introduction of a new textile, cotton, the spinning of which was mechanized from the beginning. That industry developed rapidly from 1780 on. Cotton, the premier industry of the Industrial Revolution, had important social as well as economic effects. The spinners, working together in mills and living together in overcrowded barracks provided by the capitalists, became the first real proletariat in Scotland. They were entirely dependent on their wage labor and lived in completely new circumstances in the congested slums of the manufacturing towns.

The coal industry, too, began to expand as the demand for its products rose. A new technology enabled a start to be made on exploiting the deep, difficult seams of Lanarkshire and Ayrshire. But the industry had trouble maintaining an adequate labor force. The work was hard and dangerous, and, in addition, literal serfdom had been inflicted on the colliers since the early seventeenth century. Recruitment, therefore, was difficult. To increase the supply of labor, serfdom was finally abolished in

Sir John Sinclair devoted himself to the improvement of his estates and of Scottish agriculture. He introduced such innovations as the rotation of crops, the maintaining of statistical records, the cultivation of turnips and clover, and reforestation. He worked to improve sheep-breeding, especially the Shetland flocks, and in 1793 was a founder and the first president of the Board of Agriculture. It is as a colonel in the Caithness Highlanders that Henry Raeburn portrays him.

161

1799. Ironworks were also springing up, concentrated mainly on the western coalfield in Ayrshire and Lanarkshire. The sinews of an Industrial Revolution existed, but not, as yet, an Industrial Revolution itself.

It was about to become an age of laissez-faire when the state abnegated its functions and let capitalism operate as it liked. Conditions of labor steadily worsened, and sharp conflicts arose between employers and employed. Trade unions were forbidden by law, and strikers were treated as criminals; and the able-bodied unemployed, whose numbers were growing with the trade cycle, were either denied poor relief or given the most grudging doles.

Yet with society in flux, political institutions changed hardly at all. Everything until 1832 was petrified in the mold cast in 1707. Thus, for example, in the royal burghs the corrupt closed-shop system continued; and the self-elected town councils openly embezzled the common good while taking care not to keep accounts. Edinburgh, indeed, was sunk deep in debt. Aberdeen and many other royal burghs were in broadly similar case.

Henry Dundas, first viscount Melville, was the unchallenged political boss of Scotland in the second half of the eighteenth century. His control of Scottish patronage was won through his favor of successive prime ministers, whom he served as an expert adviser on military and financial matters. This portrait is by Sir Thomas Lawrence.

So, too, with parliamentary representation. The old feudal franchises and outmoded electoral machinery were not substantially altered until 1832. Of Scotland's total population of 1,608,420 in 1801, only about 4,000 were qualified to vote, and many of these held fictitious qualifications. Yet few parliamentary politicians felt that anything was amiss.

It was decidedly awkward that, at this time of change and erosion of older values, management and corrupt practices were carried to new heights after 1784 by the younger Pitt's Scottish lieutenant Henry Dundas, who greatly extended the range of patronage and sewed up the Scottish constituencies. An able politician, Dundas was a lawyer and a member of a famous legal dynasty, but he was not a great landed magnate. He was born and long remained plain Henry Dundas, and only reluctantly did he become Viscount Melville in 1802.

Dundas's word became law in Scotland, as Henry Cockburn, a Whig who hated Toryism but was related to Dundas, vividly illustrates again and again. Says Cockburn of Dundas: "He was the Pharos of Scotland. Who steered upon him was safe, who disregarded his light was wrecked." Dundas managed to gain control of the vast patronage of the East India Company, and soon "John Company's" service was saturated with Scots; so much so that Sir Walter Scott referred to India as "the corn chest of Scotland."

To the upper classes in Scotland Dundas thus appeared as a benefactor rather than a tyrant. Nor was he a tyrant by nature. He was liberal in many ways, and this appeared most consistently in his belief in religious toleration. In 1792 he freed the nonjuring Episcopalians from their disabilities, and a year later he eased the situation of the Roman Catholics. His personality, too, helped him, for he was bluff and accessible and he knew his Scotland. He remained a Scot who was proud of his heritage, and while others of his class were torturing themselves to acquire polite English, he retained his broad Scots, which he used to remarkable effect in Parliament. Then, too, in spite of his impeachment on charges of malversation in 1806, he was personally honest and was rightly acquitted, though censured for carelessness.

It was Dundas's misfortune that, in the late eighteenth century, criticism of the political system was mounting. There was a mood growing in the country at large that the whole process of government was archaic, incompetent, and corrupt. Burns frequently touched on this theme and was later to give that mood a more cutting edge with his marvelous song, surely the great war song of democracy, "A Man's a Man for a' That."

As evidence of this growing mood of disenchantment, a movement arose dedicated to reform of the royal burghs, which were notorious sinks of corruption. The significant point about the burgh reformers was that they voiced the aspirations of a new middle class made up of merchants and professional people who bitterly resented their exclusion from the corridors of power, both local and national. Some of the county electors, too, mostly lairds, also pressed for reform of the electoral system. But the county reformers were weak and vacillating. Anyway, even so-called extreme reformers of the 1780s, like George Dempster, never advocated democracy. Indeed, to the upper classes the word democracy then meant anarchy and was something to be dreaded.

It was the French Revolution that let loose democratic political aspirations and also initiated working-class politics in Scotland. But the democratic movement was individualist and not socialist, and, like Burns, it stressed the natural rights of man. A brilliant, if biased, account of the impact of the French Revolution on Scotland is given by Henry Cockburn in his *Memorials*, where he rightly stresses its divisive effects. "Everything,"

163

says Cockburn, "rung and was connected with the Revolution in France. ... Everything, not this or that thing, but literally everything, was soaked in this one event." But Cockburn lost no opportunity of flaying the Tory government, which, horrified by the violence in France, became ultraconservative and determined at all costs to preserve the *status quo*. From 1790 on, following the publication of Tom Paine's *Rights of Man* and availing themselves of the shrill anti-Jacobinism of Edmund Burke, the authorities clamped down on democratic reform movements. Many such had arisen demanding universal male suffrage, annual Parliaments, abolition of sinecures and privileges; and with them had also sprung up a radical press.

Harsh political trials formed an important part of the government's onslaught on Jacobinism. The most famous of those trials in Scotland were presided over by the notorious judge, Lord Braxfield, later immortalized by R. L. Stevenson as Weir of Hermiston in the novel of that name. In September, 1793, Thomas Muir, a young lawyer and a leader of the extremist section of the Society of the Friends of the People, was convicted of sedition and sentenced to fourteen years at Botany Bay. Similar trials followed, as the so-called Dundas Despotism ruthlessly crushed reformers of all shades and even ostracized the Whigs. Many democrats were forced to flee from the "White Terror" in Scotland, including Alexander Wilson, a radical weaver-poet of Paisley. Like many others, Wilson sought refuge in the United States. There, to develop his manifold talents, he made a great name for himself with his monumental *American Ornithology*.

With Britain at war against France from February, 1793, the security of the realm seemed to need the repressive Tory regime, and repression appeared to succeed. Yet the whole imbroglio was a mare's nest of mutual fears and misapprehensions, for the threat of revolution so much dreaded by authority had little substance in reality, and the repression was tempered with good sense. Anyway, once Napoleon's imperialism had trampled on revolutionary ideals, patriotism effectively countered radical aspirations in Scotland. In the long years of war after 1793, however, the *status quo* that the Tories were determined to preserve became illusory, so deep were the economic and social changes produced by the titanic struggle. Economic warfare with Napoleon led to recurrent booms and slumps. A new social structure grew.

Between 1780 and 1830 the population not only increased but was beginning to be radically redistributed. Areas of hitherto restricted population, such as Ayrshire and Lanarkshire, became the main seats of industry and attracted more and more of the total population. Again the case of Glasgow was by far the most dramatic. Glasgow's commercial and industrial supremacy drew people in from the Lowland countryside, and, after 1815, as many again from the Highlands.

The depression that followed the peace of 1815 was widespread in Britain but hit the Highland economy with devastating force, ruining the cattle trade, fishing, and kelp. The dream of improvement that had haunted late-eighteenth-century thinking was rudely shattered. After 1815 the large populations in the north and west subsisted miserably on tiny holdings and became increasingly dependent on the potato crop. More and more landlords turned to sheep for salvation. Sheep-farming was not labor intensive, and sheep needed vast grazings; so massive evictions took place as one after the other Highland landlords carried out clearances. In 1846–47 the blight ruined the potato crop and thousands starved. After that the rate of emigration soared, emptying the glens and building up the populations of Canada, Australia, and New Zealand. The greatest of all Scottish Diasporas had begun. But not all the dispossessed Gaels

The GIANT-FACTOTUM amusing himself.

Dundas's financial wizardry and manipulation of Scottish boroughs and Indian nabobs were indispensable to William Pitt the Younger. The identity of this Scot as an essential supporter of the prime minister is cleverly delineated by James Gillray, who depicts him in tartan dress supporting Pitt's right foot.

went overseas. Many settled in the industrialized Lowlands, where a new Scottish breed was evolving, a blend of Highland and Lowland with a leavening of Irish. For over a century West Lowland Scotland was to be the country's powerhouse and chief moving force, a fact that has not always endeared it to other areas, where continuity has been more marked.

Political grievances, grinding poverty, and the harsh and unhealthy environment of the new industrial order combined after 1815 to spark a revival of radical activities. The Tory government tried to administer a dose of repression along the lines that Dundas had earlier used, but failed miserably.

The unrest steadily escalated, culminating in an easily suppressed armed uprising, the Radical War of 1820. Public opinion became critical of government, whose few concessions to reform were tepid and belated, and the Whigs profited from this situation. Furious at their continued exclusion from office, and hating the Tories, the Whigs posed as the champions of the democrats and were able to cement an alliance with them after the insurrection of 1820. That alliance helped to carry the Reform Act of 1832; but the Whigs were no democrats and ditched their working-class allies by withholding the franchise and refusing to introduce social legislation.

Soon the working class struck out for its own measures and supported the Chartist movement, which the Whigs, playing to perfection the role they had attributed to the Tories in the 1790s, stigmatized as revolutionary. Whig reform, however, took some cognizance of the growing class struggle by enfranchising the middle class in 1832; and a year later the burgh reform acts ended the old regime in the Scottish burghs, thus conveniently giving the Whigs' middle-class allies a forum in which to expend their boundless energy. But, limited though it was, Whig reformism broke the Tory stranglehold on Scotland, and after 1832 the Tories found Scotland uncongenial soil. That trend was reinforced by the disruption of 1843, and for the rest of the nineteenth century Scotland was to be a Liberal bastion.

At that very time, in the 1830s, the real Industrial Revolution in Scotland was beginning. Neilson's hot-blast process enabled coal to be used for smelting and blackband ironstone for ore. This breakthrough led to the creation of a massive heavy industry complex located mainly in the west of Scotland. The way had been prepared for it by improvements in communications with the cutting of canals such as the Forth and Clyde and the Monkland in the late eighteenth century; and the coming of the railways in the first half of the nineteenth century confirmed the industrial predominance of the West Lowlands. The result was that by 1850 shipbuilding on the Clyde was rapidly developing into the premier industry of Scotland, and the country's economy no longer rested on agriculture and textiles but on export-oriented heavy industry.

The new society thus created was ill-regulated and afflicted by serious problems. Urban overcrowding or rural squalor were the lots of too many, and lack of hygiene and inadequate water supplies led to increasingly poor public health. Mortality rates soared. Nor was the countryside unaffected. Too many farm laborers subsisted on the margin of destitution, and conditions of life and labor in the mines were frankly horrific. In the east of Scotland little girls from the age of eight had to carry loads of coal in creels from the wall face to the pit bottom. Many of the children, boys as well as girls, were physically deformed by the crushing, dangerous toil. Those today who believe that laissez-faire never existed should look at the graphic line drawings that illustrated the Royal Commission Report of 1842 on Children's Employment. R. H. Franks, the reporter, was scandalized and concluded that "a picture is presented of deadly physical oppression and systematic slavery, of which I conscientiously believe no one unacquainted with such facts could credit the existence in the British dominions."

The irony is that in a country that was visibly growing richer, the poor got poorer and more numerous. This was the paradox that bedeviled Scottish society in the first half of the nineteenth century and occasioned a great public controversy about poor relief. Should the existing system, which, based on the realities of the old rural society, restricted relief to the impotent poor, be reformed or not? The prevailing social philosophy frowned on reform. Thomas Chalmers, a leading Evangelical minister of the Church of Scotland, headed those who demanded retention of the old system, while medical reformer Professor W. P. Alison of Edinburgh, who believed that a better system of poor relief would effectively combat typhus, was the champion of its reform. In the end a New Poor Law Act was passed in 1845 which preserved most of the principles of the old and stood by the notion of self-help, but introduced a more secular organization. The New Poor Law was, in fact, partly the consequence of a violent upheaval that tore the Church of Scotland asunder.

The ten years' conflict that issued in the disruption of 1843 was a complex phenomenon. Many of the principles in contention derived from the days of Knox and Melville and concerned the nature of Presbyterianism itself. But past, present, and even future weighed in the ten years' conflict, and hence its bewildering complexity. In short, the conflict had to do with the church's position in an evolving society and its relationship with the state. If the church could not respond to the social challenges of the times, many, Evangelicals mainly, feared that its proud tradition as a national church would come to an end. In particular it seemed likely that, cramped in its old structure and postures, the Church of Scotland would lose its hold, tenuous as that was, on the new industrialized Scotland that was rapidly growing and seemed destined to dominate the future.

The dissenters, too, were profiting from the failure of the established church in the urban areas. So the very existence of the established Church of Scotland seemed also to be at issue. Dead-hand moderatism could make nothing of those problems, and the strength of the Evangelicals steadily grew with fears for the future of the kirk. At last, in 1834, the Evangelicals won a majority in the General Assembly. But their chief acts, the Veto Act to prevent the intrusion of unwanted ministers on congregations by patrons and the Chapel Act to give ministers in newly erected parishes full status in church courts, were challenged by the Moderates and condemned in the civil courts.

Parliament badly fumbled the issue, unable to see the Scottish establishment except through Anglican spectacles, and an act of Parliament that would meet the needs of the Church of Scotland could not be obtained. In the end the nonintrusionists refused to accept that the Church of Scotland was the creature of the state, as the legal decisions asserted, and marched out of the establishment, led by Thomas Chalmers, to form the Free Church of Scotland.

An inevitable result of the disruption was a weakening of the kirk's role as a national establishment. The Church of Scotland could no longer effectively supervise poor relief, and hence the New Poor Law Act of 1845. The kirk's ability to supervise education also declined, though sectarian battles prevented the establishment of a state system until 1872. In short, the disruption led to the emergence of a more secular approach to social administration, and led, too, to the further waning of the social discipline exercised by the kirk.

Finally, on the debit side, the fierce rancor to which the ten years' conflict and the disruption gave rise damaged the universities and helped to smother the Scottish intellectual tradition. But all was not lost. The disruption was above all a magnificent act of idealism, and not least because it was a massive repudiation of claims for the omnipotent state that were then arising.

By the mid-nineteenth century the age of laissez-faire was drawing to a close and centralization was beginning to predominate. All was to be directed from Westminster. To act or not to act was regarded as the prerogative of the omnipotent mother of Parliaments. By this time the practical home rule of Henry Dundas's prime had become a mere memory. In 1826 Sir Walter Scott, protesting bitterly in his *Letters of Malachi* against a plan to curtail the issue of Scottish bank notes, had made the first stand against London absolutism. But by mid-century the concept of North Britain that had satisfied Scott and his contemporaries was fast fading. England became shorthand for United Kingdom, and in Europe Scotland meant simply an eccentric corner of Angleterre. Those changes were noted and resented by many Scots and led in 1853 to the formation of the National Association for the Vindication of Scottish Rights.

The National Association adhered to the union but complained bitterly of excessive centralization, feeble legislation, and chaotic administration. Indeed, slackness and inefficiency had become pronounced after the fall of management in 1827.

Some of the legislation of that period was in fact ludicrously bad. The disruption had left bitter memories of governmental neglect and legislative inertia. As a remedy the National Association demanded the appointment of a Scottish secretary to coordinate administration and see to the provision of legislation that was timely and effective. Thus, the very period that witnessed the triumph of the principle of centralization also inaugurated demands for devolution. The reason is not hard to find. The condition of Scotland in the mid-nineteenth century cried out for good government, and such could not be had. Not until the 1880s did a secretary and a Scottish office begin to emerge, and, such was the onward rush of centralization that they proved to be no panaceas. The provincial status of "Scotlandshire" became more and more pronounced.

But something of the Scottish ethos remained. Its purpose in a changing world became uncertain, but in some ways it retained its influence. Two outstanding examples can be cited. On August 15, 1856, an unwanted illegitimate child was born in a squalid one-room cottage at Legbrannock, a mining hamlet in Bothwell parish in north Lanarkshire. That child, James Keir Hardie, was to do much to fashion a new ethos and provide a vision of a more just and less-tortured society.

Just five months after Hardie's birth, the greatest of African explorers returned from his first tour of discovery to be feted by the Royal Geographical Society in London. The great explorer had been born in 1813 at Blantyre in that same corner of Lanarkshire, once celebrated for its beauty but then being converted into an industrialized wasteland. Of mixed Highland and Lowland blood and of humble stock, the famous explorer was the archetype of the new Scottish strain that was being evolved in the central belt. Typically, too, he began life as a cotton-spinner in Monteith's Mill at a time when the spinners were scorned as the dregs of humanity. But, determined to become a medical missionary, that boy had toiled by day and studied by night to attain his goal. For all the acclaim that he earned, David Livingstone remained proud of his Scottish working-class background. And Livingstone, like Hardie later, was a Congregationalist, mainly because he suspected the commitment of the Church of Scotland to the gospels; and, like Keir Hardie again, he responded to the age-old and timeless democratic creed that had inspired Robert Burns. Happy would it have been for Africa had it known only explorers of Livingstone's kind and never heard of Stanley or King Leopold! For in the heart of darkest Africa Livingstone was often heard humming a song, whose message, "When man to man, the world o'er,/ Shall brothers be for a' that," he applied in his day-to-day contact with Africans.

The great changes wrought in Scotland since 1707, and the devastating social effects that so often accompanied the generation of wealth, had evidently not obliterated the idealism of the Scots. Rather, the clearances and a high rate of emigration had combined with the ancient *perfervidum ingenium Scotorum* to carry that idealism into the four corners of the earth.

This aerial view of Edinburgh shows the New Town looking east toward Arthur's Seat. On October 26, 1767, James Craig began laying out the New Town. His plan, with its parallel streets and anchoring public squares, was more than an exercise in logical Georgian city planning. It was a program in which the streets themselves symbolized the union of the two crowns and the reign of King George III and Queen Charlotte. The churches dedicated to the patron saints of Scotland and England, Andrew and George, were to be the focal points of squares at each end of the long avenue, George Street. On each side of George Street smaller streets for shops were called the Thistle and the Rose. Queen Street lies to the north and Princess Street to the south.

Glenfinnan, at the head of Loch Shiel on the western end of the great rift scoured by glaciers which divides the Highlands, is dear to many Scots for its association with Bonnie Prince Charlie. At Glenfinnan, Charles raised his standard on August 19, 1745, signaling the beginning of the rising against the English. Just eight months later and fewer than seventy-five miles away, at Culloden moor (above) east of Inverness, he lost the battle that doomed his cause.

Robert Burns's house in Dumfries was the last residence of the poet, a modest row house befitting his humble station as a tax collector. Though he tried to follow his father's livelihood of farming, he was not successful and ultimately had to seek employment in the town.

At St. Michael's churchyard in Dumfries, Burns's tomb is the white Grecian temple at the back of the churchyard. The romantic legend of Burns as a simple farmer is reinforced by the sculpture inside the tomb depicting the Muse of Poetry finding him at the plough.

Burns was not suited for crop-growing, but not until the first volume of his work was published in Kilmarnock in 1786 did he feel certain about his vocation. His popularity expanded rapidly; he was patronized by lords and established writers; but the headiness of success may have proved unsettling to his politics, and he remained in conflict about the comparative merits of English and his native Scots for the diction of his poems. Still, as a chronicler of his nation's moods, as a singer, and as a song-collector, Burns had no peer. Alexander Nasmyth painted this notable portrait (opposite).

Souter Johnnie's house, a thatched cottage, was the home of village cobbler or "souter" John Davidson, whom Burns immortalized in his spirited narrative poem *Tam o'Shanter*. It is now one of several Burns museums and displays cobblers' tools typical of those Davidson would have used.

This view from Edinburgh Castle shows the gardens at the foot of Castle Hill—once the site of North Loch—and the imposing facades of the Royal Scottish Academy (at left) and the National Gallery. Beyond, along Prince's Street, is the Walter Scott monument.

Culzean, a fortified house dating from medieval times, was transformed into an elegant Georgian castle by Robert Adam in the late eighteenth century. The spectacular site on a high cliff overlooking the Firth of Clyde near Ayr in southwest Scotland enhances the romantic image.

Mellerstain, one of the great houses of Scotland and an exceptionally fine example of the work of Robert Adam, is also notable as the work of father and son, for it was begun by William Adam for George Baillie of Jerviswood in 1725. The Mellerstain gardens were originally designed in a Dutch style. The present gardens, more in keeping with the Adam architecture and interiors, were laid out in 1909 by Sir Reginald Blomfield.

Sir Walter Scott as painted by Henry Raeburn. Scott read voraciously as a child, when illness kept him indoors. His prodigious memory served him well for the rest of his life. He worked hard as the clerk of sessions and as sheriff depute of Selkirkshire for twenty-five years; but the world remembers the literary productions that flowed from his pen for almost four decades. He began as a poet and ballad-collector, seeking to create within Scotland a counterpart to Goethe's treatment of Rhine manners and culture. Acknowledging Byron's superior talents, he turned from poetry to the writing of the Waverley novels. These fictions, dealing with the past of both Scotland and medieval England, took Europe by storm, and became the leading influence on writers in dozens of nations for more than a century.

7

The Scottish Enlightenment

Harold Orel

Art During the Enlightenment

Marilyn Stokstad

178

THE SCOTTISH ENLIGHTENMENT is extraordinary on several counts. What happened north of the border was infinitely more exciting, in an intellectual sense, than almost anything taking place in England. Yet ungrudging recognition of the distinctive Scottish character of the Enlightenment movement within the British Isles has been largely delayed until the current generation of historians. For a nation of limited population, resources, and opportunities, the length of the Enlightenment far exceeded any reasonable expectations (running, as it did, almost a full century, from the 1730s until the 1820s). Moreover, as a movement it touched practically every profession and vocation in the land. The boast of David Hume, in 1757, that the Scots had become "the People most distinguish'd for Literature in Europe," antedated the splendid achievements of Burns and Scott, and yet was fully justified at the time of its utterance. Five universities in Scotland (if we count as two institutions King's College and Marischal College in Aberdeen) may be contrasted with Oxford and Cambridge, the only two universities of England; Scotland, at the end of the eighteenth century, had only 1.6 million people, and England more than 5 million, and even if we count Trinity (Dublin) on the English side, the balance is not adjusted.

The ability of great men to flourish in the cold kingdom of the north suggests the importance of university tradition as a shaping force in Scottish life. As far back as the fourteenth century, when England and Scotland supported rival popes, it became evident that sending a young Scot to England for his higher education might serve only to alienate him from native sentiments and soil. Benedict XIII, a pope backed by the Scots, issued a bill founding the University of St. Andrews. This first university was followed by Glasgow (1451), King's College, Aberdeen (1495), Edinburgh (1582), and Marischal College, Aberdeen (1593). One should also mention St. Salvator's College at St. Andrews (founded in 1450), as well as, in the same city, St. Leonard's and St. Mary's Colleges (early sixteenth century). Scottish education tended to be much more democratic than English, and more thorough as a finishing ground for the best students from more than three thousand schools.

In the century of our primary concern, the eighteenth, Latin was dropped as the language for formal academic lectures. A development fully as striking for what it implied for the future was the abandonment of the regenting system, whereby one professor, a regent, taught several different subjects to the same class; worked with books that he approved and selected; and supervised disputations. Regenting had more drawbacks than the obvious overreliance on a single man's range of information. It is to the credit of the Scots that they perceived the true nature of the problems: the rapid dating of information in set texts that were apt to be retained long past their period of maximum usefulness, the inevitable delays in recognizing the emergence of new disciplines (such as political economy), and the difficulties faced by those who held regentships in becoming noted for scholarship in medicine, mathematics, or any single science. With the end of regenting it became possible to establish separate chairs. Scotsmen no longer had to travel to Leiden or to London to study medicine. Before the century ended Scottish doctors were tending Peter the Great, Elizabeth, Catherine the Great, and Alexander I of Russia; and Scottish medicine had become the envy of Europe. Research degrees were, for the first time, an available option. A Scotsman could take honors, also for the first time. Indeed, law and science degrees proliferated, while the number and importance of degrees in divinity inevitably diminished. The number of students multiplied over the span of a century, quadrupling at Edinburgh, quintupling at Aberdeen. And young men came from other lands to Scottish universities.

William Inglis was president of the Royal College of Surgeons and captain of the Honorable Company of Edinburgh Golfers. Golf has been played in Scotland since the thirteenth century.

Professor Dugald Stewart is the classic example of the philosopher of "common sense." Expanding further on theories developed by Adam Ferguson, who taught moral philosophy at Edinburgh, and Thomas Reid, Adam Smith's successor at Glasgow, Stewart attracted a devoted following of students. A political liberal, humane, dedicated to the idea of social progress, and a skilled orator, he passed on the concept of an intelligent and principled public morality.

Learning at the university level became more accessible, partly through the expansion of bursary funds; increasingly empirical and practical-minded; and higher in quality and more advanced than almost anything offered in England or on the Continent. In addition, it was more conscientiously taught, often by truly distinguished educators. At least a few should be named: Dugald Stewart, John Millar, John Playfair, and James Gregory. These teachers, of course, possessed what inspiring educators in every age have known how to exploit successfully—curiosity; enthusiasm; an interest in students over and beyond the classroom experience; and a strong sense of service, manifesting itself in careful preparation of lectures. But the history of European education in the eighteenth century bears witness to the rarity of this kind of dedication. We are, indeed, talking about a new commitment to education.

Universities expanded intellectual horizons in all directions, but they dealt with limited numbers of students at best. At the secondary level the Scottish church tremendously improved elementary education in the Lowlands, while a Scottish branch of the Society for Promoting Christian Knowledge (S.P.C.K.) founded hundreds of elementary schools in the Highlands. English was taught at the expense of Gaelic. Inevitably there was a serious cultural loss; but Highlands and Lowlands were beginning, perhaps for the first time, to understand and appreciate the nature of the problems shared by both. The efforts of the church to establish a school in every parish were perhaps more heroic than has generally been understood. Transference of the responsibility for general education to the state, the establishment of elected school boards, and the making of students' attendance a compulsory habit built upon the solid foundation of the preceding century.

It is only fair to note the problems confronted by those who fought to extend the boundaries, and improve the quality, of the primary schools. As in Ireland, the dominie was usually underpaid and his social status was low, so that, to make ends meet, he took second and third jobs. A girl had much poorer chances for acquiring an education than a boy. Some parishes were too poor, some too stingy, to fund adequately the schools that were needed. The sparsely populated Highlands suffered from additional difficulties, such as the unpopularity of the established church, the poor communications between settlements, and the reluctance of Gaelic-speaking parents to allow their children to learn the language of a conqueror.

Antagonism to the English language was not limited to the Highlands. Scots was no longer a viable literary language by the mid-eighteenth century. Latin was seen, more and more, as an inadequate medium for the purposes of commerce, science, and education in a modern society. The arrogance of those members of the intelligentsia who insisted on eliminating Scotticisms from polite literature had a humbling, if not a downright humiliating, effect on writers who were seeking to make their way. Even Burns, militantly patriotic though he was, never made up his mind firmly on the question as to which language best suited his genius, and *The Cotter's Saturday Night*, for all its fine achievement as a poem, comes down to us as an uneasy compromise between rival traditions of language.

Yet the forces of education at work in Scotland were powerfully consistent in their view of what needed to be done. All classes of society needed more and better educational opportunities. Education was never conceived in narrow nationalistic terms. Its leaders drew from the teachings and writings of many cultures and willingly investigated new ways of thinking, no matter where they originated. A remarkable highmindedness, an objectivity about ideas, and a respect for the ground rules of debate marked the Scottish Enlightenment. And, not to be forgotten in any review of principles subscribed to by Scottish educators, there ran a deep current of faith in the need of man to recognize his ties to a social structure. An individual possessed talents and earned a claim to dignity by the sheer fact of his existence; but his true worth could be tested only by the number and quality of his contributions to the *group*.

When we speak of Scottish education as being both pragmatic and democratic, we are not far from Burns's classic vision of the day when a Parliament of Man shall be inaugurated:

> Then let us pray that come it may,
>   As come it will for a' that,
> That sense and worth, o'er a' the earth,
>   May bear the gree,* and a' that,
>   For a' that and a' that,
>   It's coming yet, for a' that,
>   That man to man, the warld o'er,
>   Shall brothers be for a' that.
>   —"For A' That and A' That"

It may well be that this poem, composed in the full flush of enthusiasm for the French Revolution, would have been repudiated as the bloody consequences of that historical event became better known in Scotland, and if Burns had lived longer. Yet its sentiment is a natural and inevitable development of sentiments expressed by John Knox and his colleagues in the *First Book of Discipline* (1560), a work that advocated access to elementary, grammar, and university-level institutions. Knox set up no religious tests, no barriers based on either economic status or social class. Distrust of rank that based its claims upon inherited wealth was widespread in Scottish literature and philosophy. Burns was by no means the only champion of the common man; his popularity among readers of all classes testifies to the fact that the leveling he spoke of was not seen as demagogic or irresponsible.

Along with education, the Church of Scotland may be counted as a second great force moving in the direction of freer intellectual endeavor. Such a claim may seem surprising only if we believe that the institution had remained static, narrowly intolerant, and gloomy about the relationship of man to his fellow man as well as to his God. It is true that when patronage returned in 1712, after a break of more than two decades, the right of secession became an important disruptive influence. Some 90 percent of the benefices were controlled by the crown, the nobility, and the gentry. Conflicts over choices for the post of minister pitted the local landowner all too often against the congregation. It soon became clear that a great split was developing between the Moderates and the defenders of the traditional faith. The patrons were often more liberal-minded than the congregations they sought to serve.

By mid-century the Moderates were gaining control of the Church of Scotland, and the Popular party, which demanded stricter regularity and discipline, might censure the new developments, but was powerless to arrest their progress. William Robertson was perhaps as influential as any single individual in helping to work out the growing democratization of the electoral process within the church.

The eighteenth century may be characterized, overall, as an age of relative religious peace, with secession serving as an invaluable escape mechanism for those who could not abide the new leadership. The Episcopal church, of course, was in eclipse because of its Jacobite sympathies during the risings of '15 and '45, and the imposition of heavy penal laws. These

181

* A gree is a prize.

were not repealed until 1792, after which time it began to grow again in size, wealth, and influence. The great withdrawal of approximately one-third of the ministers and members of the Church of Scotland, including practically all its missionaries and scholars, an event which has become known as the Disruption, and which led directly to the formation of the Free Church of Scotland, took place in 1843; the schism did not end until 1929. The eighteenth century tolerated, even encouraged, intellectual adventuring among the clergy. The Moderates produced ministers who cultivated interests in fields often far removed from traditional theology.

Alexander Carlyle, a minister, scandalized the elders by patronizing the theater. He enjoyed Hume, Smollett, and many other Scottish writers; he played cards; was a clubman, an authority on burgundy and claret, and the author of a lively *Autobiography*. Carlyle's memoir has colored later scholarship, which has used it as part of a general attack on the lack of theological content in Moderate literature; on the encouragement of dissent (and secession) by the Moderates in order to retain their grip on church machinery; and on a new form of religious bigotry no less pernicious because it was "rational," abolished hellfire, and advertised itself as the party of the majority.

But the Church of Scotland might not have survived if it had continually waged war on heretics or opposed major secular trends; if it had restricted its clergy exclusively to religious activities; or if it had become an agent of social and political reform, as some of the dissenters wished. The fact remains that under Robertson's leadership the Church of Scotland produced two generations of scholars, orators, authors of polite

Scottish dedication to books and learning is of long standing. Here in the eighteenth-century library at Traquair House the early system of cataloging and shelving books according to names of philosophers, whose portraits appear in the coving above, can still be seen.

literature, historians, experts in agriculture, and even dramatists. The church had become, by century's end, broad in its base, reasonable about problems of faith, and certainly less dogmatic than ever before.

A third great element in national history allowing for the development of Enlightenment thought was the astonishing economic and industrial progress that was taking place, particularly during the second half of the century. Chemical and iron factories were prospering. The sense that the New World held the key to future trade accounted for the dizzying growth of trade in Glasgow, which replaced Bristol and Liverpool as the tobacco center of Great Britain. Agriculture prospered, as did the traditional industries, and, later, so did cotton, largely as a consequence of the Act of Union. Although the population increased by only 50 percent during this century, the national revenue multiplied much more rapidly: fifty-one times. If there is any truism for the age, it is that this newly earned wealth encouraged an appetite for social and cultural amenities.

It may well be, as Hugh Trevor-Roper has argued, that the original contribution of the Scottish philosophers lay in the movement from psychology to sociology. It energized thought in a number of surprising ways: the redefinition of the terms of political economy, the founding of "utilitarianism," the coining of Francis Hutcheson's phrase "the greatest happiness of the greatest number," and the adaptation of Hume's philosophy to Whig politics in a clever fashion that made possible the emergence of new doctrine in the writings of Macaulay and Mill in the early nineteenth century. Trevor-Roper has emphasized the breaking-out of Scottish intellectuals—late in the seventeenth century—from religious barriers (France), political antagonisms (England), and hatreds generated by determinedly intolerant members and leaders of the national kirk. The defeat of a narrow nationalism meant the end of isolation and the resumption of foreign contacts on a full scale.

183

In the development of centers of thought, universities, however important, played only one role among many. "Voluntary bodies" of association should be cited. The Edinburgh Speculative Society, founded in 1764, counted among its members Dugald Stewart, Walter Scott, Henry Brougham, Francis Jeffrey, and Henry Cockburn. It lasted into the next century. Though it originated as a student association, members proudly maintained their memberships after they left the university. The Medical Society began as a student organization that self-consciously imitated a society run by and for professors, but by the 1760s a substantial library had come into existence for the benefit of members; by the 1770s a building was needed to house its books and facilitate its meetings; and after it was renamed the Royal Medical Society in 1778, its considerations of topics related to the physical and natural sciences as well as medicine led to lively meetings, many of them controversial. Organizations specializing in natural history, law, and philosophy attracted enough members to justify the establishment of similar kinds of libraries, volumes of proceedings and papers, and traditions of debate. These societies included the Newtonian Club and the Aberdeen Philosophical Society, clubs for investigators of topics of both general and specialized interest, and organizations devoted to the botanical gardens and museums that are distinctively eighteenth-century phenomena.

All these societies were "learned" to some extent. They provided mutual reinforcement for members who, as individuals, could not afford to publish their own papers. They stimulated discussion. They enabled scholars working in widely scattered locations to pool their data and expertise. They strengthened the ties between academic research and the workshop or laboratory where the results of research might be put to work.

Membership was often open to the landed gentry as well as to pro-

The gentlemen of Scotland improved
their minds by study, reflection, and
good conversation. This 1773
painting was probably done at
William Fullerton's home, Carstairs
House, where Captain Ninian Lowis
lived at the end of his life. The
painter, John Seton, worked in
Edinburgh and in India.

fessionals in a given field. This broadening of interests proved beneficial
to all concerned. Names of distinction in this gallery of societies include the
Select Society, founded by the artist Allan Ramsay. The Rankins Society
of Edinburgh, founded in 1716, takes pride of place as the first true society
of the Scottish Enlightenment. It gave a tremendous push to the fortunes
of Berkeleyan philosophy in Scotland. The Political Economy Club of
Glasgow proved helpful to Adam Smith as he collected materials for *The
Wealth of Nations*. The Aberdeen Philosophical Society (the "Wise Club")
redefined its early theological concerns in a way that made possible the
investigation of "philosophical" subject matter. The Society of Antiquaries was sometimes described as "anti-Enlightenment" because it
proposed a concept of natural history opposed to the more liberal one
espoused by the Royal Society of Edinburgh. The Wernerian Natural
History Society debated the relative merits of the theories held by the
German geologist Abraham Gottlob Werner (who believed in a
"catastrophic" theory of creation, whereby giant upheavals in the earth
changed the structure of the earth) and James Hutton (whose *Theory of the
Earth* of 1783 preached the probability of a more gradual series of changes,
influenced by glaciation, weathering, and slow shifts of various formations,
a theory that has become the basis of modern geology and is referred to as
"uniformitarian"). Other convivial clubs of some demonstrable interest to
Enlightenment concerns were Simon's Club in Glasgow, and the Poker, the

Oyster, and the Friday Clubs in Edinburgh; and specialist clubs such as the Harveian Society, which met faithfully for a dinner on April 12, Harvey's birthday, and the Aesculapian Club.

Some of these organizations were self-consciously dedicated to "improving" the conditions of Scottish life as well as thought. Since one of the most important of them was related to agriculture, this seems as appropriate a place as any to record that Scottish innovations in agricultural practice rapidly supplanted the English way of doing things from the 1730s on. Scottish inventors contributed significantly to early versions of, and invented the modern concept of, the threshing machine. James Clark developed the modern horseshoe (1770), which replaced the "broad-dished" type used throughout Europe; more important, his work, *A Treatise on the Prevention of Disease Incidental to Horses* (1788), defined for the first time a rational and modern scheme for the handling of a much-abused farm animal. James Small invented the first modern plow, which eliminated two oxen from the ploughing team.

Scotland's advances in agricultural science compressed more than half a millennium into less than five decades, and the abandonment of the runrig system in favor of enclosed fields was an important development in the catching-up process. The Society of Improvers in the Knowledge of Agriculture (founded in 1723) multiplied branches and correspondents throughout Scotland. For Scots lairds, as well as for fascinated observers not directly dependent on the land for their living, ways of improving agricultural practices became a favored topic of discussion. In particular, the methods used in East Lothian, where high farming was favored (as opposed to mixed farming that combined grain and pasture in varying proportions), attracted experts from both Europe and the New World. Scottish dairy farming, the quality of beef, and sheep runs were all markedly superior to comparable industries south of the border.

There were, of course, serious problems involved in this accelerated growth of farm production. It would be a lopsided account that omitted all mention of the Levelers, who destroyed fences because of their rage at land enclosures that allowed for the expansion of black-cattle breeding; or the patchy nature of improvements, which left untouched huge areas of

Breeding and racing of horses was an eighteenth-century obsession. Careful breeding, after the introduction of Arabian horses in Stuart times, produced elegant mounts like the one shown here, ridden by the twelfth earl of Cassillis in a race from Culzean to Glasgow.

Scotland; or the rises in the cost of living which affected rural as well as city populations, and accelerated emigration from the Lowlands and Highlands both. By the time of the American War of Independence fully one-seventh (possibly one-sixth) of the population of the colonies was of Scottish blood. Benjamin Franklin estimated that one-third of the population of Pennsylvania was Scottish. These people had left Scotland to improve their lot in the New World, and the pace of agricultural improvement in the land they left behind was by no means rapid enough for them. Yet the heartening element here is that all the changes that took place in the world of agriculture were made by people open to the possibility of its improvement in long-standardized, long-static practices. The Society of Improvers had more than three hundred members, including landlords and peers, but also dukes and professors. Agricultural development was not simply a consequence of intelligent use of new inventions, but an essential element in the history of the Scottish Enlightenment.

This whole subject is intimately connected with the increasing sophistication of Scottish science. It is understandable that developments in both theoretical and applied science should have been limited during the first half of the eighteenth century, when the Jacobite wars disrupted the Highlands. Still, the name of Colin Maclaurin (1698–1746) is worth remembering in any world history of science for his original contributions to his century's extension of principles inherent in Newtonian calculus and geometry. Maclaurin became professor of mathematics at Marischal College, Aberdeen, and then, on the basis of Newton's recommendation (1725), moved to the University of Edinburgh, where some fifteen years later, he defended Newton (against George Berkeley) in his *Treatise*. After his death, his account of Sir Isaac Newton's *Philosophical Discoveries* was published. Maclaurin's Theorem is still taught; his system of generating conics, his method for distinguishing between maxima and minima in general (in the theory of the multiple points of curves), and his formulation of a concept of level surfaces gave him an international reputation. Like Michelangelo in an earlier age, he was entrusted with the defense of a city (Edinburgh). After the Jacobites took the Scottish capital by a ruse, he died worn out by exertions suffered in fleeing from Edinburgh to York.

The first half of the century produced other men of scientific talent such as James Stirling (1692–1770), whose *Methodus Differentialis* (1730) summed an infinite series; James Douglas (1675–1742), an anatomist of distinction; William Smellie (1697–1763), obstetrician and promulgator of an improved midwifery; James Ferguson (1710–1776), who designed an orrery and a number of historically significant astronomical mechanisms and instruments; James Short (1710–1768), optician and developer of parabolic mirrors for telescopes; and David Gregory (1661–1710), perhaps the most famous theoretical physicist of the age. Still, these decades were limited to a few individuals struggling heroically to make their colleagues aware of developments that were being reported in other languages.

Of the quality of Scottish scientific endeavor in the second half of the century there can be no doubt. Scotland provided the best medical education in Great Britain—in the world, some claimed. Even before the University of Edinburgh set up its own medical school, one existed which members of the Royal College of Physicians and the Royal College of Surgeons had aided in developing.

Key movers in the development of Scottish medicine were the members of the Monro family. Father, son, and grandson, all physicians, held in successive appointments the chair of anatomy and surgery at the University of Edinburgh for more than a century. Alexander Monro (1697–1767) denominated *Monro primus*, helped to establish the Royal

Infirmary, an invaluable tool in clinical teaching. Paying close attention to the teachings of Hermann Boerhaave, the eminent Dutch physician whose work had made the University of Leiden the foremost training ground for doctors in Europe, the father defined the relationship of jaundice to the bile tract; improved surgical instruments and procedures; and cooperated with the lord provost George Drummond to make the university a more attractive place for students from the North American colonies, and to open its gates to dissenters from the Anglican high church.

His son, also called Alexander, or *Monro secundus* (1733–1817), performed the invaluable task of collecting his father's papers, including an account of inoculation in Scotland; and made for himself an independent and even greater reputation as the author of *Three Treatises on the Brain, the Eye, and the Ear* (1797). He discovered how the lateral ventricles of the brain communicated, which to this day carries the name *Monro's foramen*. He was the first to use the stomach pump to puncture, surgically, a body cavity in order to drain fluid, an operation of great importance in its time. His crucial work on *Functions of the Nervous System* (1783) achieved immediate recognition as a pioneering study. His specialty, comparative anatomy, attracted so many students that, by century's end, the number of earned medical degrees had quadrupled over the number conferred in the 1730s.

The grandson, Alexander Monro, or *Monro tertius* (1773–1859), taught at Edinburgh from 1798 to 1846. Though he lacked the brilliance of his forebears, and indeed lectured from his grandfather's notes, his pupils included Sir Humphry Davy and Charles Darwin.

William Cullen (1710–1790) taught at Edinburgh as professor of chemistry and later as professor of the theory of physics. He was a gifted lecturer, clear in his expositions, and attractive to large numbers of intelligent students. Perhaps his main gifts lay in his ability to systematize, to bring order out of chaos. For example, he was the first to realize how worthless many of the pharmaceutical formulae had become in the light of advancing information about medicinal ingredients, and his *Materia Medica Catalogue* (1776) was a serious and truly revolutionary advance in pharmacopoeia. Again, he rendered like service for the medical profession by establishing, in *Synopsis Nosologicae Medicae* (1785), a system for classifying major diseases.

One of his pupils was Joseph Black (1728–1799). From Cullen, Black learned the value of original research. Though he published little during his lifetime, his work proved hugely provocative. Many of his pupils were later to claim and gain credit for discoveries that he had made. His thesis for the M.D. demonstrated, for the first time, how carbon dioxide was formed. He has been credited with founding quantitative pneumatic chemistry. He discovered the bicarbonates. He defined, though perhaps not as carefully as then-available instruments permitted, the latent heats of freezing and of vaporization of water. In 1760 he proposed the concept of specific heat. Black's work made clear that chemistry could no longer be considered a handmaiden to medicine, but was a noble science in its own right.

Black's brilliant contributions to a number of fields indicated that his polymathic mind had genuine interests in the projects of others. So it proved, perhaps never more fruitfully than when he advanced the then-enormous sum of £1,000 to James Watt to finance experiments with the steam-engine concept. Watt paid attention to Black's lecture material on latent heat, and remembered it when one day he was asked to repair a Newcomen engine. Watt perceived, as others had done, that the engine wasted steam prodigally because it did not perform with a satisfactory heat balance. The heat lost in changing the state of the substance—the

An unlikely candidate for father of the Industrial Revolution, James Watt began his career inauspiciously as an instrument cleaner and repairer at the University of Glasgow after a brief apprenticeship in London. Watt's skill and diligence quickly earned him the respect and friendship of his colleagues.

Watt's first practical introduction to the steam engine came about when he was asked to repair a model of Newcomen's engine (below left) at the University of Glasgow. The Newcomen engine was an essential but inefficient source of power whose use was limited to crude tasks and to sites where there was a plentiful supply of cheap fuel.

Recognizing the shortcomings of Newcomen's engine, Watt designed a revolutionary modification of the engine. By creating a separate condenser (below right), he dramatically increased the efficiency and power of the engine.

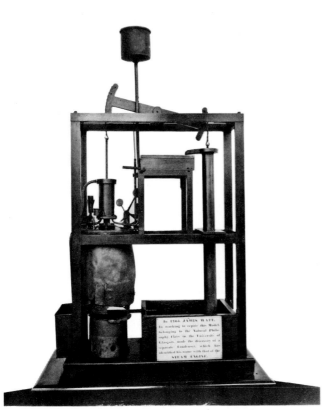

Once the basic invention had been made,
Watt spent the balance of his career
developing refinements, adaptations, and
improvements to the elementary design.
One such example, and one of the
earliest of its kind, is the double-acting,
rotative beam engine (above) with its
separate condenser and air pump made at
the Soho factory near Birmingham in
1788. It was known as the lapp engine
because of its employment in driving
machinery for "lapping" or polishing
steel ornaments.

At right is a detail of the engine.

latent heat—had to be trapped. In the Newcomen engine, steam was forced into the cylinder, an action which forced the piston out to the end of its stroke. A jet of water would then be injected into the cylinder to cool it and to condense the steam. Atmospheric pressure would, at that point, return the piston to the position from which it had begun its movement. Watt's contribution to the steam engine, made after protracted and often disheartening experimentation, was the concept of a condenser, separate from, yet connected to, the cylinder. But such a bald statement hardly begins to note the brilliance or the multiplicity of his achievements.

Watt invented a sun-and-planet gear to enable a shaft to make a double revolution for each stroke of an engine; a double-acting engine which created pushing as well as pulling movements for a piston; parallel motion, or a rod connection that, by perpendicular motion, guided the piston rod; and a novel means of applying the centrifugal governor to control engine speed automatically. Watt may well be the best-remembered Scottish scientist of the age. His genius did not depend on university training, and indeed he thought of himself as a journeyman. Nor was he the inventor of the steam engine, though he is often credited as such; yet the modern world, and the Industrial Revolution in which Scotland figured so prominently, is hardly conceivable without Watt's contributions.

Watt's genius found expression in improvements for a combustion furnace; an ink designed for the copying of letters; a machine that sculptured busts and figures; a means of press-copying letters and drawings; a screw propeller; and (independently) the identification of the elements composing water. He was one of the first to use, and to popularize, the slide rule. And perhaps he has never been given full credit for adapting the process of the French chemist Berthollet for bleaching by chlorine to the finishing processes involved in the linen industry. Watt's contribution to the history of the steamboat was critical, for though models of a steamboat had been built very early in the eighteenth century, only the improved steam engine made possible the developments of the 1780s.

The gallery of major contributors to the history of science and medicine in the eighteenth century is very crowded. John Brown (1735–1788), in *Elementa Medicinae* (1780), created a milestone in medical literature because it effectively discredited the universal practice of bloodletting as a cure-all for illness. Robert Whytt (1714–1766), a member of the Edinburgh Medical School, demonstrated the importance of the sympathetic nervous system. James Carmichael Smyth (1741–1821) discovered how to use nitrous acid gas to prevent the spread of contagion in fever cases, and another Scot, Sir Gilbert Blane (1749–1834), drew up the rules of the Quarantine Act of 1799. James Lind (1716–1794) learned, much earlier than anyone else, that lemon juice could be used as a specific against scurvy, and Sir Gilbert was responsible for persuading the Admiralty to issue a ration of lemon juice.

Sir John Pringle (1707–1782) is the founder of modern military medicine. He paid close attention to the role of putrefactive processes in spreading disease; he was deeply interested in antiseptics. Because he believed that hospitals ought to be treated as neutral by all belligerents, he is an acknowledged ancestor of the Red Cross philosophy. *Observations on the Diseases of the Army* (1752) was a revolutionary study, firmly based upon observations made while he served as physician general to the British forces in the Low Countries during the 1740s, when the War of the Austrian Secession raged. Sir John's work in analyzing the nature of dysentery, typhus, and influenza, as well as his enlightened views on how a military camp should protect its hygienic facilities, and thus its personnel, insure him a permanent niche in medical history.

We are really talking about men who founded entire sciences. William

One of the pioneer teachers of anatomy, Dr. William Hunter was one of the key figures in the advancement of surgery.

Hunter (1718–1783), for example, almost single-handedly created the profession of gynecology, by transferring obstetrics from midwives to doctors. His book, *The Anatomy of the Human Gravid Uterus, Exhibited in Figures* (1774), built upon the work of William Smellie, and his anatomical and pathological preparations became one of the great collections of the University of Glasgow. John Hunter (1728–1793), his brother, has been called the father of scientific surgery. He amassed a collection of more than ten thousand specimens (biological, pathological, and anatomical); served as physician extraordinary to King George III; and performed high-quality medical administration in his capacities as deputy surgeon general to the army (1786) and inspector general of hospitals (1790). One of his most important students was Edward Jenner, who is credited with the discovery of vaccination. Matthew Baillie (1761–1823) published *Morbid Anatomy of Some of the Most Important Parts of the Human Body* (1793), the first book in English that treated pathology as a separate subject, and systematized its study. Thomas Charles Hope (1766–1844) identified the new element strontium (named after a lead mine at Strontian, Ardnamurchan). He was the son of John Hope, professor of botany at the University of Edinburgh, who had founded the New Edinburgh Botanic Gardens (1776).

An embodiment of European Enlightenment, David Hume epitomizes those qualities of rationality, logic, and dispassionate examination which made the eighteenth century the foundation of contemporary thought. His sense of moderation and his healthy skepticism were famous then, and are admired now.

Scots were prime movers in the creation of the chemical industry. John Roebuck (1718–1794) developed the lead-chamber process and helped to start the huge sulphuric-acid plant at Prestonpans and, later, the Carron Iron Works, the first modern iron-smelting plant in Scotland. Francis Home (1719–1813), in his *Principles of Agriculture and Vegetation*, made clear for the first time many of the principles underlying plant nutrition and helped to found the paleotechnic bleaching industry. Charles Tennant (1768–1838) discovered bleach solution (1798). Scotsmen promoted air navigation. The Montgolfier brothers, famous for their heated-air balloon experiments in France in the 1780s, were heavily dependent on the gas research of Joseph Black. Black's pioneering work on CO_2 led, within thirty years, to preparation of hydrogen, chlorine, oxygen, and nitrogen by other investigators and to definitive statements on the composition of both air and water.

In two other fields, philosophy and literature, the Scottish honor roll, long as it is, must be limited in prudent observation of the space available here. At least one criterion for remembrance of specific philosophers at this late decade in the twentieth century must be the singular importance of these individuals for their times, though much of their work has inevitably diminished in importance as their disciples and later generations of thinkers built upon their works. Any history of the eighteenth century must look at the following individual men, if we are to understand why Scottish philosophy attracted the attention of students from many European nations as well as from across the Atlantic Ocean.

Francis Hutcheson (1694–1746) has often been called an English philosopher because his major works were published first in London, and because he began his career by quarreling with the writings of Hobbes and Bernard de Mandeville, thinkers whom he considered cynical, materialistic, and champions of selfish causes. In fact, Hutcheson was born in Ulster, where his father, like his grandfather before him, served as a Presbyterian minister. Though for a full decade he led an academy for the children of dissenting Presbyterians in Dublin, his own education was secured at the University of Glasgow (1711–17), and there he returned in 1730 as professor of moral philosophy, teaching and exerting an increasingly wider influence until his death. Adam Smith was one of his students, and *The Wealth of Nations* is deeply imbued with convictions about an innate moral sense, an essential element in Hutcheson's teaching. The writings of Hutcheson were well known to John Adams, Thomas Jefferson, and James Madison; their influence is traceable in documents ranging from the Constitution to the Federalist Papers.

Hutcheson's views on aesthetics, though of historical significance, were considered inoffensive by the divines. Hutcheson called attention to the existence of beauty in universal truths, and claimed that beauty affects our understanding of morality. Hutcheson stressed the likelihood (a certainty in his mind) that men possess a moral sense. Though he qualified his theory to suggest that the moral sense might be defective in some individuals, the presbytery of Glasgow, shocked by what it considered dangerous teaching that contravened the Westminster Confession, tried him for "false and dangerous" doctrines.

Specifically, it accused Hutcheson of preaching that the standard of moral goodness is the promotion of the happiness of others, and that one may know good and evil without knowing God, or even prior to a knowledge of God. The charges, brought in 1738, did not hold. Hutcheson has been seen as the great breaker-down of superstition, as one of the first rebels against ascetic and depressing Calvinist doctrine.

Henry Home (Lord Kames, 1696–1782) was one of Hutcheson's allies. *Essays on the Principles of Morality and Natural Religion* (1751) emphasized the importance of education and culture in refining the moral sense; but that the moral sense was innate he, too, had no doubt. In a number of stimulating and wide-ranging works that touched on aesthetics, the fine arts, and theology, Lord Kames advanced our appreciation of the role of reason in apprehending the glories of God. Reason enables us to see more clearly the relationship between beauty and pleasure as well as the need for postulating, within man, a sense of deity. Like Hutcheson before him, Lord Kames ran into strong opposition from some members of the Church of Scotland, and for a time *Essays* had to be withdrawn because of its implication that free will was an illusion. Lord Kames was also highly regarded as a historian and as a compiler of legal cases.

The distinctions between such terms as "philosopher" and "historian," or "economist" and "sociologist" were less clear-cut in the Enlightenment than they have since become. We are here considering various models of what Emerson was to call "man thinking." More of these "models" settled and worked in Edinburgh than in any other city of Scotland. Edinburgh was and remained the intellectual center of Scotland throughout this long period. No name shines more gloriously than that of David Hume (1711–1776), and this despite the fact that suspicions of his "atheism" prevented him from succeeding to the chair of philosophy at either the University of Edinburgh or the University of Glasgow.

Hume was known in his own time primarily as a historian. His philosophical treatises had been dismissed as the product of a skeptical mind. The antiobscurantist tone of Hume's writings may be appreciated best in his writings in both philosophy and history. Hume regarded the

David Hume is portrayed here by his celebrated contemporary, James Tassie, the gem engraver and sculptor.

Middle Ages as mostly given over to superstition and barbarism. He disliked the religious controversies that had impeded human progress, and he thought of himself as a rationalist, and of his philosophy as empirically based. Like his contemporary Voltaire, he respected the newly rediscovered tradition of skepticism as one of the chief avenues to true knowledge.

David Hume was not only the chief luminary of the Scottish Enlightenment, but in our imagination he remains today what he was during his lifetime, a most attractive and generous type of human being. Everyone liked him. Gibbon cheerfully and repeatedly confessed to having been influenced by Hume, and James Boswell called him "the greatest writer in Britain." The French spoke of him as "le bon David." And many Scots took pleasure in calling him "St. David," a tribute first offered by Voltaire. Such tributes can be multiplied: they came from Diderot, Montesquieu, Kant, and all who saw beyond his infirmities and corpulence to his astonishing mental faculty and his determinedly affirmative courage.

Hume's writings concentrated on philosophical problems, some political issues, and a history of England. He believed that logic, morals, criticism, and politics constitute the four main divisions of the science of man. Despite the objections of early reviewers that he was being willfully obscure, even egotistical in his use of the first person, his emphasis on the importance of learning how to define fundamentals proved salutary. What, after all, is knowledge? Whence does it originate? How reliable is it? Like Francis Hutcheson before him, Hume redefined the mind as "a heap or collection of different perceptions," or ideas. Though this destroyed "matter" along with "mind" and made increasingly difficult any argument for freedom of the will, Hume, in the *Treatise*, went further. Reason by itself could not motivate the will, and is (or ought to be) "the slave of the passions." The moral sense of man comes from sympathy, from a sense of identification with our fellowman. Men, from the beginning of time, have been social. Everything must be tested by reason, we must be able to judge, we must examine skeptically conflicting claims to our credulity. Hence his sweeping rejection of miracles, and his somewhat dry remark that "it is nothing strange...that men should lie in all ages."

Hume anticipated the doctrine of natural selection. In *Dialogues Concerning Natural Religion*, he suggested that God, in creating the universe, may have bungled by making so many species, all so deadly and hostile to one another. On political questions, Hume, in later writings, was to consider, with some sympathy, both communistic and democratic schemes for government, though he finally rejected them as overly facile answers to social problems. He stressed the paramount importance of labor, and the dangers of printing more money than an economy could accommodate.

Taken altogether, these works were increasingly widely recognized as constituting a body of doctrine for all who sought to modify, or expand, or even refute the main teachings of British empiricism. But Hume found his largest public with his complete *History of England* (1762), a work that began with two volumes on Stuart England (1754, 1757); continued with two more volumes, on Tudor England (1759); and concluded with two volumes dealing with Julius Caesar's invasion and continuing down to the Tudor period. There were immediate objections to his sympathetic portrayal of Charles I, for he described his execution as an overreaching by Cromwell, one that had established a dangerous precedent. But the Tories appreciated Hume's daring to say what was unpopular, while the Whigs admired the style of a history that Voltaire pronounced as possibly the best that had been written in any language.

As the monumental work wound slowly to its conclusion, it became clearer that Hume's insistent demands for documentation of the "ancient constitution" that sanctified demands made upon the king by the House of

Commons were inevitably bound to erode the folkloristic basis of conventional eighteenth-century history. Hume's analysis of the feudal social structure introduced by William the Conqueror into England, of the true nature of the victory won by the English over the Spanish Armada, and his masterful use of Clarendon's history of the English civil wars, make for stimulating reading more than two centuries later. Of special note is Hume's characterization of Sir Isaac Newton as "the greatest and rarest genius that ever rose for the ornament and instruction of the species."

Another writer whose achievements made Scottish historiography internationally respectable was William Robertson (1721–1793). His three great works, including *History of America* (1777), demonstrated a keen awareness of the value of primary sources, and an unwillingness to rest content with the judgments of earlier historians. Like Hume, he regarded the medieval period as *dark*. His anti-Jacobite sympathies focused, with a surprising sharpness of detail, on the untrustworthy behavior of Mary Queen of Scots, a woman who had become deified by generations of Scots who opposed the union of 1707. Again like Hume, his reputation in his own time rested largely on his historical writings.

But Robertson was also of the establishment, more centrally positioned than Hume ever was. Under the patronage of Lord Bute (also a Scotsman), Robertson served as chaplain of Stirling Castle (1759); principal of the University of Edinburgh from 1762 to 1792, a very long period indeed; as moderator of the General Assembly of the Presbyterian kirk (1763 on), as a recognition of the services he had rendered as a leader of the "Moderate" party since 1746; and as historiographer royal for Scotland, an appointment made by King George III (1763). The cant of religious fanaticism found one of its most implacable enemies in Robertson. He believed in property, government, law, freedom, and culture, and he saw the condition of all these things improving during his century.

Another of the great defenders of common sense as a guide to human conduct was Adam Ferguson (1723–1816). He served as chaplain to the Black Watch (1745–54), and participated in the battle of Fontenoy, in Flanders. Resigning from the ministry in 1754, he became Hume's replacement as keeper of the advocates' library in 1757, and then tutored the sons of the earls of Bute and Warwick. His tenure as professor of natural philosophy (from 1759), of moral philosophy (from 1764), and of mathematics at the University of Edinburgh provided him with the time needed for his imposing studies in moral philosophy and Roman history. Yet it is not for these that he is remembered today. Rather, his *Essay on the History of Civil Society* (1767) represented, at the time of its writing, one of the crucial first investigations of sociological theory.

Ferguson may be accounted the father of modern sociology. He differentiated between the nonpolitical aspects of a civil society and the state itself, and argued that the former helped to determine the nature of the latter. What he called the "social appetite in human souls" became "the great spring and source of human actions." Like Hume, he rejected the idea of a social contract. Kinship was more important. Individuals were less important than groups (or should be less important) to the historian endeavoring to trace the history of his nation. Ferguson's ideas were developed further by Saint-Simon, and they were assimilated in Marxist theories of social class during the next century.

One of Ferguson's admirers should be mentioned at this point: John Millar (1735–1801), who studied under Adam Smith and who shaped for himself a notable career as a professor of civil law (1761–1801) at the University of Glasgow. His important works stressed economic considerations in the history of man. First the necessities, then a growing sense of property. After that, laws are promulgated to distribute justice and recognize and protect "the various rights of mankind." When he dedicated *An Historical View* to Fox, he used, for the first time anywhere, the phrase "constitutional history," which was to become so important in later discussions of the prerogatives of the crown as opposed to those of Parliament.

The lasting fame of Adam Smith (1723–1790) is directly due to the major book of his career, *An Inquiry into the Nature and Causes of the Wealth of Nations* (1776). It would never have been written if the young Smith had not come under the influence of Hutcheson at the University of Glasgow; if he had not read Hume's *Treatise of Human Nature*, a work thought to have dangerously heretical content; and if he had not been supported in his early career by Lord Henry Kames. He summed up within his life many of the best elements of Enlightenment thought: a fearlessness about saying what may often have been said before, but saying it with originality and forcefulness of style; a timeliness of subject matter that appealed directly to a rising economic class of businessmen; and a personal attractiveness that endeared him to men of diverse interests.

We know less than we would like to know about Smith's childhood. At the age of four, he was kidnapped by gypsies; it is an odd episode in an otherwise placid life. Hutcheson's strong personality, as well as his exciting views on the economic basis of life, formed a rich educational experience for Smith, who was only seventeen at the time of his graduation. The high quality of his Scottish education did not prepare him for the slack, world-weary, and unimproving education that he encountered at Oxford. There he remained for six years, educating himself in preference to sitting at the feet of dons who did not care to teach. His lectures on rhetoric and polite literature, delivered at Edinburgh in 1748, led to a professorship of logic at Glasgow (1748) and moral philosophy (1749), also at Glasgow. His teaching made a strong impression on his students and on fellow Scots.

Smith's first published work, *The Theory of Moral Sentiments* (1759), announced several themes of importance to *The Wealth of Nations*, such as that of the "inner man" who acts as a moral judge of his own actions as well as those of others; the importance of sympathy as the basis of all our moral sentiments; and the importance of the rational faculty. The growing awareness that Smith in himself constituted a moral force for good led the wealthy Charles Townshend to offer him a handsome pension and the responsibility for tutoring his stepson and ward, the young duke of Buccleuch. The writing of his masterwork lasted from 1763 to 1776.

Although publication of *The Wealth of Nations* met a sympathetic reception, its sales were modest. Its influence, however, was enormous. It established a whole school of political economy. It became a justification for a doctrine of laissez-faire and industrial growth. Its optimistic, carefully reasoned style made it instantly—as it has since remained—a classic work of the Scottish Enlightenment. After its appearance, Smith was appointed commissioner of customs for Scotland, and was later elevated to the rectorship of the University of Glasgow (1787). Before his death, Smith destroyed most of his unfinished work and personal papers. After his burial in the churchyard at Canongate, the destruction of other manuscripts was carried on by others.

The doctrine preached in *The Wealth of Nations* has often been misunderstood. It would have been difficult, in the years preceding the outbreak of the American Revolution, to discern the true form of the emerging Industrial Revolution that would so soon transform the world. Adam Smith had little or nothing to say about huge corporations that might base their pyramiding wealth on scientific enterprise, differentiated labor skills, and a ruthless unconcern with the commonweal. But he anticipated problems that would inevitably arise if employers misunderstood the primary value of labor in establishing the market price of commodities, and his sympathies were much more often with the oppressed, the workers, than with those who benefited handsomely from their exertions. No man would have been more distressed than Smith by the way in which his theory so swiftly became dogma, justified middle-class arrogance toward the "lower orders," and led directly to nineteenth-century arguments (by Marx and others) that the world is a jungle of competing economic interests, and that the invisible-hand doctrine (the self-restraint which leads to harmonious adjustment between the interests of the individual and those of society) will not work in the absence of intelligent government constraints.

Yet it is clear, even after the passage of two centuries, that much of *The Wealth of Nations* makes good sense and represents enlightened doctrine. Smith did not blink from the likelihood that American resentment of unfair taxation policies might lead to an armed movement seeking independence, but, more important, he approved of the revolution. His definition of the three duties of the state—to protect a society from violence and invasion, to protect individuals from being exploited or oppressed by other individuals, and to establish "public works and public institutions" which the more limited resources of individuals could not afford—reverberated with an understanding of obligations owed by the state to those it sought to represent. He argued for the suppression of monopolies, the right of labor to organize, and the benefits of high wages. He was also an early champion of the necessity for abolishing slavery.

Thomas Reid (1710–1796) taught philosophy at King's College, Aberdeen (1751–64), after which he succeeded Adam Smith at the University of Glasgow as professor of moral philosophy. Reid became indignant about Hume's philosophy in the 1740s and spent much of the rest of his life attempting to refute its skepticism. Reid's *An Inquiry into the Human Mind on the Principles of Common Sense* (1764) denied that men can be sure only of their knowledge of their own senses and ideas. It proposes as an alternative the doctrine of common sense, or "original instinct," to reassure us of the reality of the external universe. Reid's work made it possible for philosophers to reaffirm the continuity of personal identity. Reid's attack on "the enchantment of words," i.e., contemporary metaphysics, and more specifically Hume's theory of ideas in which (Reid believed) the original error lay, heightened the awareness of the intelligentsia that Hume's work contradicted what they thought they knew about the everyday world, the nature of perception, and the relationship of reason to the passions. Reid's writings became critical to the teaching of Dugald Stewart and to Sir William Hamilton (1788–1856), the distinguished professor of logic and metaphysics at the University of Edinburgh; to the Frenchman Victor Cousin; to Italian and Belgian thinkers; to Ludwig Wittgenstein and G. E. Moore in this century; and to C. S. Peirce in the United States.

Of Scottish literature during this century books may be written, and have been written; but let us concentrate on four names only: John Home, James Macpherson, Robert Burns, and Walter Scott. The Scots Presbyterian minister John Home (1722–1808) was born at Leith, a fighter against the Jacobites in the rising of '45, and a preacher in the parish at Athelstaneford, Haddingtonshire. Home sought inspiration both in the legendary materials of his homeland and in classical literature. On the one hand, he was a key figure encouraging and persuading James Macpherson to publish his "translations" of Gaelic poems, which, perhaps as much as any single literary event, made possible the full flowering of English Romanticism. On the other hand, he adapted a theme from Plutarch in a tragedy, *Agis*, and wrote declamatory blank verse in a more successful, romantically flavored play, *Douglas*.

The event was noteworthy if only because any minister writing for the stage ran a calculated risk at a time when the theater was generally considered immoral. The play, which dramatized the grief of Lady Randolph, who had lost her infant son and had never reconciled herself to the event for some twenty years, had an extraordinary cast. William Robertson, David Hume, Alexander Carlyle, John Home (as Douglas), Adam Ferguson, and Hugh Blair, all important figures of the Enlightenment, were the principal players. Production and success led to a furious pamphlet war between Moderates and Evangelicals. The presbyteries of Glasgow and Edinburgh condemned, then formally accused, a number of those involved. Home decided to resign his charge the next year, but only after, in London, the theater management of Covent Garden staged it. Opening night was a tremendous success, and James C. Dibdin's *Annals of the Edinburgh Stage* (1888) recounts an oft-told anecdote about an event of that evening: when Young Norval "was busily employed giving out one of his rodomontading speeches, a canny Scot, who had been observed to grow more and more excited as the piece progressed, unable longer to contain his feelings, called out with evident pride, 'Whaur's yer Wully Shakspere noo!' "

Home, indeed, was to become known as the Scottish Shakespeare, and *Douglas*, to this day, resembles no other English play of the century. Many critics described it as a "perfect" example of the genre, and it remained popular in America for fully half a century. It may be that an important element in eighteenth-century praise of *Douglas* was the fact that the play's success gave an important victory to religious Moderates. Writing for and attending the theater were no longer such hazardous enterprises.

James Macpherson (1736–1796), an obscure schoolmaster from Inverness-shire, was genuinely interested in the fragments of primitive poetry still known and recited in the Highlands. The stimulus needed for his great life's undertaking—the collection and publication of these materials in *Fragments of Ancient Poetry Collected in the Highlands of Scotland and Translated from the Gaelic or Erse Language* (1760), *Fingal, An Ancient Epic* (1761, dated 1762), and *Temora, An Epic Poem* (1763)—was provided by John Home and by Hugh Blair, the fashionable Presbyterian divine who served as pastor of the High Church, Edinburgh, and as the first occupant of the chair of rhetoric and belles-lettres in Edinburgh. Macpherson did not translate directly from Gaelic originals, but embroidered and wrote reminiscences and echoes of numerous manuscripts that he consulted while touring the Highlands. He exaggerated, for reasons of his own, the difficulty of publishing the originals on which he had based his work. Though Wordsworth censured Macpherson for falsifying not history but nature, there was grandeur in many passages of the "translations." Western Europe responded with enthusiasm to the primitivism and sentimentalism of the poetry, which appeared in the form of a rhythmic prose and which frequently exploded in stirring exhortations and exclamations.

Macpherson may well have been the most important poet of Europe for fully half a century. The provenance of the original materials, despite the spirited controversy that they provoked, was ultimately less significant than the impact of the Ossianic "poems" on a large number of creative geniuses: Goethe, Herder, Schiller, Blake, Coleridge, Scott, Byron, Diderot, and practically every French Romantic poet of the nineteenth century. The Italian translation by Cesarotti was carried everywhere by the young Napoleon, who thought that Macpherson's work was superior to that of Homer.

The muse of Caledonia, Robert Burns (1759–1796), was the greatest

James Boswell achieved his greatest fame as the biographer of Dr. Samuel Johnson in a book that Thomas Macaulay described in the *Edinburgh Review* of 1831 as "assuredly a great, a very great work." But Boswell's Scottish roots go deep, and it was no casual impulse that led him, a son of Lord Auchinleck, to attempt to revise Dr. Johnson's prejudices against the Scots and Scotland. Ultimately, he persuaded the elder man to visit the northern kingdom and the result of that trip, as written by Boswell, has become one of the great classics of travel literature, *The Journal of a Tour to the Hebrides*. Boswell has earned a belated and quite extraordinary second fame in the twentieth century, based on the discovery in 1927 and 1928 of the hordes of his private papers at Malahide Castle near Dublin and Fettercairn House in Aberdeenshire. Publication of these writings, beginning in 1950, has revealed a lively, witty, and lusty personality that has made some of these editions into bestsellers. In the portrait, Boswell is portrayed in 1865 as a serious young man of twenty-five by the noted portraitist George Willison.

poet of his age, and in many readers' minds remains the best poet Scotland ever produced. Yet the number of popular misconceptions about Burns remains almost as high today as it was in his lifetime. Burns was never an illiterate peasant or the "poetical ploughman" that Edinburgh enthusiasts described him as being after the publication of *Poems, Chiefly in the Scottish Dialect* (1786, the Kilmarnock edition). The honest sentiment of his poems has led more than one biographer to sentimentalize his life. The degree of his moral turpitude or laxity is wildly exaggerated. He did not die from excessive drinking; he did not mistreat or neglect his wife and children. He was not a flaming radical. Though devoted to Scottish song, he believed his best poem to be *The Cotter's Saturday Night*, a work filled with King James cadences and echoes of more than a dozen English poets. And, finally, he must not be accounted either a "Romantic" poet or a pre-Romantic poet, a term that unfortunately implies he acted as some kind of John the Baptist, preparing the way for one greater than himself.

The poems that Burns added to the Edinburgh edition of 1787, the

Among his many other accomplishments, Sir Walter Scott was one of the great collectors and preservers of Scottish ballads, one of the glories of the literature of the fourteenth and fifteenth centuries. Most ballads were meant to be sung, though their musical settings have often been lost. In some ways the most important body of artistic work left behind by border tensions, they recount events of great violence. Their composers, for the most part illiterate, were not always at ease in their attempts to re-create a world of aristocratic manners, but the ballads nevertheless contain invaluable information about social conditions and historical events. Of the great ballad-collectors— including Scott, Thomas Percy, Robert Jamieson, and Francis James Child—Child, whose five-volume work appeared between 1882 and 1898, helped to fix the canon most definitively, and of his three hundred examples, fully one hundred and eighty come from north of the border. These include "Lord Randal," "Sir Patrick Spens," "Thomas Rymer," and "Edward." A Scottish ballad is compressed, and often omits pre-history for the startling event that forms its subject matter; usually it is unmarked by editorial judgment. "The Battle of Otterburn," along with such famous companions as "The Wife of Usher's Well," "The Lass of Roch Royal," "The Twa Corbies," and "Lady Maisry," helped to shape the tastes and determine the themes of more than a dozen generations of poets.

posthumously published poems, and the songs are read and loved by millions; they constitute an extraordinary body of work. The satires indicate that Burns, in his own person, incarnated the spirit of moderatism. Yet Burns's attacks on bigotry, on sham of all kinds, are delivered from a conviction that the strengths of Scottish life will overcome the extremes of doctrine. In such poems as *The Holy Fair*, *Address to the Unco Guid*, *Epistle to M'Math,* and *Address to the Deil,* Burns indicated that, unlike many Moderates, he could never be at ease in Zion. His satires assume—perhaps overoptimistically—the existence of an audience interested in discovering the truth about themselves as well as about religion.

We may regret Burns's genteel imitation of English models and the "solid vote for English" cast by Scottish intellectuals, specifically those who were in a position to influence Burns's development. But it may be that for most readers Burns's greatest achievements lay neither in his satires nor his English-styled poems, but in his songs. Perhaps Burns did not think of his songs as poetry. They were, after all, adaptations, reworkings of airs and lyrics gathered from all corners of the land. But William Butler Yeats marveled at the artistry of "The wan moon sets behind the white wave, / And time is setting with me, Oh!"

Millions have sung Burns's modernized songs, and loved them, without knowing the full extent of Burns's contribution. Burns wrote most of his songs for inadequate or no compensation. He undertook the restoration of long-neglected songs as a patriotic duty. Far more than any of his contemporaries, he may be credited with having created the body of Scottish songs that constitute what is one of the proudest elements of a national literature.

It would be a mistake to move toward the end of our review of the Scottish Enlightenment without acknowledging the importance of Sir Walter Scott (1771–1832). He came late, after many of the greatest names of the eighteenth century had completed their work and passed from the scene. Yet Scott's attraction to his nation's past was stimulated by the stories and legends recounted by members of his family, by a self-education "in every branch of knowledge," by his admiration of Alexander Fraser Tytler (his history professor at the University of Edinburgh), and Dugald Stewart, his professor of moral philosophy.

Scott, in brief, was a child of the Enlightenment, and his works would never have been written without the influences operant in the Scotland of the final decades of the eighteenth century. Moreover, critical and popular opinion agree that Scott's best fiction deals with Scottish history. He recounted many of the events still vivid within the memories of his elders. Any of his fictions which might go back more than two hundred years is seriously limited by a lack of imaginative sympathy and (perhaps) of historical information; but the Scottish novels—*Waverley, Rob Roy, The Antiquary,* and *Old Mortality,* to name four of the finest—are filled with alert sympathy and vivid understanding of what had made modern Scotland. If he praised William Osbaldistone, the merchant of *Rob Roy,* as a man who understood the future, he did so because he recognized the inevitability of a trade-oriented Scotland and understood that the cause of the Pretender had been destroyed forever on the field of Culloden. Scott's fictions always deal with the divided self. The protagonist wavers between conflicting loyalties (hence the singular appropriateness of the name Waverley). No cause is wholly virtuous. The future (no matter how glittering) comes in at the expense of much that is worth preserving. Scott himself, acknowledging that the union of 1707 had brought tremendous benefits to Scotland, could not resist shedding a tear for the Stuart cause.

Scott, before he turned to the writing of novels, was the most popular poet in the British Isles, with his tremendously successful recastings of Scottish legends in *The Lay of the Last Minstrel* (1805), *Marmion* (1808), *The Lady of the Lake* (1810), and *The Lord of the Isles* (1815) to his credit. He exploited his antiquarian interests to produce *Minstrelsy of the Scottish Border* (1802–13), a collection that provided a firm base for later scholarly investigations of medieval British poetry.

He represented, in his life, his writings, his sense of humor, and his limitless capacity for friendship, a rational man's response to rapidly changing conditions. No stranger to sentiment, he nevertheless refused to oversentimentalize the past, and in his old age he became something of a Tory. But he was more than an oarsman rowing with the stream. He transformed the literary scene, and his influence on the nineteenth-century novel was incalculable.

Finally, let us give full credit to one of the principal agents for diffusing Enlightenment thought not merely in Scotland but throughout the civilized world, the *Encyclopaedia Britannica,* published first in three volumes in 1771 and then, in a new edition, in ten volumes in 1778. The editors were all Scotsmen: Andrew Bell (1726–1809), Colin Macfarquhar (c. 1745–1793), and William Smellie (1740–1795). Smellie, a printer, was later to become the secretary of the Society of Scottish Antiquaries. The *Britannica* was originally intended to cover the arts and sciences, but with its second edition history and biography became subjects of inquiry. Continual expansion of relevant fields of knowledge continued in the third edition of fifteen volumes (1788–97) and the fourth edition of twenty volumes (1801–10).

This new reference work represented a compromise between systematic encyclopedias, popular up through the sixteenth century, and encyclopedic dictionaries, which, concentrating on contemporary matters, came into favor in the seventeenth century. It had become obvious that the heightened timeliness of the latter form was secured at the expense of a clear sense of the interrelatedness of human knowledge. The *Britannica*'s solution—forty-five principal subjects, alphabetically arranged, with numerous cross-references—enabled leading authorities to write at length on their disciplines and to suggest fruitful lines of inquiry for readers interested in tracing connections between various arts and sciences. The *Britannica* began as a derivative work, based largely on already published materials, and the second edition was accused of plagiarism in a court case. But the quality of its engravings, its shrewd marketing, and the fact that experts wrote its survey articles increased its respectability as a reliable source of information.

Under the shrewd directorship of Archibald Constable, one of Scotland's great publishers of the early nineteenth century, the *Britannica* became, and has remained, one of the supreme reference works of the English-speaking world. The Scots have put all of us in their debt for their contributions to three main types of general reference books: encyclopedias, atlases, and dictionaries. These works make human knowledge, so painfully acquired over a period of centuries, more easily accessible and better known. They explain to us the exact nature of what we know, and equally as important, the limitations on our knowledge. Both the grandeur of the endeavor and the pragmatic realism of the results are characteristic of the Scottish Enlightenment.

HOW COULD SCOTLAND in the eighteenth century, torn as it was by the risings of '15 and '45, have produced the scholars, artists, and supportive public required for that flourishing intellectual movement known to later generations as the Age of Enlightenment? The tranquillity required for reflective creative thought, the wealth and stability for the patronage of the arts, do not characterize Scottish history; and yet, in defiance of all expectations, the Scottish Enlightenment shines, to borrow a description of the Cathedral of Elgin, like "the lamp of the north."

By the Act of Union, the "Scottish achievement" was to become the "British achievement"; even the *Encyclopaedia Britannica*, as we have seen, was a Scottish project. So too *Vitruvius Britannicus*, that great visual statement of the classical ideal in British architecture, was produced by Colen Campbell; and later the Adam family gave their name to the style that still forms our ideal of the gracious life. Allan Ramsay's witty essay on the arts, *A Dialogue on Taste* (1755), predates Hogarth's *Analysis of Beauty* (1757) and Reynolds's *Discourses* (1769–90). Sir Joshua Reynolds delivered his *Discourses* to the Royal Academy of which he was president and the Scot James Boswell was secretary; but a generation before the establishment in 1768 of that august symbol of taste and education in the arts, the Scots had founded three art academies: the Academy of St. Luke (Edinburgh, 1729), Richard Cooper's Winter Academy (Edinburgh, 1735), and Foulis Academy (Glasgow, 1753). The first school of applied arts and design in Britain was the Trustees' Academy (1760) in Edinburgh; later (1798), John Graham established a school of fine arts for the study of "the elegant arts of design," also in Edinburgh. Meanwhile Scots and Englishmen finished their education with a grand tour to Rome, where Gavin Hamilton and other Scottish artists and antiquaries acted as guides, teachers, and friends.

The Academy of St. Luke in Edinburgh, named after the great academy in Rome, lasted only from 1729 to 1731. The academy had eighteen members, who met eight hours a week for the four winter months and two months in summer to draw from casts and models and to copy engravings of old master paintings. Four years later Richard Cooper, an English engraver who had served as treasurer of the Academy of St. Luke, set up his own academy, the so-called Winter Academy since it only met in the winter. His own collection of engravings must have formed the basis of instruction, and one of his pupils, Robert Strange (1721–1792), became the greatest reproductive engraver of the eighteenth century.

The most important of these early attempts to establish a permanent academy in Scotland was made by the Foulis brothers, Glasgow printers and booksellers. The Foulis brothers are remembered as bookmen, not academicians, for they had one of the finest presses in the British Isles. Through superb typography they made their books works of art, rather than publications about art. (Their rival, R. Urie, on the other hand, became an important publisher of books on art—including the English translation of Winckelmann's *Reflections Concerning the Imitation of the Grecian Artists in Painting and Sculpture*, 1766, and Voltaire's *Temple of Taste*, 1751.) In 1753 Robert Foulis brought a collection of old master paintings, drawings, and engravings to Glasgow, where he opened an academy for instruction in the fine arts. In 1772 he added more paintings and some sculpture to his collection. In a contemporary illustration of students working at the academy, paintings cover the walls while books on anatomy, perspective, and the classics are scattered on the floor. Students work at copying the masters, and one is drawing a bust of Plato. In spite of the opportunity provided by the Foulis brothers, few first-rate artists studied at their Glasgow academy. David Tassie and David Allan are its only noteworthy

Sir John Halkett is portrayed by David Allan with his daughter by his first wife and his second wife Mary Hamilton and their thirteen children. Their home, Pitfirrane House, can be seen through the trees at the right; the tower of Dunfermline Abbey rises on the horizon. In the eighteenth century, the country became a place for the enjoyment of pastoral pursuits and the cultivation of leisure. Family activities included outdoor games, music, and dancing.

With the union of 1707 and the consolidation of the most important offices of state in London, Edinburgh and Scotland were reduced to political backwaters. In the absence of any other instrument of representational government, the general assembly of the kirk of Scotland became the chief forum for matters of Scottish concern. Budding politicians, such as the young James Boswell, shown at the left addressing the group, welcomed the opportunity to speak before the august body. This engraving is from a painting by David Allan.

students. The academy began to have financial problems in the 1770s and closed in 1775.

In Edinburgh the Select Society, as part of its program for improving the arts and sciences, gave prizes for drawing flowers and fruit. The members suggested that if the quality of drawing were to be improved, a school would have to be established. In 1760 the Board of Trustees for Improving Fisheries and Manufactures in Scotland established such an academy—the first school of design in Britain. The students, listed by trade, included carvers, gilders, coach painters, house painters, cabinetmakers, calico printers, embroiderers, goldsmiths, engravers, and designers of wallpaper and carpets. In time, and in reaction to the industrial emphasis of the Trustees' Academy, a drawing academy was established (1798) by the painter John Graham. After two years of rivalry and some scandal, the two academies joined to become a true school of fine arts, with Graham remaining as master until his death in 1817.

Twenty students of each sex were taught on alternate days. Graham consciously patterned his academy on the Royal Academy in London; students concentrated on the perfection of technique, drawing from casts and copying old master paintings and engravings, and on developing the skills needed to produce historical compositions. Portraiture was less esteemed, although it provided a lucrative income for the artists, and the painting of landscape and still life stood at the bottom of a hierarchy of types. Alexander Runciman, with his paintings of themes from Ossian and the life of St. Margaret for Penicuik House (after 1771), became one of Scotland's major history painters; Gavin Hamilton and David Allan turned to themes from classical or Biblical antiquity. David Allan, a fine portraitist, developed genre narrative themes in his conversation pieces. Alexander Nasmyth and his family are now admired as early exponents of pure landscape painting and the "picturesque." The first exhibition of Scottish artists was held in Edinburgh in 1808.

Of all these artists, the man who epitomized the Enlightenment in Scotland was Allan Ramsay (1713-1784). He changed the art of portrait painting in Scotland from the rather derivative Jacobean portraits in the Van Dyck tradition characteristic of Scottish seventeenth-century painting, to the polished elegance of the Italian and French Rococo style. As a scholar he worked to establish an intellectual basis for his art.

Ramsay was a widely traveled artist. Economic necessity sent many Scottish artists abroad. Scots lairds might live comfortably in their tower houses, but most of them lacked the ready money with which to buy paintings. Scotland was not altogether without a native tradition in painting. Walls and ceilings of houses were usually painted, and pride in kin and clan also assured a market for portraits. The painter of faces had a market in Scotland just as he did in the American colonies, and an occasional Scottish artist made a successful career in the New World. John Smibert (1688-1751), for example, became one of the most important colonial artists after he settled in New England in 1728.

Allan Ramsay was the son of the poet and bookseller Allan Ramsay, who had written *The Gentle Shepherd* and established the first circulating library in Edinburgh. The young Ramsay seems to have inherited his father's combination of practical and aesthetic sense. Ramsay studied at the short-lived Academy of St. Luke, moved to London (where he worked with Hogarth), and in 1736 made his first trip to Italy. On returning to London in 1738, Ramsay set himself up as a portrait painter. His portrait of *Francis, Second Duke of Buccleuch* (1739) established him as a leading portrait painter, and in the 1740s and 50s Ramsay dominated the London art scene. In the 50s he began to develop an interest in landscape, an interest that may be seen in the 1753 painting of *William, Seventeenth Earl*

205

As Scotland's first important land-scape painter, Alexander Nasmyth left records of Scottish cities and scenery which evoke the romantic grandeur of the country. At left above, he pictures Culzean Castle; below at left he depicts Old Edinburgh and the castle towering four hundred feet above the Nor'Loch, which was filled in 1816.

In 1753 Allan Ramsay portrayed William, seventeenth earl of Sutherland, in Highland dress, holding a basket-hilt sword and standing elegantly posed in a mountainous landscape. The rugged beauty of Scotland began to attract artists as early as the 1750s.

207

of Sutherland. Although the painting is a portrait—and a fine one—the viewer's attention is drawn to the Highland scenery. The detailed representation of majestic trees, mountains, and loch provides a splendid contrast to the elegance of the earl. The contrast of elegance and rug-gedness recurs in Scottish art.

In 1754 Ramsay made another trip through France to Italy, after which the elegance of French and Italian art becomes more apparent in his work. At the same time his Italian sketchbooks show that he had begun to study nature for its own sake; nevertheless, he continued his work as a portraitist. On his return from Italy he painted a splendid portrait of the Prince of Wales. When the prince became George III in 1760, he appointed Ramsay as painter-in-ordinary to the king, the highest honor an artist could achieve. Ramsay's portrait of George III and Queen

John Stuart, third earl of Bute, is best remembered today as the notorious favorite of George III, who succeeded as prime minister after engineering the resignation of his popular predecessor, William Pitt the Elder. His unpopularity and early removal from office adversely affected the prestige of Scots in public service. Though a poor politician, he patronized the arts and learning, and deserves the resplendent image that portraitist Allan Ramsay provides.

The western Highlands at Loch Ewe (opposite) are characterized by largely treeless, rugged terrain, riven by a series of geological faults which were subsequently enlarged by glacial action to form valleys (glens) and lakes (lochs). The valleys provide small, protected patches of arable land.

Charlotte became the official royal portrait and was often copied and widely distributed; Ramsay set up a workshop with assistants to produce these copies. After the 1760s royal portraiture became his principal source of income.

The finest Ramsay portraits date from the 1750s and 60s. *John Stuart, Third Earl of Bute* (1758), wearing court robes and the Order of the Thistle, illustrates Ramsay's ability to combine dignity with grace, the trappings of power seen in dress and setting with a fine characterization in the face. The vanity of the earl, as he shows off his elegant legs, gives a charming human quality to what could have been a cold Thistle portrait. That Ramsay was more than a painter of physical surfaces, but could penetrate to the character of his sitter, can be seen in his later portraits—and nowhere better than in the portraits of his friends, the philosophers Rousseau and Hume. In the portrait of *Hume* (1766), the philosopher is shown with his arm resting on his books looking like a well-fed tradesman rather than a philosopher. The sensible brilliance of the man is captured by Ramsay by means of a contrast between homely flesh and fashionable dress.

That Ramsay and Hume could be friends and not merely painter and

The Kyle of Tongue (above, and at left), a sea loch leading to Tongue Bay in the far northern region of Sutherland, opens out toward Scandinavia. In the eleventh century Tongue was the center of Norse settlement; later it became Mackay county. The photograph at left shows the mountain Ben Loyal.

211

Highland cattle are a unique breed, native to the region and characterized by shaggy coats and heavy dewlaps which afford them protection from the harsh climate.

On the following pages Ben Hope is seen from Loch Hope in Sutherland: the highest point in northwestern Scotland, Ben Hope rises to a height of 3,040 feet. The countryside is famous for its grouse.

work. The remodeling of Syon House for the duke of Northumberland began in 1762 with the rebuilding of the interior into a sequence of variously shaped rooms, inspired by Roman baths and villas. The central square space, which was to be covered by a dome, was never completed, and the dome was never built. In 1768 the Adams began an ambitious real-estate scheme, the Adelphi (brothers) Terrace (1768–72), planned as a complex of individual houses along the Thames. Streets of houses were built at right angles to a riverside terrace, raised over warehouses at the water's edge, and united by a single sweeping palace facade. The project became a financial disaster, and the brothers moved back to Scotland.

There, Robert Adam at last had a chance to challenge Chambers in the designing of official buildings when he gained the commission for the Register House in Edinburgh (1772–90), which gave him the opportunity to experiment with the theme of the circle in the square. There he built the central dome planned for Syon. Syon's Doric hall may also have influenced his design for Edinburgh University (1789–92), a building left unfinished at his death. On the Ayrshire coast he built for Lord Cassillis Culzean Castle (1777–90), a superb mock castle on the site of the ancient Kennedy keep. Here Adam must have also been inspired by a Scottish prototype, Inveraray Castle. Inveraray and Culzean may be seen in relation to the Middle Ages in much the same light as Scott's *The Lay of the Last Minstrel, The Lady of the Lake*, or the Waverley novels. In architecture as in literature, a romantic surface medievalism is laid gracefully over the delicate perfection of the classical core.

Adam also excelled as an architect of public spaces. Adelphi Terrace may have been a failure, but Charlotte Square is an undoubted success. The square stands in dramatic juxtaposition to old Edinburgh, a contrast of classical and medieval on a grand scale such as we saw in miniature at Culzean. Charlotte Square is part of James Craig's New Town. The

221

The mastery of Adam's engineering and the originality of his artistic skills combine to produce this breathtaking oval staircase in Culzean. Its utilitarian function has been transformed into an aesthetic delight.

David Octavius Hill is better known for his pioneering work in photography with Robert Adamson than he is as a painter. His record of Edinburgh as seen from the walls of the castle provides a bird's-eye view of the city which highlights the dramatic contrast between the old and new towns. The Royal Mile crosses the center of the painting with the spire of St. John's and the crown of St. Giles's Church as the focal points.

The elegant eighteenth-century extension of Edinburgh on the other side of the North Loch is a model of town planning with few precedents in Europe. Fresh from his triumphs in south Britain, Robert Adam created for the planners a city square of extraordinary beauty. Charlotte Square, a series of individual dwellings united behind a common facade, gave each owner the advantage of a private residence in a setting of the utmost grandeur, fit for a merchant prince.

The houses of Charlotte Square are as celebrated for their tasteful interiors as for their exteriors. The back drawing room of Number 7 Charlotte Square (left) was an informal room for family activities.

The elaborate fittings of the kitchen of 7 Charlotte Square (below), with its battery of utensils and cooking implements, testify to the richness of the middle class in Georgian Edinburgh.

223

Artists as well as soldiers and explorers carried Scottish culture abroad. James Hamilton, born about 1640 in Murdieston, was a renowned still-life painter. He left Scotland for the Continent during the years of the Commonwealth and spent the rest of his life in Brussels. His careful handling and attention to detail, the impeccable clarity of his composition, and his delicate drawing appeal to contemporary taste.

233

be made for 1707, the year of the Union of the Parliaments of Scotland and England, when the United Kingdom of Great Britain was created and the Scots were given freedom of trade and shipping throughout its area and its overseas possessions. Although the immediate stimulus of the Treaty of Union to Scotland's trade and emigration can be overestimated, there is no doubt that it increased both of them significantly. Scots of all classes and cultures, in the ensuing two and a half centuries, took full advantage of the opportunities for individual and communal advancement which the formerly English empire afforded them.

But claims could also be made for 1560 as a midpoint from which to gain perspective on the Scots abroad. This was the year of the Treaty of Edinburgh, which terminated French attempts to dominate Scotland and brought to an end two and a half centuries of the Auld Alliance with France. Up to this time, Scotland enjoyed something of a special relationship with France. The 1560 treaty spelled the end of this period. It also put Scottish Protestants in a strong position; and it is not surprising that, with the meeting soon after this Treaty of the Scottish Parliament which repudiated papal supremacy, the seal had been set on the Reformation in Scotland.

This, some would argue, was the end of the medieval period in Scotland, when the Scot with ambitions abroad looked to Europe rather than further afield. Yet it could also be claimed that the ending of the Middle Ages in Scotland needed something more than the snapping of the links with Catholic power overseas. It also depended on the destruction of feudal ties at home; and this was not achieved until the abolition in

Buffeted by winds of the North Atlantic, a peat-walled cottage on the island of South Uist in the Outer Hebrides shows the bleak, treeless environment in which the island crofters lived. It is no wonder that so many took the opportunity to emigrate to the colonies of the New World when the chance was offered.

1747 of heritable jurisdictions after the suppression of the Jacobite rising of 1745 which led to increased emigration.

Whichever of these three midpoints one chooses, 1560, 1707, or 1747, they constitute in themselves an era of transition in the nature and extent of migration from Scotland. This was a period when Scotland began to think of building up its own empire of trade and colonization overseas. It was the start of a very different vision of the Scot abroad from that which had dominated Scotland in the Middle Ages and before.

At that time, as far as the evidence available allows one to make judgments of size, there were no very substantial communities of Scots abroad. Certainly, following the medieval lines of penetration into Europe of Scottish mercenaries, students, craftsmen, and traders, communities of Scots were emerging overseas. Few of them, however, seem to have been as substantial as the Scottish community at Rotterdam, which was estimated to number about a thousand at the start of the eighteenth century. Yet, in the larger cities of the Continent, especially in France, the Low Countries, the German states, Denmark, and Sweden, groups of Scots were familiar sights.

But Europe at this time, for the enterprising Scot, was no frontier, as North and South America, southern Africa, and Australia were to become toward the end of the eighteenth century. Opportunities for substantial Scottish settlements on the Continent were limited; and there is, therefore, an individualistic character about the wandering Scots in Europe at the end of the Auld Alliance and later. Individual traders made their fortunes. Individual soldiers of fortune made reputations for themselves: the earl of Douglas, for example, became lieutenant-general of the French armies and duke of Touraine in 1424; the Scottish general, Patrick Gordon, until his death in Russia in 1699, rendered distinguished service to Peter the Great.

But, looking back on the Scots in medieval and early modern Europe, it is perhaps the scholars and the philosophers who deserve to be remembered most. The great age of Scottish enterprise in Europe may be said to have started with John Duns Scotus (c. 1265–1308), that subtle doctor of philosophy, who studied and taught in Paris and who is to the thought of the Franciscan order what Thomas Aquinas is to the philosophy of the Dominicans. And it ends with George Buchanan (1506–1582), who studied and taught in France, Portugal, and Italy and returned home to distill his political thinking in his *De Jure Regni apud Scotos* (1579) which was a textbook of the opponents of absolutism for a long time and may be said to point toward the Scottish contribution, two centuries later, to the emergence of democracy in America and elsewhere.

If the continent of Europe can hardly be called a frontier for Scottish settlers overseas, nevertheless the frontier spirit was displayed by Scots abroad well before the settlement of the New World. From the fifteenth to the sixteenth centuries, settlers from the Lowlands were moving to Orkney and Shetland; indeed, this process had begun before these northern islands, originally dependencies of Norway and Denmark, were transferred to Scottish rule in 1468.

The Scottish frontier was extended in the first decade of the seventeenth century as a result of the Plantation of Ulster. From the original Plantation by James I, through the Cromwellian period in Ireland in the seventeenth century, culminating in the largest settlement under William III between 1692 and 1697, Scots (mainly Protestant Lowlanders) settled in the north of Ireland. They brought with them the fortitude of those who had struggled with Rome in the Reformation: plain and pious living; the ability to work desperately hard; a stubbornness never to compromise when they were convinced that they were right; and the belief that those who did not share their religion were destined to be ruled by them. In their settlement of northern Ireland, the Ulster Scots developed a typical frontier spirit which many of them and their descendants took to the British American colonies in the early eighteenth century.

Perhaps, indeed, it was this Scottish frontier spirit breaking out of the confines of Europe that made many Scots determined either to have their own overseas trade and settlement or to play a leading part in the development of another's empire. But, in spite of James IV of Scotland's attempts in the early sixteenth century to build up an independent Scottish fleet, and the successes of Scottish privateers in European waters during the wars of the Reformation, it soon became clear that the genius of the Scottish frontier spirit was by land rather than by sea.

From 1621, when Sir William Alexander of Stirling received a grant of territories from the king to establish a New Scotland, Nova Scotia, across the Atlantic, to 1695, when the Company of Scotland trading to Africa and the Indies was set up with one of its objects to create a New Caledonia, an emporium on the isthmus of Darien near Panama, a Scottish overseas empire seemed possible to many Scots. Experiments in colonization were made in Cape Breton, Virginia, East New Jersey, and South Carolina as well as in Nova Scotia and the Panama regions. But they all came to nothing. They were not empires in the making but enclaves, and they were destroyed by or passed into the hands of the hostile or more successful empire builders who surrounded them: the French, the Spanish, and, above all, the English.

The total failure of the Darien scheme by 1700, only five years after its ambitious beginnings, was a deathblow to any remaining dreams of an independent Scottish overseas empire. Seven years later, one of the provisions of the Treaty of Union of the Scottish and English Parliaments

James Edward Oglethorpe, an Englishman, was responsible for the settlement at Savannah, Georgia, among many others in the middle states of North America. In 1733 he sent groups of English, German Lutherans, Piedmontese, Portugese Swiss, Jews, and Scottish Highlanders into Georgia. In this nineteenth-century engraving, he appears properly kilted as he visits his Highland colonists.

Macdonnel, piper to the Highland regiments, was tried in the Tower of London for desertion in June, 1743, and sent to Georgia. Hundreds of Scottish soldiers and supporters of Bonnie Prince Charlie were sentenced to transportation for their complicity. Many of these luckless victims who survived the rigorous crossing to the New World went on to found families and to build substantial fortunes.

was compensation for Scottish investors who had lost heavily in the Company of Scotland trading to Africa and the Indies. It was becoming clear to ambitious Scots that the road to empire lay through turning the English into a British Empire.

It has often been said that the Scottish genius overseas has been displayed most notably in North America, in what became the United States and Canada. Although Scots had settled in the seaboard areas and beyond in this vast area before Union, the extension of the Acts of Trade and Navigation opened up opportunities for legitimate commerce from Scotland to the American colonies, and this went hand in hand with increasing crossings of the Atlantic. At the same time, fundamental changes were taking place in Scottish life: the destruction of the clan system in the Gaelic-speaking areas; the swing of commerce away from the east coast to the west, stimulated by the growth of the tobacco trade from the Glasgow-Clyde region to Virginia; and the emergence of the Industrial Revolution in Scotland, symbolized by the growing power of the Carron ironworks, still to be seen in its light cannon (the famous "carronades") on the walls of old Quebec City.

These changes intensified the pace of traditional patterns of migration within and without Scotland: from Highlands to Lowlands; from Scotland to Ireland, Wales and, above all, England; and overseas to areas where Scots had already settled, such as Pennsylvania, the Carolinas (especially North Carolina), New Jersey, and to scattered settlements north of the St. Lawrence River. The Scots, as a result of the Knoxian Reformation with its emphasis on schooling, were a literate people; and their relations abroad were not backward, when they could afford the cost of postage, in writing home to tell their "ain folk" of the prospects for them in the New World. Through this commerce of information as well as of goods and capital, the way was open for a commerce of ideas to the New World from Scotland, as it moved into the age of its distinctive contribution to the Enlightenment in the second half of the eighteenth century.

Some of these Scots in the New World in the eighteenth century crossed the Atlantic through no will of their own. After the 1715 Jacobite rising, six hundred political prisoners were sent to the Caribbean island of Antigua, South Carolina, Virginia, and Maryland as indentured servants. As a result of the defeat of Prince Charles Edward's forces in 1745, about eight hundred of his followers were banished to the colonies. And, because of the reputation of the Scots in the North American settlements as hard workers, it was not uncommon, through trickery or undisguised force, for Scottish males and females often at a very early age to be thrust onto ships bound for the colonies. Indeed, the origin of "to kidnap" is the illegal capture of young people for the American plantations. (*Kidnapped* is the title of one of the most popular of Scottish novels; and in its seventh chapter Robert Louis Stevenson takes pains to point out that its captured hero, David Balfour, was to be transported to the Carolinas.)

The center of the Scottish kidnapping industry was in Aberdeen. It was from this city's harbor in 1740, at the age of ten, that one of the most colorful characters of Scottish-American history, Peter Williamson, was enticed on board ship and carried to Philadelphia, where he was sold into service for £16. After nearly twenty years in the American colonies, he returned to Aberdeen, where he published an account of his experiences and managed to wring compensation out of the Aberdeen city government.

Although they reached the New World in a different manner from the Jacobite prisoners and the beguiled indentured servants, Scottish soldiers, many of whom served in Highland regiments, had no say in where they were sent to fight in the widening conflict between the British and the French. A distinguished example was the Seventy-eighth Regiment of the Line, composed of fourteen hundred Highlanders recruited by Simon Fraser, the master of Lovat. This regiment was prominent in the defeat of the French at Quebec in 1759. With some of the Black Watch, the Forty-second Highlanders, they formed a nucleus of Scots in Quebec and Montreal.

The Highland migrations have always held a special place in the affections of North Americans; and the result has often been a romanticized, sentimentalized *Brigadoon* type of picture of Highland society. The original motivations behind the migrations were much less romantic. James Boswell, when he visited Skye in 1773 with Dr. Samuel Johnson, made an entry in his diary for October 2 which showed the heartbreak beneath the Highland hilarity. "We performed," he wrote, "with much activity a dance which I suppose the emigration from Skye has occasioned. They call it 'America.' . . . It shows how emigration catches till all are set afloat . . . last year when the ship sailed from Portree for America, the people on the shore were almost distracted when they saw their relations go off . . . This year not a tear was shed. The people from Skye seemed to think that they would soon follow. This is a mortal sign." Toward the end of the century, Robert Burns showed another savage side of the emigration from the Highlands of Scotland when, in his *Address of Beelzebub*, he attacked the earl of Breadalbane, president of the Highland Society, for his organization's efforts to stop five hundred Highlanders "emigrating from the lands of Mr. Macdonald of Glengarry to the wilds of Canada, in search of that fantastic thing—Liberty."

The Highlanders were to be found in many parts of America on the eve of the War of Independence. The greatest concentration of them was in the Upper Cape Fear region of North Carolina. It was to this area that Flora MacDonald, the Highland heroine who had helped Prince Charles Edward after his defeat at Culloden in 1746 to escape over the sea to Skye, went with her husband, Allan, in 1774 to seek a new life abroad.

Like many Highlanders they were prepared, through their attachment to the principle of monarchy, to support George III. When, therefore, the American rebellion against the king broke out two years later, Allan MacDonald, supported by Flora, assisted in the raising of a force of over three thousand Highlanders in the royal cause. They were defeated at Moore's Creek Bridge in February, 1776, captured and eventually, with other Highlanders, released to swell the Loyalist numbers in Nova Scotia. The MacDonalds went back to Scotland after this; but many remained in Canada. Their language, Gaelic, remained with them; and on Cape Breton Island today it is still a living force.

Gaelic might have survived to a small extent in the United States. However, as the fate of Highland immigrants in other parts of America suggests, its chances of expansion, in an all-prevailing English language environment, were slender. This was certainly the fate of the Gaels in Pennsylvania. The most notable of them, perhaps, known only through his Christian name, was Andrew, the Hebridean, whose sterling qualities are displayed in the second part of the famous third letter extolling the promise of American life in Hector St. John de Crèvecoeur's *Letters from an American Farmer* (1782). In this "short history of a simple Scotchman," Andrew advances "from indigence to ease; from oppression to freedom; from obscurity and contumely to some degree of consequence—not by virtue of any freaks of fortune, but by the gradual operation of sobriety, honesty, and emigration." This could, of course, be the story of many immigrants to America, whether in the eighteenth century or later. Is it, however, accidental that Crèvecoeur, the French author of a classic of early American literature, should have chosen a Scot as his example of the realization of the promise of American life? His words might be applied

238

The loyal service of Scottish regiments in both colonial conflicts and the Napoleonic Wars won them the right to wear once more the colorful dress of their forefathers. Here, the Edinburgh photographers Hill and Adamson capture a group of 92nd Gordon Highlanders in 1845 (above).

John Thomson, tailor of Arbroath, who emigrated to the United States, poses in an elaborate "Highland" outfit he devised for himself (left). Thomson became a renowned fiddler for the Scottish Dancing Society in Janesville, Wisconsin, in the 1850s.

to thousands of other successful Scots in America who had started with little. And yet was it not the very standardizing nature of American life, its "Americanism" (a word first employed by another Scot, the eminent John Witherspoon), which replaced Andrew the Hebridean's native Gaelic by the language of the majority?

The Scotch-Irish, the Ulster Scots, however, brought little or no Gaelic to America; they were, in the main, Presbyterians, and they stood by the English language of the 1611 authorized version of the Bible. This King James version of the Bible occupies an important place in the social and religious history of the United States; and it is arguable that the Ulster Scots, with their devotion to it, did much to implant it in the affections of the emerging American nation.

In the growth of American independence, the part played by the Ulster Scots is indisputable. Although, in small numbers, their emigration had started in the seventeenth century, its effective beginnings were in 1717, and it mounted steadily throughout the eighteenth century. The number of Ulster Scots in the United States by the time of the early national period was substantial. In the half-century before 1776, some 250,000 people left northern Ireland, mainly for America; after the end of the Revolutionary War (which stopped most immigration into America) in 1783, almost 100,000 Ulster Scots came to the United States in two decades. They had come first to Maryland and New England; and, as the century rolled on, Ulster Scots were to be found all along the American frontier, moving westward and southward down the Ohio Valley.

Unlike the Scottish Highlanders, the Ulster Scots had no religious or sentimental attachment to the institution of monarchy. On the eve of the American Revolution, most of them were already inclined toward a break with Britain. To the British government, indeed, their Presbyterian churches were "sedition shops," for from the Ulster Scots on the frontier of Virginia and North Carolina came some of the first advances toward a declaration of American independence.

If such Scots introduced the frontier spirit into the making of an independent American government, others brought the sophistication of the Scottish Enlightenment and the pragmatic force of the "Common Sense" philosophy from the churches, universities, and schools of eighteenth-century Scotland. Typical of this process were the two most notable Scottish signers of the Declaration of Independence: jurist James Wilson and the Presbyterian minister, John Witherspoon. Whether at home or in America, Scots of this kind exercised a powerful influence on the minds and hearts of young Americans in the days of the making and consolidation of the American Revolution.

The American Revolutionary era was a long one: from 1776 to 1815. During these four decades, Scottish emigration to the United States was severely reduced in numbers. Furthermore, Scots were drawn to the loyal provinces of Upper Canada, Prince Edward Island, and Nova Scotia. It was not until the middle of the nineteenth century that Scottish emigrants across the Atlantic began to show a preference for the United States.

Workers from Scotland, many of whom were thrown out of their jobs by the introduction of steam machinery into traditional industries or by the invisible hand of the trade cycle, flocked to the United States, either directly or by going first to Canada and then over the border and into the States. Their labor power, skill, and technical inventiveness helped to promote the new industrial economy of America; and some of their children, such as the fabulous Andrew Carnegie, became major instruments of the Industrial Revolution in the United States.

Andrew Carnegie came of Chartist, republican stock, from parents unorthodox in their religious opinions. He was not unique in the

Born into a working-class family, Andrew Carnegie (opposite) emigrated to the United States, where his industry and luck created one of the great success stories. From telegraph clerk to railway superintendent, and then from sleeping-car promoter to factory owner, his enterprise and investments in oil and steel made him a huge fortune. After consolidating his holdings into the U.S. Steel Company (which he created), he retired from business to disburse his wealth in philanthropic endeavors.

The magnitude of Carnegie's personal achievement is strikingly illustrated by the contrast between his birthplace in Dunfermline (right) and the sumptuous Fifth Avenue mansion to which he retired at the end of his business career (below, opposite). Given to the American people complete with furnishings, it now houses the Cooper-Hewitt Museum of Design.

democratic heritage of his family. The nineteenth century in Scotland, as elsewhere in Europe, was a time of profound questioning of all social, political, and economic values. Scots from this radical milieu sought opportunities for the exercise of their opinions and theories in the United States; and they, in their turn, left their mark on reform movements in the New World. In the 1820s and 30s Frances Wright from Dundee spoke out in America for women's rights, contraception, free education, a fair division of wealth, and the independent attitude in philosophy and religion. Her utopian-socialist colleague, Robert Dale Owen, whose father, Robert, emigrated to the States in 1825, became a member of Congress, was active in the New Harmony Community in Indiana, and instrumental in organizing the Smithsonian Institution.

Radical Scots, down to the beginning of the twentieth century, often sought a new vision of society in the North American West. Roland E. Muirhead, secretary of the Scottish Home Rule Association, was one of them; and he worked for a time in social democratic and anarchist communities on the Pacific coast. Radicalism, however, sometimes turns into conservative channels, as the American career of Allan Pinkerton demonstrates. Originally a radical Chartist, his political opinions obliged him to leave Scotland for the United States, where he organized a private detective agency to protect the property of railroads and other corporations, outstanding among which were the steel plants at Homestead, Pennsylvania, owned by his fellow Scot, Andrew Carnegie.

By the beginning of the twentieth century, Scots had distinguished themselves in many forms of American life. In addition to labor and technical skill, investment from Scotland helped to build the American economy, especially in the West. It has been claimed that, by the 1880s, Scotland provided American ranching with three-quarters of its foreign investments. Perhaps this was the call of the wild again appealing to the Scottish spirit overseas. Certainly, from the time of the pioneer study by Scottish-born Alexander Wilson, *American Ornithology*, to the attempts to preserve the forests and wildlife of the West by the explorer and naturalist from Dunbar, John Muir, some Scots have sought to conserve the wonders and resources of the natural environment of the United States, while others have been determined to change it drastically in the interests of science, technology, and a consumer society.

The staircase in the Carnegie mansion.

The garden front of the Carnegie mansion.

Born in Paisley, Scotland, in 1766, Alexander Wilson turned from the weaver's trade of his father to become an itinerant poet and satirist. After imprisonment for publishing a libelous satire, he set sail for America, where he supported himself as a schoolmaster. A devoted naturalist and increasingly expert draftsman, Wilson attracted the attention of the great William Bartram, who encouraged him to specialize in ornithology. Wilson's monumental *American Ornithology* was published in seven volumes between 1808 and 1813 and though later overshadowed by Audubon, his work is notable for the accuracy of its observation and its lifelike presentation. The plate shown here is an engraving made from his drawings after nature.

John Muir, born at Dunbar on April 21, 1838, was brought by his family to Wisconsin at the age of eleven. After leaving the University of Wisconsin before completing his studies, Muir set out on a long series of walking journeys that took him from the Gulf of Mexico to Alaska. His writings of those travels, his deep love of the western natural scene, and his acute observation have led to his eminence as the father of American conservation philosophy. Enormously influential in the national parks movement, Muir has a glacier in Alaska named for him as well as a sequoia wood in California and numerous other places of great natural beauty.

This same mixture of ruthlessness and romanticism has characterized the contribution of the Scots to Canada. If the wide open spaces challenged the Scots south of the St. Lawrence River, they presented them with an even greater opportunity to the north of it. Until the Confederation of 1867, Canada was a geographical rather than a political expression. Scots took a leading part in its exploration: Alexander Mackenzie from Stornaway discovered, in 1789–90, the river into the Arctic Ocean which now bears his name; Simon Fraser, born in Vermont of Scots ancestry, explored the Canadian west extensively in the first two decades of the nineteenth century and lent his name to the river which flows into the Pacific Ocean; and Robert Campbell from Perthshire made major discoveries in the Yukon between 1840 and 1851. These are only three of the many Scots who left their mark on the map of Canada.

In the work of binding the whole vast land together, men of Scottish origins did not lag behind: railroad builders such as Donald Alexander Smith and George Stephen, who promoted the Canadian Pacific Railway in the 1880s; communications experts such as Alexander Graham Bell, inventor of the telephone, who, although he became an American citizen in 1874, emigrated originally to Canada and kept up his interests in both countries.

In the peopling and the politics of Canada, men and women from Scotland have also performed a distinctive role. Although Sir William Alexander in the early seventeenth century had put the name Nova Scotia on the map, it was not until the province passed into British hands from the French at the end of the Seven Years' War that Scottish settlement could begin properly. About two hundred Highlanders sailed for Pictou in July, 1773, in the rickety *Hector*: the *Santa Maria* of the Gaels in Nova

A man whose motto was "Trees and more trees," John McLaren created El Camino Real and Golden Gate Park in San Francisco as well as many estates in San Mateo County. Born on a farm near Stirling, Scotland, McLaren (above left) served California and San Francisco for nearly fifty-six years as superintendent of parks.

Alexander Graham Bell (above right) was born and educated in Edinburgh. Embarking on a career as a professor of vocal physiology in Boston, he pursued an interest in the transmission of sound into the invention of the telephone.

John Galt was a friend and rival of Scott, although his literary works are no longer popular. As a founder of the Canada Company in 1826, he planned and directed the settlement of Ontario. One son, Sir Alexander Galt, became premier of Canada.

Scotia. Highlanders were to the fore again when, in 1803, Thomas Douglas, fifth earl of Selkirk, obtained a grant of land in Upper Canada and on Prince Edward Island on which to settle men and women from the distressed Gaelic areas of Scotland. Until his death in 1819, Lord Selkirk had a difficult and discouraging career in Canada; but through his work for the Red River Colony (in what is now Manitoba) he laid the foundations of western Canada. Thanks also to the effort of Scots such as the novelist John Galt and his Canada Company in the 1820s and 30s, Scots were attracted to wide regions in and around Ontario.

An amusing but incisive picture of what many would consider to be the Scottish-Canadian heartland is given by Professor John Kenneth Galbraith, who was born on a farm at Iona Station, Ontario, in 1908, in his book *The Non-Potable Scotch: A Memoir on the Clansmen in Canada* (1967). Like many Americans who were born in Canada, Professor Galbraith's career illustrates the ties that bind Scotland, Canada, and the United States of America; as, in the reverse direction, does that of George Brown (1818–1880), whose family moved from Edinburgh to New York and then on to Toronto, where he started the *Globe* newspaper, took a leading part in the formation of the Liberal party, and became one of the founding fathers of the Canadian Confederation in 1867.

Sir John A. Macdonald, who emigrated from Glasgow to Kingston, Ontario, perhaps best illustrates the Scottish style in Canadian politics. "His face," it has been said, "was hewn on rugged Scottish principles"; and similar Caledonian characteristics dominated his career in the Canadian Conservative party, his period as first prime minister of the

Dominion of Canada (1867–73), and again from 1878 to 1891—after another Scottish premier for five years, Alexander Mackenzie, the stonemason from Dunkeld—and his determination to stamp out any opposition to the advance of the new dominion westward. Macdonald was a centralizing force in the making of Canadian federalism.

Scottish names of places and persons are to be found all over Canada, perhaps even more than in the United States. And yet Anglophile Canadians are still uncertain about the distinctive elements in their national heritage. Stephen Leacock underrated the influence of Scotland on Canadian culture when he wrote in 1941, "We use English for writing, American for conversation and slang and profanity, and Scottish models for moral philosophy and solemnity." From the early nineteenth to the twentieth centuries, there is a Scottish motif running through Canadian literature. Names such as Thomas McCulloch, Hugh McClellan, Frederick Niven, and Graeme Gibson stand out prominently. Figures such as Alexander McLachlan from Renfrewshire, who was called by his admirers "the Burns of Canada," have been well aware of it; and McLachlan sounds the Scottish literary motif in many of his verses.

In the West Indies and South America, where Hispanic influences were pronounced, Scots have been less predominant than in North America. Yet in the Caribbean islands, as indentured servants, plantation owners, soldiers, doctors, Christian ministers and missionaries, and educationalists, Scots have also made their mark. By the middle of the nineteenth century, about a third of the European population of Jamaica was of Scottish descent; and this island attracted Scottish settlers until well into the nineteenth century. It is worth noting that it was to Jamaica that Robert Burns thought of emigrating in 1786 before his first volume of poems brought him fame at home. Presbyterian ministers were scattered all over the islands of the West Indies; and it was one of them, Hugh Knox, in St. Croix in 1771 who was so impressed by the young Alexander Hamilton that he set him on the road to higher education in America. In a different way, Scottish influence is to be seen in the West Indies, as it is in the United States, in the dispersal of Scottish names among the descendants of the slaves: Robeson, Douglass, and many more.

In Hispanic California, the first non-Spanish settler was a Scots sailor; and, as Martha Vogt points out, "the first book written and printed in Los Angeles was produced by a Scottish author, the finest account of the Southern California Indians was written by a product of the schools of Cardross, a Scot was *alcade* (mayor) of Monterey, California's capital." Chile, Peru, and Argentina have attracted small groups of Scottish immigrants down to the twentieth century. Scottish agricultural workers went to Latin America throughout the nineteenth century. Latin America has tended to absorb the Scots into its Hispanic-American way of life. R.B. Cunninghame Grahame, the Scottish traveler, writer, and nationalist, saw this process at work in an outlaying settlement of Buenos Aires, to which Gaelic speakers from Inverness-shire had migrated in 1745. Only a little of their Gaelic survived; and they pronounced their names in the Spanish manner: Camerón, Fergusón, McLéan.

A similar process, although one that was not so pronounced, was at work among Scots who emigrated to South Africa's Cape Colony after it fell finally into British hands at the end of the Napoleonic Wars. Some of them have been assimilated into the Dutch-derived, Afrikaner way of life, but South Africa is the only part of Africa where Scots settled as communities as they did in North America. The Scottish 1820 settlers to the Cape are typical of several who tried their luck on what was as much of a frontier in the early nineteenth century as anywhere in North America.

The spokesman, who is often considered to be the founder of South

A missionary and explorer who tried to end the slave trade in Africa, David Livingstone opened central Africa for commerce through his exploration of the Zambezi River.

African poetry and prose in English, was Thomas Pringle. Pringle was no missionary but he soon fell foul of the Afrikaners and other whites through his criticisms of their treatment of the indigenous inhabitants. Pringle's poems, especially *The Emigrant's Cabin*, employing standard English, Scots, Cape Dutch, and Xhosa (a multilingualism characteristic of many educated Scottish emigrants in the eighteenth and nineteenth centuries), evoke the nostalgia of the Scots on the Cape frontier, and the duty which some of them felt toward the native Africans who were less well qualified than they for the struggle with the laissez-faire economy of their time. Like many Scots overseas, Pringle softened the blow of leaving home through the practice of verse. Charles Murray, from the time he went out to South Africa in 1888 as a partner in a firm of architects and engineers in Johannesburg until he returned home after his retirement in 1924, expressed himself in nostalgic verse in the Scots of the northeast, which has contributed to the Scottish literary renaissance of the twentieth century.

In tropical Africa, often in the vanguard of the extension of the British Empire into these ill-charted regions, Scots were conspicuous. James Bruce of Kinnaird, wanderer in Egypt, Ethiopia, and the Sudan from 1768 to 1774, and Mungo Park of Foulshiels, traveler in the Gambia and Niger areas between 1795 and 1805, were typical products of the Scottish Enlightenment, and their inveterate curiosity to know more of the so-called Dark Continent stimulated not only other Scottish explorers but also men of science and learning around the world. David Livingstone, in spite of his missionary orientation, had the same scientific bent. Toward the end of the century, the Edinburgh-trained geologist, Joseph Thomson, between 1878 and 1891, led expeditions to east, west, and north Africa which made valuable contributions to geography and natural history.

In the last quarter of the nineteenth century, many Scots went to Africa for long periods in search of missionary and commercial opportunities. Sir William Mackinnon's Imperial British East Africa Company had an eye on philanthropy as well as profits when, for example, the East African Scottish Mission was founded in 1891. The African Lakes Company ("Mandala"), associated with the brothers John and Fred Moir from Edinburgh, worked closely with the Scottish Presbyterian missions at Blantyre and Livingstonia, both of which took their names from the Livingstone heritage, in what is now Malawi.

It was in the Livingstonia Mission, under the Scottish missionary Robert Laws, on Lake Nyasa, that the extension of the Scottish conception of the Protestant ethic into central and southern Africa produced several of the first African political leaders of the twentieth century. And, on the other side of the continent, the career of Mary Slessor, the Dundee mill girl who went out in 1876 to the United Presbyterian Church mission in Calabar in what is now Nigeria, showed what Scottish grit and competence could do in laying the foundations of modernization overseas.

Modernization, as is now realized, is a complex process, and it changes its meaning and methods with the passage of time. But, however it is defined, there is no doubt that the Scots in Southeast Asia, especially in India, from the mid-eighteenth to the twentieth centuries, have speeded the advance of what the Victorians liked to call "Progress." From the time of the Treaty of Union in 1707 and the beginnings of a British rather than an English Empire to the independence of India, Pakistan, Sri Lanka, and Burma in 1947, the participation of Scots in the development of British rule and influence in the Indian subcontinent and many parts of Asia as far as China which came into the orbit of the East India Company and its heirs was remarkable.

There were times, indeed, when it seemed that there was a Scottish rather than a British Empire in Southeast Asia. Up to the Indian Mutiny of 1857, which marked the ending of the East India Company's powers and brought India directly under the British Crown, Scottish soldiers, speculators, traders, missionaries, teachers, and administrators were all over the Indian subcontinent and its adjacent areas. When the Scottish politician Henry Dundas was a member of the Board of Control for India from 1784 to 1801, the process was accelerated because he used some of his power to put his countrymen into lucrative positions in India; and they, in their turn, tended to keep appointments within the clan.

Before 1857, the pace of centralization and modernization was advanced by men of Scottish descent such as Thomas Babington Macaulay, when he was a member of the Supreme Council for India, in his *Minutes on Indian Education* of 1835; and, above all, by James Andrew Broun Ramsay, first marquis of Dalhousie, when he was governor-general of India between 1847 and 1856. However, in spite of those Scots who lent themselves to the process of anglicization in Southeast Asia, there were others who clung fiercely to their Scottishness. A representative of these was John Leyden from Denholm in the borders, who had assisted Sir Walter Scott with his *Minstrelsy of the Scottish Border* and trained in medicine at Edinburgh University. He went out as assistant surgeon to Madras in 1803 and in 1811 accompanied another Scot, Lord Minto, to Java, where he died. Leyden made contributions to the study of Indian languages and literature; and it is characteristic of his attachment to local cultures that, when his friend Sir John Malcolm advised him in India to modify his dialect and learn

Scottish explorers ensured the extension, survival, and prosperity of the British empire during the nineteenth century. James Andrew Ramsay (above left) was only thirty-five when he took up the post of governor-general of India, the highest position in the colonial government. He proved to be a brilliant administrator who contributed to the development of the country through his improvement of communications and transportation.

Douglas Haig, Earl Haig (above right), a member of a border family (and, like Scott, buried at Dryburgh Abbey), commanded the British forces in France and Flanders in World War I. He founded the British Legion, the largest benevolent society in the British Isles, served in India and Africa, and was chief of staff of the Indian Army.

some English, he exclaimed, "Learn English . . . no, never. It was trying to learn that language that spoilt my Scotch."

After the passage of power in India directly under the British crown, Scots continued to influence the subcontinent at every level. Building on the work of such missionaries as Alexander Duff and John Wilson, they gave a distinctively Scottish tone, from the schools and colleges of the country of the Knoxian Reformation, to the Indian educational system. The great Scottish trading houses extended their power beyond India and brought into their service generations of Scots and their families. Scots strove to secure positions in the prestigious Indian civil service; and one of them, Allan Octavian Hume, was a founder of the Indian National Congress and worked for the greater participation of Indians in their country's government. The last Scot at the center of power in India was the second marquis of Linlithgow, who was viceroy from 1936 to 1943.

Men and women of Scottish descent brought many improvements to the medical services in the countries in which they worked. It would not be difficult to argue that perhaps the most important service of any Scot to the tropical countries was Ronald Ross's discovery, while he was a member of the Indian medical service in 1897, of the role of the anopheles mosquito in the transmission of malaria. He came from ancient Highland stock from Ross-shire; one of his forebears was a director of the East India Company; and his father was a general in the Indian army. Like other Scots abroad, he turned to poetry in times of tension. A verse from one of his poems, *Indian Fevers*, written five years before his great discovery, illustrates the compassion and the compulsion which drove him on to seek to ease the suffering of those less fortunate than himself:

The painful faces ask, can we not cure?
    We answer, No, not yet; we seek the laws.

O God, reveal thro' all this thing obscure
　　The unseen, small, but million-murdering cause.

In the extension and development of the British Empire further afield
than Southeast Asia—in Australia, New Zealand, and the Pacific Ocean,
and in the postimperial period there—Scots have not lagged beyond.
The archetypal castaway (the real-life model for Defoe's *Robinson Crusoe*),
Alexander Selkirk from Largo, was a member of Captain William Dampier's
expedition to the South Seas in 1703. Scots were included in the
transportation of convicts to early Australia. The most famous name of
this period is Thomas Muir of Huntershill, one of several Scottish reformers
who were sympathetic to the French Revolution, who was sentenced in
1793 to fourteen years at Botany Bay.

A soldier of Scottish descent, John Macarthur, an officer in the New
South Wales Corps, has been described as the founder of Australia's
independence because his introduction of merino sheep into the southern
continent in the nineteenth century laid the basis for its economic
prosperity. However, the growth of sheeprearing in Australia had
disastrous effects upon the Scottish industry which, in its turn, stimulated
further emigration from Scotland. Although Australia was much farther
away from Scotland than the United States and Canada, it provided
plenty of chances, in its very wide open spaces, for Scottish enterprise.
Several Scots, such as John McDougall Stuart from Dysart, Fife, who was
the first man to cross the continent from south to north and back again
in 1861–62, pioneered the exploration of Australia.

Scots, when they could scrape up enough money for the long journey
by sea, flocked to the Australian goldfields in the 1850s; and, as the
Australian economy started its expansion, they helped to keep up its
momentum. Pioneers of the Presbyterian church "down under," like John
Dunmore Lang from Greenock, encouraged their fellow Scots to join
them in the land of the Southern Cross; and they played an important
part in the achievement of responsible government in Australia. When it
was ready for federation in 1900, with the creation of the Commonwealth
of Australia, it seemed natural to many that it should be a Scot, the
seventh earl of Hopetoun and first marquis of Linlithgow, who should
become its first governor-general. And it does not seem accidental that
one of the first statesmen of the new Commonwealth of Nations should
be a politician whose ancestors went from Weem in Perthshire to Ballarat
in Victoria in the middle of the nineteenth century: Sir Robert Gordon
Menzies, twice prime minister of Australia (1939–41 and 1949–66).

New Zealand, although it was even more difficult to reach than
Australia, had its attractions for Scots. Some came directly from Scotland
in the early colonizing experiments in the 1820s and 30s; and it was
symptomatic of Scottish interest in the far-off islands that, by 1839, there
should be a New Zealand Emigration Society in Paisley. As early as
1842, a Scottish sculptor, George Rennie, conceived the idea of starting a
"New Edinburgh" in New Zealand. The Disruption of 1843 in Scottish
ecclesiastical history and the creation of the Free Church of Scotland
delivered this scheme into the hands of zealots who favored a strictly
Free Church settlement in the Antipodes. Two hundred and forty-seven
Scots, headed by Thomas Burns, nephew of the poet, sailed for Otago
from the Clyde in 1847. Other parties followed; and in 1848 what was
intended to be a highly Scottish city, Dunedin, was established eight
miles southwest of Port Chalmers (named after Thomas Chalmers, the
leader of the Disruption in the Church of Scotland) in Otago Harbor.
The plan of the town and the naming of its streets were based upon
Edinburgh.

249

Dr. Elsie Maud Inglis studied medicine in Glasgow and Edinburgh and
later founded a medical school for
women in Edinburgh. During World
War I she organized hospital units
staffed by women, and led one of
them as it accompanied the Serbian
forces. This bronze bust of Dr.
Inglis, made in 1918 by Ivan
Mestrovic, was presented by Serbia
to Scotland in recognition of a
deeply appreciated contribution.

Sir Walter Scott's poem *The Lady
of the Lake* was published in 1810,
and in the same year an unau-
thorized edition became available in
Philadelphia. Two years later, a
melodrama based on the poem was
produced in the Chestnut Street
Theatre in Philadelphia. Thomas
Sully painted Miss C. Parsons in the
title role on a commission from
James McMurtrie, who paid three
hundred dollars for it.

With other settlements in the South Island of New Zealand, the Free
Church experiment succeeded in creating one of the most determinedly
Scottish enterprises in the British Empire. A no less determined Caledonian
community, this time Gaelic-speaking, was started in 1853 at Waipu in
the north of the North Island. Led by the individualistic and dominating
Norman MacLeod, this resolute group of Gaels had been nearly forty
years finding a place which suited their strict religious temperament. They
went first to Nova Scotia in 1817, then on to Australia in 1849, and
started the final stage of their odyssey in 1853, which was completed seven
years later when about a thousand Highlanders came to rest at Waipu.

But Scots of other temperaments were to be found in New Zealand,
adding to the growth of this faraway country the distinctive Caledonian
traits of hard work. Scots have made important contributions to New
Zealand politics, particularly to its labor movement. Peter Fraser, a left-
wing emigrant from Easter Ross in 1910, helped to form the New Zealand
Labor party. He was a member of the New Zealand Parliament from
1918 and prime minister from 1940 to 1949.

Elsewhere in the Pacific, the Scottish presence has been dispersed
among the many scattered islands. New Caledonia in the western Pacific
and the New Hebrides in the southwest owe their Scottish names to
Captain James Cook, who charted them, perhaps because he had a
Scottish father. But Scottish potentialities were virtually eliminated in
New Caledonia in 1853 when the French annexed it; and although
Presbyterian missionaries were active in the New Hebrides from 1848 on
and demonstrated their distrust of French intentions, the archipelago
became an Anglo-French condominium in 1907.

Nevertheless, the Pacific has provided a sphere for the exercise of
Scottish missionary courage, notably in the martyrdom in 1901 of James
Chalmers, the Congregationalist missionary in New Guinea. Scottish
traders and shippers have been active among the islands. And, through
the liberal policy of such officials as Sir Arthur Gordon, governor of Fiji
from 1875 to 1880, Scottish administrators have helped to preserve the
rights and customs of some of the indigenous inhabitants of the Pacific
islands. The Scot, however, who perhaps did most to uphold the rights
of the islanders against European imperialism in the nineteenth century
was Robert Louis Stevenson, not only by his actions against white
rapaciousness and politicizing in Samoa, where he lived for four years
and where he died in 1894, but also by the power of his pen.

Was Robert Louis Stevenson, with his travels in Europe, America,
and the Pacific, one of the last of the old type of wandering Scots?
Certainly by the time of his death in the last decade of the nineteenth
century, when the British Empire still had half a century before it, it
would not have seemed so. But, looking back from the vantage point of
the last decades of the twentieth century, the frontiers of empire, even
when they seemed to be expanding rapidly in real power and potentiality,
may now be seen to be contracting. Rudyard Kipling, who knew his
Scots (his mother was a Macdonald), wrote in 1893 *McAndrew's Hymn*,
his poem in praise of the wandering Scot on the high seas of the world.
Four years later, however, Kipling published his *Recessional*:

> Far-called, our navies melt away;
>   On dune and headland sinks the fire:
> Lo, all our pomp of yesterday
>   Is one with Nineveh and Tyre.

By the close of the nineteenth century, the end of the British Empire was
in sight. And with it would go the wandering Scots. Perhaps the last

The Right Honorable James Ramsay
Macdonald was secretary and then
leader of the Independent Labour
party. He was prime minister and
foreign secretary in Britain's first
Labour government, and was premier
again between 1929 and 1935.

From earliest childhood Mrs. Mar-
jory Kennedy Fraser and her entire
family toured the world singing and
playing folk music. After the death
of her husband she devoted herself to
the folk music of the Hebrides. In
1905 she began to collect songs in
Eriskay, and her lectures and
recitals made the "auld Scots song"
known throughout the world.

lad o' pairts of the authentic Scottish type to carve out a distinguished career for himself on the closing frontiers of empire was John Buchan, whose novels from *Prester John* in 1910 to his *Sick Heart River*, published in 1941, the year after he died in office after five years as governor-general of Canada, reflect not only Buchan's career in Africa and North America but also the increasing challenges to a declining British Empire which he, as a loyal Scottish son of the manse, had done so much to uphold.

This decline was apparent in 1937, when the Scottish jurist and nationalist Professor Andrew Dewar Gibb published his survey of Scots overseas in the imperial service, formal and informal. In his last chapter of *Scottish Empire*, he rightly noted that the "existence of the Empire has been the most important factor in deciding the relationship of Scotland and England in the last three centuries"; and he went on to speculate about what this implied for Scotland when the British Empire came to an end. He suggested that Scotland "might seek to form and justify a new conception of her function in the framework of European civilization."

Some Scots now envisage this new overseas function for their country within the structure of the European economic community of which Great Britain became a member in 1972. Others are less optimistic about Europe and seek a fresh international part for Scotland inside the new multinational, multicentered Commonwealth which has arisen from the ashes of the British Empire after World War II, and to whose emergence Scots such as Philip Henry Kerr, eleventh marquis of Lothian, made no small contribution. Yet other men and women of Scottish descent, at home and abroad, can see no future for their country which will enable it to revive many of its best characteristics that were dispersed abroad during the imperial centuries, other than through absolute independence and the destruction of the Treaty of Union with England, which touched off those centuries.

In 1962 Dean Acheson made his famous comment on contemporary British history: "Great Britain has lost an empire and has not yet found a role." Of no part of the United Kingdom, in the opinion of the present writer, is this truer than of Scotland, now that the epic of the Scot abroad has come at last to an end.

9

❦

Romantic Images of Scotland-Words and Music

Henry L. Snyder

Romantic Images in Art

Marilyn Stokstad

Nineteenth Century Literature

Harold Orel

ROMANTIC IMAGES OF SCOTLAND—WORDS AND MUSIC

by Henry L. Snyder

SCOTLAND, so far as the rest of the world is concerned, is essentially the creation of the Romantic age and if one can point to a single work that inspired the romantic image of Scotland in the eyes of Europe in the late eighteenth and nineteenth centuries it is the *Poems of Ossian*. Though its originality may still be disputed, it unquestionably owes most if not all its creation to James Macpherson (1736–1796). In an age which admired the simple and the natural and which extolled the noble savage, the apparent effusions of a humble, medieval Gaelic poet who endured the intense hardships of the rocky coast of western Scotland seized the imagination of Europe. Ossian, Robert Burns, and Sir Walter Scott created the Scotland we know and love. To round out that picture, its image in other genres cannot be neglected.

It took Europe by storm. It is surely no coincidence that a taste for the rugged grandeur of Scotland in general and the islands in particular was reflected in voluminous travel literature describing the glories of that country. The first notable accounts were those of Thomas Pennant's two tours of 1769 and 1772, which appeared in 1772 and 1774 respectively. The most famous is undoubtedly Samuel Johnson's *Journey to the Western Islands of Scotland, Performed in the Year 1773*. Eagerly awaited, its appearance in 1777 evoked a storm of commentary, including printed tracts because of the Englishman's outspoken and critical remarks about the country and its inhabitants. Of equal subsequent fame is the Edinburgh-born James Boswell's version of this journey, published as his *Journal* in 1785.

From Pennant onward accounts appeared almost yearly, sometimes two or more in a year. These accounts were in English, principally of Englishmen who were now willing to ignore the discomforts of poor if not absent roads and indifferent accommodations to enjoy the natural beauty of the north. Some, such as that of John English (1762), outdid the later work of Johnson in abusing the Scots. Mrs. Mary Hanway (1775), on the other hand, was ecstatic in her praise, reflecting the appeal to the burgeoning Romantic age with such descriptive phrases as "most romantic views," "ruinous beauties," "horrid gulph," and "terrifying noise." The novelty of Vincent Luardi's account (1786) was that his were "aerial voyages," for he was transported by balloon. The discovery by Englishmen of their long-neglected northern neighbor was quickly followed by similar rapturous accounts by Europeans. *Ossian* was, if anything, more popular on the Continent than it was in England, and continental visitors to Scotland were as intent as their English counterparts on making the pilgrimage to North Britain to pay homage to the land of the immortal Celtic bard. Only the wars of the French Revolution and Napoleon put a temporary cessation to the procession of visitors.

The impact of *Ossian* was notable in many other ways. It became one of the most widely admired and imitated works of literature in history. In 1774, when Goethe wrote his passionate *The Sorrows of Young Werther*, often regarded as the first romantic novel, he quoted Ossian. In Jules Massenet's operatic masterpiece *Werther* (1892), that poem becomes the text for one of the most beautiful arias in all opera—"Pourquoi me reveiller?" (Why awaken me?).

The verses of Ossian inspired many other composers. Etienne-Nicolas Mehul, a French composer of the revolutionary period, composed his *Uthal* (1806) on a subject from Ossian, while his contemporary Jean-François Lesuer also capitalized on the enduring popularity of this work in his *Ossian, ou Les Bardes* (1804). The vogue for national subject matter in opera was a direct result of the similar trend Ossian sparked in literature so that the romantic German operas of Carl Maria von Weber, to name only one, may be reckoned a lineal descendant. *Ossian* continued to inspire operas more than a century after its composition, again invoking a national spirit or identity as in the *Ossian* (1905) of Frederick Corder, one of the most devoted Wagnerites in England.

Ossian's influence was not limited to opera. The poems of Ossian, either directly or through imitation, also enriched the art-song literature of Europe. Franz Schubert set eleven songs from Ossian in the years 1815–17, including *The Night* and *The Maiden of Inistore* (the Gaelic name for the Orkney Islands). His *The Death of Oscar* is viewed as "proof of Schubert's great desire to write an Ossian-opera."

Still another form of music touched by Ossian was literature for the orchestra. In 1829 Felix Mendelssohn made his first journey to the British Isles and included Scotland on his itinerary. He took in the Hebrides and made a pilgrimage to Fingal's Cave, on Staffa. The wild scenery and rough weather he experienced excited his imagination, and he penned a brooding, restless overture, reminiscent of the wind and waves of the Western Isles. The *Fingal's Cave Overture* is one of his most inspired works. Staffa exemplifies how recently Scotland was "discovered." When Dr. Johnson visited Scotland in 1773 he made a similar pilgrimage, only to be denied a landing because of rough weather. Yet, remarkably enough, Staffa had only come into the consciousness of Englishmen and all but local natives the previous year. It was called to the public's attention by Sir Joseph Banks on his visit en route to Iceland in 1772.

The elemental, rough, and natural quality of the landscape and the people was what attracted the jaded residents of the salons of London, Paris, and Berlin. Gothic imagery, rugged scenery, precipitous slopes, raging storms, and white-capped water made the Highlands and islands of Scotland irresistible, as were the Alps of central Europe or the fjord country of Norway. The taste for the exotic—the chinoiserie of the eighteenth century, the Turkish motive in the music of Mozart—gave way to the unspoiled naturalism of the mountain landscape. These images and others inspired Mendelssohn again in his *Scotch Symphony* (1842) twelve years later and Max Bruch in the twentieth century in his *Scottish Fantasy* for violin and orchestra.

The increasing interest in folk literature and poetry, best exemplified in the collections of the brothers Grimm, also extended to Scotland. Due to the interest first inspired by *Ossian*, other Scottish poetry was collected and set to music. In 1791 the Scottish musician and music publisher William Napier persuaded Joseph Haydn (1732–1809) to set a collection of Scottish songs. George Thomas, an Edinburgh publisher, made a similar appeal to Ludwig van Beethoven, and another set of Scottish songs was favored with the compositional skills of a celebrated continental composer. Scottish ballads were set with great dramatic effect by the German lyricist Carl Loewe, notably his *Edward* (1818), in a translation by Herder. Loewe also set a song by no less than Mary Queen of Scots.

Following Ossian, Robert Burns was the next major Scottish poet to attract international attention. The setting of his poems by continental composers is not as well known as those of Ossian, but one must record that Robert Schumann, among others, found his poems worthy of his attention. Even more than Ossian, one Scottish writer stands out above all others in his influence upon European literature and music—Sir Walter Scott. The musical translations of Scott's poetry are not so familiar as those of his novels, but they include some of the most beautiful of German art songs. In the case of Schubert the consummate beauty and simplicity of one of these has made it a folk song of a rare international kind—his "Ave Maria" (1825), set to a poem from Scott's *The Lady of the Lake*. Aside from the singular beauty and universal love for this song, the most notable settings of Scott's stories or texts have found their place

The rebel barons who forced the abdication of Mary Queen of Scots were hardly so deferential and regretful of their act as this 1850 painting by Joseph Severen would indicate (opposite). The romantic historicism of costume and architectural setting is a contrast to the actual crude stone tower prison on the island in Loch Leven.

in some fifty works for the operatic stage. One opera based on a Scott novel has an unquestioned place in the normal season—Gaetano Donizetti's *Lucia di Lammermoor* (1835). It is the sole survivor and presumably the best of at least six works written to Scott's *Bride of Lammermoor*. The specter of the blameless but unbalanced Lucy Ashton descending the grand staircase of her family home on her wedding night, wearing a bloodstained bridal gown and carrying the dagger with which she has just murdered her husband, is etched in the mind of the general public whether opera fans or not. The story line has become almost secondary, but the gloomy setting of a Scottish castle and the gothic starkness of the Wolf's Crag scene are characteristic stereotypes of the Scottish landscape.

Other Scott-inspired operas are in a lighter vein, like François Boieldieu's *La Dame Blanche* (1825), based on both *Guy Mannering* and *The Monastery*. Set in the eighteenth century, it evokes the Jacobite invasions and the exiled Stuarts. The outdoor settings are described in the inevitable terms of rocky, mountainous landscape. A run-down castle is another stock setting. Further, there are operas by Friedrich von Flotow and Reginald De Koven on *Rob Roy*. *The Heart of Midlothian* has no less than five settings, while *Ivanhoe* can count seven, including one by Gioacchino Rossini and another by Sir Arthur Sullivan. One version, Heinrich Marschner's *The Templar and the Jewess*, is said to have influenced Wagner. One other Scott opera is occasionally revived and has taken on a new lease of life in the current revival of bel canto works—Vincenzo Bellini's *The Puritans* (1835). The story has been so guyed around and is historically so inaccurate that Scott would undoubtedly forswear any responsibility if he could be taken to see it, but the fact remains that it was loosely based upon *Old Mortality*. Even ballet did not escape the Scottish influence in the late Romantic age. The Michel Fokine classic set to the music of Frédéric Chopin, *Les Sylphides* (1909), opens in a Scottish castle, the corps de ballet appropriately clad in tartan costumes.

If Ossian and his successors inspired the romantic writers and composers, and Scottish mountain scenery was taken as the epitome of wild, untamed nature, Scottish history also evoked powerful responses in Europe in the nineteenth century. Mary Queen of Scots is one of the classic *grandes dames* in European literature. Her unhappy fate, her death at the hands of her cousin and fellow queen, her unhappy love affairs, were natural subjects for the romantic artists. The classic retelling of her story is that by Friedrich von Schiller in his drama *Maria Stuart* (1800). In this play the Scottish queen is clearly the heroine, her English cousin Elizabeth I the villain. The climax of the drama is reached when the two queens confront each other, a fiction of the writer, never occurring in fact. The story has been the basis for several operas, from Donizetti's *Maria Stuarda* to the recent *Mary Queen of Scots* by the Scottish composer Thea Musgrave.

The two most discussed figures in Scottish history are not necessarily the most important. Yet Mary Queen of Scots and Bonnie Prince Charlie have evoked more literature, and more bad history, than any other figures in the history of that country. In Mary's case especially the interest in France seems to have been great. It may well relate to the Auld Alliance between the two countries and Mary's steadfast allegiance to her Roman Catholic faith in defiance of her Presbyterian countrymen. The studies include the editions of her letters and instructions by Prince Alexander Labanoff (1844) and Alexander Teulet (1859), and biographies by François Mignet (1851), Baron Kervyn de Lettenhove (1889), and more recently Roger Chauvire (1937). Her descendants—James VII (II of England), his son the Old Pretender, and his grandson Bonnie Prince Charlie—have also spawned an enormous literature. In their case the

fact that their royal heritage passed to a German branch of the family and that James's second wife and the mother of the Old Pretender, Mary of Modena, was Italian may account for the still greater international character of the literature about them. The ardent Catholic convert and German historian Onno Klopp, who spent most of his life in Vienna, devoted no less than fourteen volumes to the later Stuarts. The French historian François Guizot edited and published twenty-five volumes of memoirs relating to the revolution of 1688 in 1825. The marquise Campana de Cavelli published two massive volumes of documents on the exiled Stuarts in 1871, while in this century study of the last of the Stuarts has attracted the Spanish historian Maria Josefa Carpio.

Though the inspiration was varied, the fascination of Scotland for Europeans and Americans alike has never waned. Words and music combine to intensify the romantic image of Scotland both on the lyric stage and in the art song. But for many, especially those sons and daughters of Scotland who have left their homeland, the nostalgia and beauty their native land invokes are best exemplified in the songs of Robert Burns. In such lyrics as "My heart's in the Highlands," "My love is like a red, red rose," and "Auld Lang Syne," the Jacobite song "Charlie, he's my darling," or the Scottish anthem "Scots, wha hae wi' Wallace bled," he has created a national ethos and identity which have won universal recognition as the art of Scotland.

IF SIR WALTER SCOTT created the romantic image of Scotland, Queen Victoria fixed it in the public eye, and generations of Scots "over the water" have carried traditions to new worlds. Romantic imagination has changed a bloody history into a pageant of youth, beauty, and tragedy: from William Wallace to Mary Queen of Scots, from Bonnie Prince Charlie to Robert Burns, from border ballads and lyrics to legends of fairies and monsters, from the fine art and high tragedy of *Lucia de Lammermoor* to the simple nostalgia of *Brigadoon*. Romantics everywhere love stories of youthful idealists destroyed by the uncontrollable forces of nature, fate, or history, but in Scotland romance has a decidedly literary cast. In what other capital does a monument to a novelist and man of letters, rather than a politician, dominate the city?

Antiquarian studies did not begin with Sir Walter Scott, nor did he alone "rediscover" the Middle Ages. But he did stimulate the popular enthusiasm for all things medieval, beginning with the publication of *Ivanhoe* in 1820. The Middle Ages, the Scottish Baronial period, the early eighteenth century, all provided settings for novels. Scott and his readers seem fascinated by minutiae; they delight in physical details—proper armor for their heroes, or the look of a great hall decked out for a festival. Through novels and antiquarian studies, Scott fostered the Gothic Revival in art and architecture and the development of the Scottish Neobaronial style. In 1818 he found the Scottish regalia in Edinburgh Castle; later he convinced George IV to return the great fifteenth-century cannon, Mons Meg, to Edinburgh. (Andrew Geddes recorded the event in a painting, *The Discovery of the Scottish Regalia*, 1818.)

Through such tangible, visual symbols Scott fostered national pride. Seeking to re-create the image of a Scottish border laird in his own life, he bought the farm called Cartley Hole in 1811. There, on the banks of the

Walter Scott was an indefatigable promoter and preserver of the traditions and history of his country. The wealth he acquired from his writings allowed him to indulge his fancy in this romantic version of a Scottish baronial castle overlooking his beloved river Tweed.

A Gothic extravaganza, designed by George Kemp in 1840 and rivaled only by the Albert Memorial in London, the Scott Monument in the heart of Edinburgh is the largest and highest (200 feet) monument to a writer in the world.

J. E. Alexander, an amateur painter, faithfully recorded the details of Scott's funeral on September 26, 1832, in the ruins of Dryburgh Abbey. The simple dignity of the procession, with the coffin carried by Sir Walter's servants, contrasts with the ostentation of the monument to Scott in Edinburgh.

river Tweed, he built a magnificent medieval house which he filled with antiquities and rechristened Abbotsford. There was some justification for this; undoubtedly some abbot at some time forded the Tweed near this spot, for Dryburgh and Melrose Abbeys lay nearby. In his armory and his library Scott kept such treasures as a Celtic pony cap (a combination of a faceplate and two drinking horns, an incorrect "restoration" designed to create a fantastic horned headdress), mementoes of Rob Roy MacGregor, the door of the Edinburgh Toll Booth prison, and a cast of the skull of Robert the Bruce. At Abbotsford Scott wrote novel after novel. In his last days he could only lie on a couch in front of his dining-room window, looking over his beloved Tweed Valley. He was buried at Dryburgh, a last romantic gesture that turned the ruined choir of the Cistercians into a place of literary pilgrimage.

Edinburgh's monument to Scott dominates the heart of the city, challenging the modern world of the railroad, symbolized by Waverley Station. The monument seems a point of balance between the old and new towns, important to both the busy shopping street and the public gardens. Designed by G. Meikle Kemp and built by public subscription in 1840–44, this incredible Gothic shrine stands two hundred feet high; its lofty pinnacles are filled with sculptured characters from Scott's novels rather than saints and angels; it is the largest literary memorial in the world and predates the Albert Memorial in London by over twenty years. The huge open pinnacle dwarfs the sculptured portrait of the writer, just as Scott the man disappeared behind the medieval facade of the house and the literature he created. Scott's sense of theatricality surely would have been satisfied.

Scott knew the value of symbolic gesture and display. He staged one of

George III was the king commemorated by Glasgow's George Square, but the column which was to have supported his statue bears instead the figure of Sir Walter Scott. Behind the column is the cenotaph, a war memorial. The square itself was laid out in 1781 and still forms the modern city center. The city chambers by William Young, an Italian building with a tower, dominates the square.

The visit of Queen Victoria and Prince Albert to Hawthorden in 1842 was recorded in paint by William Allan. The royal couple, accompanied by the duchess of Buccleuch, overlook the river Esk, where the prince read an inscription to the poet William Drummond. The queen's love of Scotland and her conversion of Balmoral Castle into a royal residence stimulated an enthusiasm for all things Scottish.

the finest pageants of the day, the entry of George IV into Edinburgh, a scene painted by Sir David Wilkie. He reestablished Scotland on the world stage by bringing a reigning monarch again to Holyrood House and persuading him to appear in full Highland regalia, swathed in the tartan of the Royal Stuarts. The creation of a mystique around the formerly proscribed tartan and plaid and the national masculine dress, the kilt, together with the enthusiasm for the Scottish "baronial" image defined by the architecture, spread quickly from royalty and Scotland to people in all walks of life around the world.

George IV's successor Victoria was caught up in the new enthusiasm for Scotland. Scotland was exotic but no longer threatening; a distant land, but not too distant; foreign, but still British. The wild beauty of the Highlands could stimulate romantic thrills without real dangers; and the natives could be seen as picturesque fixtures on the moors while the poverty of their lives was overlooked. In 1848 Victoria and Albert leased Balmoral, a small Gordon estate in the Dee Valley, after they had been impressed by a painting of the old house by James Giles. Four years later the royal family bought the property, and Prince Albert, assisted by William Smith of Aberdeen, began to build a grand country seat. With its tower and turrets one hundred feet high joining residential and service wings which could house over a hundred people, Balmoral became a symbol of the royal family's Scottish connection. The interior of the castle,

The reconciliation of Scotland with England emerged
in the nineteenth century as an aggressive partnership.
Yet the full recognition of Scotland and her place in
the kingdom awaited the return of the monarch to the
ancestral home of the Stuarts. One of George IV's
earliest acts as king was to make a formal journey to
Scotland to acknowledge the northern kingdom. The
royal visit was stage-managed by Scott and painted
by David Wilkie, who also portrayed the monarch in
full tartan regalia.

Balmoral Castle, the royal residence in Scotland since Prince Albert bought it in 1853 and later bequeathed it to Queen Victoria, is situated about six miles north of Braemar and the river Dee. Built of granite, the stately house takes its name from the Gaelic for "majestic dwelling." This photograph is one half of a stereopticon pair by George Washington Wilson which was no doubt circulated in its original form to thousands of late-nineteenth-century Scottish and English homes.

fitted out with Royal Stuart tartan, set the fashion not only for Scottish lairds but for nostalgic Scots in Scotland and abroad. "Balmoralizing" and "tartanizing" became nineteenth-century decorators' plagues.

Scottish Neobaronial architecture, however, should not be dismissed as a mere aberration in the history of building design. Dunrobin Castle (1844–50), the seat of the duke of Sutherland, on Dornach Firth, is a magnificent essay in the Baronial style by Sir Charles Barry and W. Leslie. William Burn of Edinburgh created superb country houses throughout the British Isles; and Burn's pupil, the Edinburgh-born architect Richard Norman Shaw, became the leading late-Victorian designer of country houses and churches in a vernacular style.

If the words Scottish Baronial conjure up images of ornamental turrets and crow-stepped gables or towers with loopholes and battlements, then the impression must be balanced with one of sound underlying structure, rugged strength, fine craftsmanship, and architectural composition based on well-proportioned masses. Wealthy financiers and industrialists might play at being earls and barons, but they demanded comforts in their castles. Even that prince of romantics, Sir Walter Scott, installed gas lighting at Abbotsford. People did not want to live in real tower houses, climbing ladders into second-floor entrances. Grand staircases led to drawing rooms; billiard rooms replaced guard rooms; Balmoral had an enormous ballroom. Tartans and border tweed are very beautiful fabrics, even if Balmoral was filled with tartan curtains, upholstery, and carpets. Horns and antlers, or twisted sticks, make strange furniture, but suggest a virile, rustic society.

With the enthusiasm for Baronial architecture came a taste for flamboyant Gothic decoration inspired by the ruins of Melrose Abbey and Rosslyn Chapel (immortalized in Scott's *The Lay of the Last Minstrel*). Gothic was the style adopted and reinterpreted in the Scott monument. Flamboyant Gothic ecclesiastical architecture continued to inspire builders well into the twentieth century, including the great Edwardian architect Sir Robert Lorrimer. Lorrimer was a master of many styles from the pristine classicism of the St. Andrews University library to the bristling baronial of his country houses. In the Thistle Chapel at St. Giles, Edinburgh, Lorrimer recaptures the richness of the Sinclairs' Rosslyn Chapel. Commissioned by John David, twelfth earl of Leven, and his brothers in 1909 (finished by 1911) as a chapel for the Knights of the Thistle, it was the most elaborate "medieval" building erected since the fifteenth century. The tiny building was literally encrusted with sculptured ornament. The addition of the Thistle Chapel to Edinburgh's town kirk was a grand gesture of romantic historicism, just as the Thistle robes of rich green velvet powdered with silver thistles provided costumes for the ultimate fantasy of the nostalgic adult.

Sir Walter Scott re-created the Middle Ages and inspired Scots to relive their history as it should have been, not as it was. Another literary figure, Robert Burns, through his life as well as his poetry, provided a model of the star-crossed romantic hero. (What other people celebrate the birth of a poet, January 25, Burns's night, as something approaching a national holiday?) Burns, a handsome youth, was a poetic genius: barely surviving as a farmer and an excise man, irresistible to women, admired by men, and, of course, as a true romantic hero, tragically dead at an early age. Youth, beauty, genius, and early death define a typical hero. William Wallace striking the first blow for liberty, then drawn and quartered; Mary Queen of Scots beheaded; Bonnie Prince Charlie and Flora MacDonald pursued through the Highlands—their legends still capture the heart. Mary is never a scheming, dangerous politician; Charles Edward Stuart is never an elderly debauched exile. They live in the imagination as beautiful tragic figures.

Mary, the legend, still inspires sympathy: a child-queen of France, widow at seventeen, sent from the luxurious French court to austere Edinburgh, a pious Catholic confronted with the Calvinism of John Knox, bereft of friends and married to political opportunists, executed on the orders of another queen. Painters have immortalized the great tragic moments of her life: Mary's last look at France (William Frith), Mary denounced by John Knox (Sir William Allan, William Frith, William Beattie, Robert Herdman), the murder of David Riccio (John Graham, John Opie, William Allan), Mary resigning her crown (Gavin Hamilton, Joseph Severn, Alexander Johnston), her escape from Loch Leven (David Wilkie, John Graham), or the innumerable versions of her execution (John Opie, John Graham, Robert Herdman). Roy Strong's list of historical paintings exhibited at the Royal Academy in London includes seventy-four on the theme of Mary Queen of Scots.

Later, another dashing subject for history painting arrived in Scotland from France, Prince Charles Edward Stuart. Prince Charles came not as a ruler in triumph but as an exile, a twenty-five-year-old Scottish general intending to lead Scottish troops into battle for their country. His dramatic raising of the standard and the rising of the clans led by the MacDonalds and the Camerons was pictured by W.S. Cumming and C.D. Johnson, the ball at Holyrood House, the triumphal entry into Edinburgh by Thomas Duncan, and the final defeat at Culloden by Charles Lidderdale and John Pettie. The prince's months of hiding and escapes with the aid of Flora MacDonald provided wonderful subjects for paintings by Thomas Duncan,

Curling, a kind of golf on ice, was the great winter sport in Scotland from as early as the sixteenth century, and this Victorian-era genre painting captures the look of its early days.

This painting (below) by George Harvey was called *School Dismissing* when it was exhibited at London's Royal Academy in 1871, but its real title in Scottish dialect is *A Schule Skailin'*. Harvey gained fame as a painter of scenes from Scottish history, but he was also a master of genre painting.

David Wilkie's first major painting (below) after his student days in Edinburgh was an imaginative re-creation of the annual May fair held in Pitlessie village near his home. Many of the 140 figures were based on sketches he had made during his father's sermons, and through them he captures the spirit of the popular entertainment of the ordinary people in rural areas. Wilkie sold this painting for £25 and with the money continued his studies in London. Within a year he had become a famous and successful artist whose scenes of daily life among the Scottish peasants established a new school of genre painting in Britain.

Alexander Johnston, John Brodie, John MacDonald, and Allan Stewart.

David Scott, John Pettie, and others often interpreted Scottish history in visual form. Scott gave us a splendid William Wallace in a huge triptych, painted in 1843 (now in the Paisley Art Gallery): *Sir William Wallace Planting the Shield of Scotland upon the Body of Cressingham, who was Defeated and Slain at the Battle of Stirling, and Staying the Progress of Edward*, with its flanking wings, *Scottish War: The Spear*, and *English War: The Bow*. The very title embodies the sweep of history. Scott was fascinated by the personal element in the tragedies of history and painted memorable images of the *Murder of Riccio*, *Mary Receiving the Warrant for Her Execution*, and the *Execution*. John Pettie also painted Jacobite themes, from *Bonnie Prince Charlie* to the melodramatic *Hunted Down*.

The illustration of literature as well as history provided stimulus and employment for many artists. Scott's novels were an endless source of inspiration for artists, such as Robert and James Lauder. Because of Scott's passion for topographical accuracy, the artists and their patrons could visit famous sites and re-create the events in their imaginations. Furthermore, the popularity of antiquarian studies meant that the painter could give his work a historical aura by depicting the correct armor, costume and jewelry, castles, window tracery, and gates, while he painted the landscape. The contrast between Gavin Hamilton's *Mary Queen of Scots* in the eighteenth century and Herdman's carefully researched paintings is evident.

The distant past, too, began to exert a fascination. Interest in the Picts and other early inhabitants of Scotland had been awakened by Sir Walter Scott. In *The Weird Wife* by the Aberdeen painter James Giles a witch moves through an eerie landscape filled with standing Pictish stones. Scott's articles on demonology in the *Phrenological Journal* (1824) awakened the romantic imagination at its richest; such a mood may be found in Faed's depiction of *Tam o' Shanter*'s wild night with the witches.

The beauties of Scottish landscape became more accessible after the opening of the country by railroads and roadways. Dorothy and William Wordsworth traveled through Scotland in 1803, recording their impressions. Victoria and Albert were painted and photographed in the Highlands. By the end of the century middle-class travelers had discovered Scotland. The landscape painters of the nineteenth century found in the Scottish Highlands all the drama of the Alps. Early landscapists had painted crisp and elegant topographical views, or idealized golden-hued trees and castles. Now the power of creation and the drama of destruction caught the imagination. A Glasgow painter, Horatio McCulloch, painted sweeping scenes such as *Glencoe*. His monochromatic panoramic views emphasized the wild crags and ruined castles in which the viewers could read the frailty of human works in the face of untamed nature. If such images of mountains and glens seem larger than life, so too was the emotional reaction to the scenery. The viewer expected to tingle with emotion at the spectacle of Ben Nevis, to recall Tam and the witches at the Grey Mare's Tail, or to follow in the footsteps of the lone hunter—or the stag at eve— by Ellen's Isle.

Scots abroad, whether in London or in distant America, provided a steady market for paintings of Scottish scenery, border abbeys, Highland cattle, baronial towers, and kilted pipers. The Faed brothers, John, James, and Thomas, developed genre painting as a major direction in Scottish art. Thomas's imaginary scene, *Sir Walter Scott and His Literary Friends at Abbots-ford* (1851), was an immediate success and enabled the artist to settle permanently in London. John remained in Edinburgh, painting miniature portraits and creating very fine illustrations that continue to delight. James, a mezzotint engraver, reproduced his brothers' paintings and gave their work its worldwide audience. The Faeds were masters of pathos. Thomas's

In this painting by Alexander Carse we see not only the interior of one of the fine houses of Edinburgh's New Town, but the family and their possessions. The contrast between the bashful daughter and her elegant city cousins suggests scenes from the novels of Jane Austen. The house could be one of those in Charlotte Square.

The Mitherless Bairn (1855), *Sunday in the Backwoods of Canada* (1859), and the *Last of the Clan* (1867) are well composed and beautifully painted, even though the anecdotal detail and sentimentality seem cloying today. He received plaudits from Longfellow for a painting of *Evangeline* ("very beautiful and very pathetic").

Popular taste and public enthusiasm for visual images can be judged by advertisements for engravings of paintings. Hodgson and Graves's advertisement in *Art Union* (1829) suggests that enthusiastic salesmanship of reproductions of works of art for homes is not a modern phenomenon. They offered both *John Knox Administering the Sacrament in the Castle of St. Andrew's* by William Bonnar, and for those of a different taste, a scene called *The Highland Whiskey Still*. There was also *The Highland Gamekeeper's Hut* by G.S. Cooper, "the celebrated cattle painter . . . wherein will be introduced every description of dogs and game peculiar to Scotland—the whole being painted from Nature."

Such engravings in the nineteenth century spread an image of Scotland around the world. As Scots sought and found their fortunes abroad, they perpetuated the romantic image of a land they only half-remembered and a history which was at least in part fantasy.

MOST LITERARY HISTORIANS describe Scottish literature after Burns and Scott as a Scottish "contribution" to the development of nineteenth-century British literature. They do not think of it as a distinctively Scottish literature. Such a judgment, however nettling, is understandable. One can argue for the creative talents of John Gibson Lockhart, Scott's son-in-law (1794–1854), who wrote a number of entertaining but minor fictions and who painted a gallery of Edinburgh portraits in *Peter's Letters to His Kinfolk* (1819), a primary document for anyone interested in the sociology of the intelligentsia in the first quarter of the century. It may be easier to champion the literary talent of James Hogg, the "Ettrick Shepherd" (1770–1835). His great satirical novel, which sets Faust firmly in Edinburgh, has devoted readers to this day: *The Private Memoirs and Confessions of a Justified Sinner* (1824) is a genuinely important statement about Calvinist piety running amok. John Galt (1779–1839) exercised firm control over a realism that records, with humor and shrewdness, the changing social classes of Scotland, particularly in *Annals of the Parish* (1821), *The Provost* (1822), and *The Entail* (1823).

But Lockhart and Hogg more readily created an audience for their literary criticism and journalism than for their fiction; Galt's audience outside his native land has always been limited; and the development of Scottish poetry never rose much above the sentimental, stereotyped poems of *Whistle-Binkie, A Collection of Songs for the Social Circle*. The writing of fiction generally spiraled downward until, late in the century, the Kailyard

NINETEENTH-CENTURY
LITERATURE
by Harold Orel

269

James Hogg, known as the "Ettrick Shepherd," was born in Ettrick Forest, the land of Wallace and the Bruce. Almost entirely self-taught, he was inspired by reading Allan Ramsay's *Gentle Shepherd* to write songs himself. Hogg knew the old border ballads and assisted Sir Walter Scott in collecting materials for *Minstrelsy of the Scottish Border* in 1802. The men remained friends throughout their lives.

school of storytellers—referring to the cabbage or borecole, with wrinkled leaves, that grows in common gardens—made it impossible for readers to see behind the isinglass of idealized country life. The two greatest Scots writers of the century were Thomas Carlyle (1795–1881) and Robert Louis Stevenson (1850–1894), but there were many arid years between the former's decline and the latter's rise to fame.

Nevertheless, the world of literature owes much to Scottish genius in the nineteenth century, for this was the age of great quarterlies, periodicals edited and written by reviewers, journalists, historians, and political scientists who, though they wrote anonymously, always spoke with great authority for clear-cut points of view. The influence that they exerted was enormous, the excitement they generated almost inconceivable to a generation distracted by audio-visual entertainments.

In the first half of the century, three of the most important periodicals in the United Kingdom were Scottish enterprises, organized, edited, and largely written within the environs of Edinburgh. The first was the *Edinburgh Review,* which made its initial appearance in two installments only, during the years 1755 and 1756, before it disappeared. Its efforts to review all books that had been published in Scotland, to advertise recent developments in the sciences, and to draw upon a very limited number of contributors who knew and were comfortable with each other's ideas marked it as an Enlightenment phenomenon, though one that was needlessly provincial in its coverage.

The second incarnation began in 1802, and, like the first, was marked by an interest in adult education. Its editors saw themselves in much the same light as "improvers" of the previous century had seen their societies as responsible for spreading the good word on agricultural and scientific innovations. Three men shaped the destinies of the *Edinburgh*: Francis Jeffrey (1773–1850), who held conservative literary tastes and Whiggish political ideas; Henry Brougham (1778–1868), who later became an activist and a controversial Lord Chancellor; and Sydney Smith (1771–1845), a witty reformer and satirist. Jeffrey's slashing reviews have become notorious in the light of our knowledge that his early reviews of Romantic poetry were unbalanced, but he did write at length on poetry that he did not care for, thereby guaranteeing struggling writers a serious audience. There was far more to his appreciation of Wordsworth than his magisterial "This will never do."

During the first five years of the *Edinburgh,* Walter Scott contributed ten important essays, until the journal's liberal political ideas dismayed him, and he took his talents elsewhere. But it was more than a periodical of brilliantly edited essays, many of them condensed and rewritten against the wishes of their authors, and more than a journal which aimed to please a well-defined readership. It prized independent judgment, and it argued heroically for standards of taste and decorum in both political and literary criticism. "The *Edinburgh* has but two legs to stand on," Jeffrey said in the course of his quarrel with Scott. "Literature is one of them, but its right leg is politics."

Jeffrey's essay of 1809 on French politics in Spain, with its emphasis on "popular" doctrine, alarmed a number of readers, to the point that establishment of a rival, Tory-oriented journal, *The Quarterly Review,* became inevitable. With the backing of John Murray, an eminent English publisher, and essays by Scott, Southey, Rogers, Moore, and a number of talented contributors, the circulation of *The Quarterly* rose, by late in the second decade, to fourteen thousand copies, approximately the same number as that of the *Edinburgh*. A third journal, *Blackwood's Edinburgh Magazine,* began publication in 1817, and found its footing when Lockhart and Hogg joined up with John Wilson (more famous as Christopher

Thomas Carlyle, often called *the* Victorian sage, derived much of his rhetorical power and harsh view of the human condition from a specifically Scottish background. His *Sartor Resartus*, one of the most original books of the nineteenth century, appeared in 1833–34; then followed an astonishing cascade of essays, character sketches, jeremiads, and historical surveys. Carlyle did not like the modern world, which he believed had become a man-destroying machine. He preached the need for heroes who would triumph over the political democracy corrupting the land.

271

North, his pen name) to write slashing reviews; a scandalous and sensationally successful satire on Edinburgh personages, *The Chaldee MS.*, written in Biblical language; and *Noctes Ambrosianae*, a series of conversations between real and imagined figures. *Blackwood's* may have been the most consistently entertaining of the three journals, and its allegiance to Tory principles meant that the *Edinburgh Review* fought with two formidable competitors for the attention of the reading public.

Yet David Daiches is fully justified in noting that these reviewers were not concerned with Scottish literature as such and did not seek to promulgate the notion of a distinctive Scottish literary tradition. Their contributions "represented," in the words of Daiches, "a major part of the literary life of Edinburgh, a minor phase of the history of English criticism, and no definite part at all of the history of Scottish literature or criticism, if by Scottish literature we mean literature that is part of a Scottish tradition extending back to the Scottish Chaucerians and beyond."

The Victorian seer who, perhaps more than any other writer, embodied the sense of authority and wisdom that has since become a cliché of the age was Thomas Carlyle (1795–1881). Born in Ecclefechan, in the Lowlands, Carlyle attended Annan Grammar School and later the University of Edinburgh; after some tentative, disappointing experiences in teaching at Annan and then Kirkcaldy, he came back to Edinburgh. Within a few years he had met and fallen in love with Jane Baillie Welsh, who possessed an intelligent, restless temperament that was more than a fair match for his own.

Carlyle in many ways is not an attractive figure for our age. His career consisted of a series of attacks on the spirit of Moderatism, indeed on the Scottish Enlightenment as a whole. He became increasingly intolerant of conflicting viewpoints, and his defense of Governor Eyre, who bloodily suppressed a rebellion in Jamaica in 1865, outraged liberal opinion. His *Shooting Niagara: and After?* (1867) was provoked by the passage of the second Reform Bill, and hysterically predicted anarchy within half a century, as a consequence of legislation that was long overdue.

Carlyle's enthusiasm for the "God-inspired hero," one who could do no wrong because of his efficiency in advancing toward his goals, made him a popular figure in Germany. His monumental *History of Frederick II of Prussia* (1852–65) was a logical extension of his interest in German mysticism, romanticism, and *Kultur*. The Prussian government bestowed its Order of Merit upon him in 1874. Much later, Hitler admired his teachings, and Carlyle's writings sold in hundreds of thousand of copies in Nazi Germany.

Carlyle as a struggling young man, as a suitor of Margaret Gordon

Skerryvore Lighthouse, Argyll, stands ten miles out at sea off the island of Tiree. It was built in 1843 by Robert Stevenson, a Glasgow engineer and the grandfather of Robert Louis Stevenson. He built twenty-three lighthouses and invented the flashing light.

(the romance is idealized in *Sartor Resartus*), as a wretchedly underpaid translator of Goethe and other German writers, as an unsuccessful aspirant toward the law and later toward a professorship, is a far more attractive figure because his opinions were still malleable, because he exhibited the vulnerability of a man of genius unrecognized, hence uncorrupted by public adulation; because he was still moving toward a definition of self. Carlyle's Calvinism was shaken by readings in eighteenth-century history and philosophy, by his understanding of Newtonian physics, by increasing disgust with modern ethics and materialist doctrine, and perhaps even by the first signs of the dyspepsia that was to torment him for a lifetime. It is impossible to calculate how many young men have since identified with Carlyle's tracing of the three stages of his hero's movement toward a new faith suitable for the age: the Everlasting No, the Center of Indifference, and the Everlasting Yea.

Although Carlyle moved permanently to London in 1834, and thought of himself thereafter as an English writer, it is possible to argue that the most ingratiating elements in Carlyle's career are precisely those that remain intractably and recognizably Scottish. The universe, he argued, was essentially spiritual. Though his concept of God was idiosyncratic his distrust of current orthodoxies, his hatred of sham and hypocrisy, and his fierce espousal of the doctrine of hard work and of a sense of duty, remind us of the subject matter in the satires of his great predecessor, Robert Burns.

One of Carlyle's most important essays deals with Burns (in *Heroes and Hero-Worship*, 1841), and there one Scotsman describes another as attempting to write a poetry of "wisdom and religion," and generously accepts Burns, faults and all, for the sake of his manliness and his message. It is possible to trace Carlyle's indebtedness to Goethe, Fichte, and the German Idealists, but Carlyle's view of life is a characteristically Scottish retention of Calvin's tenets.

Carlyle's importance for his time cannot be minimized. Kingsley, Ruskin, Dickens, and Browning dedicated books to him. His sense of history as an exciting discipline was manifested first, and perhaps most strikingly, in the epic rhythms of *The French Revolution* (1837). *Past and Present* (1843) made studies of the medieval period popular. Carlyle's prose style was hugely influential on younger writers, and it was as a teacher that Carlyle primarily saw himself. The fact that his reputation fluctuated during his lifetime and after his death suffered more than one blow should not distract our attention from his accomplishments: his inculcation of "truths" that more than one generation found congenial, his rhetorical skills, his elevation of the poet to the status of hero, his sense that true history is dramatic and the story of men, and his courage in saying what he knew (well in advance) would be unpopular.

He paradoxically functioned both as the first and greatest of the Victorian prophets and as the most eloquent, and thunderous, of the anti-Victorians. In George Meredith's phrase, Carlyle was "a heaver of rocks, not a shaper." But he was also a moral force. No student of the Victorian Age can ignore the value of his contributions to the spiritual and intellectual life of more than half a century, not only in England but throughout the Western world.

More approachable as a human being, and indeed one of the more fascinating masculine temperaments of the century, was Robert Louis Stevenson. He was, in several ways, an original. The grandson and son of civil engineers who specialized in lighthouse design, he was raised by his mother to appreciate the virtues of religion and the contributions of the Covenanters to Scottish history. Illness afflicted him from an early age; he was carefully nursed and protected by his parents and by "Cummy,"

Alison Cunningham, who fed his remarkably receptive imagination with folk tales, songs, and scraps and tags of Scottish tradition. The University of Edinburgh was primarily valuable to him as the home of the Speculative Society, which helped him to master elements of writing and public oratory, and the *Edinburgh University Magazine*, to which he contributed. His pamphlet *The Pentland Rising, A Page of History* (1866) was published while he was still sixteen.

Any review of his life must note the restlessness of his travels in search of a congenial environment, or one that might be converted into journalism. Some of his finest achievements in literature are cast in the form of travel essays or books—about Belgium, France, California, and the South Seas. Those who in their youth have read *Treasure Island* (1883), *A Child's Garden of Verses* (1885), *Kidnapped* (1886), or *The Black Arrow* (1888) may find it difficult to believe that the author of such books ever grew up, because he seemed to be writing so directly and unaffectedly for children, from a child's perspective.

Yet there is a darker, and possibly more interesting, side to Stevenson. It was long obscured by the admiring sketches and memoirs that appeared after his death and that fixed in many people's minds the image of a "seraph in chocolate." There is, for one thing, his turbulent relations with his father, expressing rebellion through aborted careers in engineering and law and through somewhat startling statements of religious doubt. He wasted a gift of £1,000 given him by his father, and it was not until the mid-1880s that Stevenson became reconciled to his need for parental love. He had uneven relationships with women and with his collaborators, and he may never have been an easy writer to work with.

Remarkably candid in self-assessment, he knew that his jointly written plays and stories tended to fall below the literary standard he had set for himself. But even more nagging was his suspicion that his talent was more modest than his admirers would allow, and that the reputation of some of the writers whose "realism" he denounced as depressingly photographic would last longer than his own. It is difficult to read that extraordinary pamphlet written in defense of Father Damien, the priest who had given his life to the lepers of Molokai, without recognizing the fact that the anger expressed therein against oppression and exploitation of a native culture is an anger that moves just below the surface in a very large number of his works on criticism and travel. He is, for example, one of the first writers about the South Seas to diagnose the dangers inherent in colonial attitudes. The gloominess in much of his writing is attributable to frustration in establishing satisfactory personal relationships as well as to pain and ill health.

It is unjust to dismiss Stevenson's books aimed at a juvenile audience as in some way subliterary; they are among the finest and most deservedly popular classics of children's literature. But much of his fiction is openly, admiringly imitative of earlier masters. And yet, despite all the reservations one might have about the originality of Stevenson, adult readers can find much to admire, even gasp at, in the macabre retelling of Deacon Brodie's story (*Dr. Jekyll and Mr. Hyde*, 1886), "Thrawn Janet" (in *The Merry Men*, 1889), "The Beach of Falesa" (in *Island Nights Entertainment*, 1893), *The Master of Ballantrae* (1889), and the unfinished *Weir of Hermiston* (published in 1896, after his death). These tales are grimly cognizant of the powerful attraction that Calvinist doctrine exerts over men and women. Hyde, Stevenson wrote, "is the essence of cruelty and malice and selfishness and cowardice, and these are the diabolic in man—not this poor wish to love a woman, that they make such a cry about." It is precisely this emphasis upon the diabolic that makes Stevenson an important contributor to modern fiction.

Robert Louis Stevenson, in an age of great storytellers, proved his mastery in short stories, novels, and plays; but he was a superb essayist, his word-pictures of smoky Edinburgh have never been bettered, and he wrote the immortal *A Child's Garden of Verses*. His biography includes problems of parental disapproval, debilitating ill health, a romance with an older woman, and the flight to Samoa, where he died of a cerebral hemorrhage. The scandals of his life, often exaggerated, are less interesting than the truth. This portrait bas-relief is by Augustus Saint-Gaudens.

Stevenson's widely collected essays, graceful, compulsively readable, and remarkably consistent in their tone, did much to win him a large audience, but that kind of readership inevitably fell away as more rigorous standards of literary analysis came into favor. He expended the major part of his creative genius on his fiction, and its faithful re-creation of Caledonian scenes and manners fully justifies the pride that his fellow countrymen take in the productions of their best storyteller since Scott.

Like Carlyle, he was a moralist, and his stories resonate with his personal involvement in the painful, perhaps insoluble conflicts created by moral issues. Like Carlyle, too, he had a clear sense of wherein a man's duties lay. He was an agnostic who had not found a way to set himself free from obligations imposed by Calvinist ways of thinking, a romancer who disliked the British prudery that prevented him from writing in a more realistic mode, and a diffident artist whose firm control of narrative technique repays close analysis.

10

Twentieth Century Literature

Harold Orel

Art in Modern Times

Marilyn Stokstad

The National Revival

Henry L. Snyder

BY THE END of the nineteenth century, Scottish sentimental fiction had earned twice over its unpleasant reputation: escapist, irresponsible, untrue to domestic life, artificially wrought, and amiably disinclined to confront real problems of the late Victorian Age. Fatuities and commonplaces might be disguised by dialect. Easy writing led all too often to easy reading. And the term used to describe these fictions—the Kailyard school—acknowledges the writer's condescension to an audience that presumably wants no challenge in its entertainment.

The Reverend John Watson (1850–1907) and Samuel Rutherford Crockett (1860–1914) were expert practitioners; the former, better known as Ian Maclaren, secured large audiences with *Beside the Bonnie Brier Bush* (1894), a moral, optimistic, and pathos-choked narrative, while the latter exploited a similar vein of village humor (and humors) in *The Stickit Minister, and Some Common Men* (1893). The grandfather of all these novels had appeared in 1828: David Macbeth Moir's *Autobiography of Mansie Waugh*. But Moir was humorously opening up materials that Galt had handled with some distinction and gravity, while the Kailyard novelists were all too obviously manipulating fictional ingredients to make preconceived points about the nature of Scottish character.

Yet of them all the best and most commercially successful was a writer of genuine distinction, Sir James Barrie (1860–1937). He began his professional life as a writer of leaders for the *Nottingham Journal*, and blossomed with a series of sketches that exploited his memories of Kirriemuir, in Forfarshire. Barrie's tone was forever retrospective and more than a little complacent. He liked his fictional creations: Tommy Sandys, a young Scot who enjoyed the finer things of life (e.g., himself); John Shand, a railway porter who enjoyed reading and eventually became famous and influential (hero of *What Every Woman Knows*); Andrew Riach, Mary Rose, Peter Pan, and—in a number of disguises—his own mother, who is written down most directly in that charmingly readable memoir *Margaret Ogilvy* (1896).

Barrie turned from prose fiction to drama shortly after the turn of the century, and Tommy, hero of both *Sentimental Tommy* (1896) and *Tommy and Grizel* (1900), was the last protagonist of his serious novels. But, of course, Tommy is recognizably the creation of a writer skilled at sketching, humorously and swiftly, the idiosyncrasies of a national type, and he belongs to the same universe as the old charwoman of *The Old Lady Shows Her Medals* (1917) and the butler who triumphs, by virtue of inner grace, over effete aristocrats in *The Admirable Crichton* (1902). In Barrie's art, humor is always commingled with pathos, the village gossips are more picturesque than malicious, true love has the odds in its favor, and manliness is depicted as being somehow a Scottish birthright.

The combination of craft, genuine belief, and refined sentimentalism proved irresistible or ingratiating for more than one generation of readers. Indeed, in an age of alienated art there is much to be said for Barrie's sense of rapport with his audience. Even when we concede that the master truths of his fiction do not grapple with ultimate questions, he pioneered in depicting supernatural events on the stage, contributed significantly to a rich literature for and about children, defined a mother-son relationship with disarming candor, and created a gallery of Scottish men and women who are, all things considered, fun to know.

But Barrie, despite his obvious superiority to Watson and Crockett, was often accused of falsifying the grim realities of the Scottish hinterland. If any one book may be said to have ended the Kailyard school it was George Douglas Brown's *The House with the Green Shutters* (1901). Brown (1869–1902), who died a year after its publication, despised the commercial concoctions that purported to tell the truth about ordinary

Sir James Matthew Barrie has often been described by the subtitle he gave to his play *Peter Pan*: "the boy who wouldn't grow up." But the characterization underestimates his achievements as a journalist very much of this world, a calculatingly sentimental exploiter of Scottish materials, a shrewd dramatist and theatrical figure in an era of flamboyant actor-managers, and a creator of character.

279

Scots. His novel is aflame with a passion that far transcends the immediate circumstances of the story it tells. It is as if Brown were scoring off a lifetime of unhappiness; memories of his own childhood as an illegitimate son born as an Ayrshire "uneducated, short-coated peasant" lurk not far beneath the surface of this brutal, uncompromising picture of a community named Barbie. But inhabitants of Ochiltree were no more shocked by Brown's portrait than were Scots throughout the land and overseas. Brown's pages described a community brutalized by a bully, John Gourlay, and his increasingly successful competitor, James Wilson. Gourlay's wife is dimwittedly resentful of her fate. His son is too stupid to take advantage of the education at Edinburgh University that his father underwrites; eventually he is responsible for his father's death; and the concluding chapters dramatize, with an amazing power, the total destruction of the Gourlay family.

Even those who correctly note that "not a character in the book is likeable," and that "it is all meanness, ugliness, coarseness," do not deny its power as a social document. As a blast against sentimentality in Scottish fiction, *The House with the Green Shutters* achieved complete success. Though we dignify the novel unreasonably to speak of its theme as the fall of a Scottish House of Atreus, there is more than a small measure of truth in its sour portrayal of frustration, and in its expectably tragic ending.

Scottish literature of the twentieth century is much more committed to invoking and praising the spirit of charity than it was in any earlier age. As a consequence, it seems more human, more interestingly hesitant about the

The late nineteenth century saw the beginnings of industrial labor organization and social agitation in Britain. The speaker here may be James Keir Hardie, a key figure in early union development. This etching is called *Socialists*.

answers it proposes. Not for our century—or for the free taste of most Scottish readers—is the gnarled, bitter blank verse of John Davidson (1857–1909), who, like Nietzsche, praised the right of the strong man to rule those less self-confident than himself. Yeats admired Davidson, and Eliot learned from him; there was even a possibility, for a brief heady period, that Davidson might become the poet laureate; but Davidson's anger at a world that withheld success and full recognition could turn nowhere, finally, save in upon itself, and Davidson's suicide by drowning showed a recognition that Scottish literature would not willingly develop further in the direction he had marked.

Scottish literature of the modern age, however, is best represented by Christopher Murray Grieve (1892–1978), better known as Hugh MacDiarmid. Not that he wrote well at all times, or fully earned his right to be cranky, mean-tempered, and egotistical. He brought not peace but a sword to the cause of Anglo-Scottish relations. His efforts to revive Lallans (Lowland Scots dialect) as a literary medium earned him plaudits within an understandably restricted circle, while larger audiences were appalled by such works as *Three Hymns to Lenin*, which certified the existence of the phenomenon of Scottish communism by excusing "the Chekha's horrors" as necessary. In his vast outpouring of autobiographical materials, two of his most important books, *Lucky Poet, A Self-Study in Literature and Political Ideas* (1943) and *The Company I've Kept* (1967), mix astonishing insights, Swiftian invective, and near-insufferable name-dropping. Cursed by total recall, he could never forget what he had read or whom he had met.

Nevertheless, as Kenneth Butlay wrote in the *Writers and Critics Series* (1964), Hugh MacDiarmid "is the scourge of the Philistines, the ruthless intellectual tough looking for a rumble, the catapulted stone amongst the stool pigeons. Not for him the prolonged agony, in the words of Kierkegaard, of 'being trampled to death by geese.' " He died having accomplished less than he hoped to achieve, the founder of no internationally influential movement, and more isolated from the mainstream than he himself may have realized. But he was impossible to ignore while alive. His lively prose, his dynamic poetry, and his extraordinary personality made him a Scot of high visibility, and Scottish literature a palpable body of work with its own respectable tradition and masterpieces.

Born near the border, in Langham, he was to derive grim satisfaction from his origins, working-class over several generations. He found exactly what he needed in the library left by Thomas Telford, the engineer. It consisted of several thousand books and was housed in the post-office buildings where the Grieve family resided. He read "almost every one of them," learned more about American literature than Scottish, and acquired an enormous range of information.

He became actively identified with Socialist societies as he moved into Scottish journalism and conducted research on "the rural problem" for a Fabian Committee on Land Problems and Rural Development. In 1915, as a member of the Royal Army Medical Corps (R.A.M.C.), he went to Salonika, Italy, and France, at the end of which service (1920) he launched himself furiously on a career that combined politics and literature for the rest of his life. He became a Labour member of the town council and a J.P. He helped to found the Scottish Centre of P.E.N. and the National party of Scotland. He announced his leadership of a Scottish Renaissance Movement. His reputation as Scotland's leading author was firmly established by the early 1930s. All the more disturbing, therefore, was his turbulent relationship to Communist party affairs.

The rights or wrongs of his political beliefs seem less important now than the poetry he created. Though much was dedicated to ephemeral causes, and the plea for the Scottish vernacular as an official literary language no longer rings in our ears so stridently, one easily appreciates the service that MacDiarmid rendered readers everywhere by his attack on a sentimentalized Burns tradition, his faith in a serious Scots literature, and his attempt to make his countrymen aware of larger currents of European thought. He was able to argue, immediately after publication of *Ulysses*, that a similar service for Scottish culture was necessary, and he functioned, for much of his life, as a cultural ambassador; the similarities between himself and Yeats as a somewhat self-conscious bringer of light to the benighted heathen are striking.

His masterpiece remains *A Drunk Man Looks at the Thistle* (1926). This book-length poem treats a theme which MacDiarmid returned to in various works: "a beautiful soul in the making," or, more specifically, a man passing through hell to self-knowledge. It is often an uneasy mixture of English and experimental Scots.

MacDiarmid could write fine poems in straightforward English, and a casual-seeming lyric like *Dytiscus* or an impassioned reply to A. E. Housman, *Another Epitaph on an Army of Mercenaries*, will remind us how impassioned occasional poems may sometimes rise to the level of artistic documents. Beyond the tiresome shows of erudition, beyond the propaganda for causes of varying merit, and even beyond the bad jokes and sophomoric demands that everyone march to the beat of the same drummer, lies a body of major poetic work.

The best of MacDiarmid's contemporaries and admirers was William Soutar (1898–1943), whose declining years were spent in invalidism and were marked by a courageous determination to persevere. He began as a poet writing in conventional, and occasionally tired, English. But he moved beyond Georgian influences to his own idiom in *A Handful of Earth* (1936), *In the Time of Tyrants* (1939), *But the Earth Abideth* (1943), and *The Expectant Silence* (published in 1944, after his death).

Some of Soutar's finest work may be found in *Seeds in the Wind* (1933, expanded in 1943), and though he never surrendered some reservations about Scots as his *one* language, he rose, time after time, to self-imposed challenges in his exploitation of a colorful, synthetic Scots that no one save MacDiarmid knew how to handle as well. Readers of works written by other members of the Scottish Renaissance—Douglas Young (1913-1973), Robert Garioch Sutherland (b. 1909), Alexander Scott (b. 1920), Sydney Goodsir Smith (1915-1975), Alastair Mackie (b. 1925), and George Campbell Hay (b. 1915)—will want to return, sooner rather than later, to Soutar and MacDiarmid as prime exemplars of two propositions: Lallans, skillfully employed, is exportable, and its range is fully as wide as that of English.

If Scottish literature is to be seen as worthy of international recognition, perhaps it is not so controversial after all to insist that its greatest distinction arises from a preoccupation with Scottish subject matter, the use of Scottish locales, and a pride in Scottish speech and folkways. Much as some critics may admire Eric Linklater (1899-1974) and Compton Mackenzie (1883-1974), as well as a number of writers who originally hail from Scotland but have since gone forth to other lands, making rich contributions to literature there, they are best seen as members of that vast army of Scots abroad rather than as writers of fiction, essayists, dramatists, and poets who thought that their homeland, in fact as in their literary production, was Scotland itself. This standard allows us to turn to the achievements of James Bridie (1888-1951), Lewis Grassic Gibbon (1901-1935), and Edwin Muir (1887-1959). Their contributions to Scottish literature are varied, willingly experimental as well as traditional in form, and agreeable in the best sense. They remind us of how much good writing in this century has been shipped south and west to other English-speaking nations.

Bridie is the pen name of Osborne Henry Mavor, who was born in Glasgow and educated in that city's university medical school. Like MacDiarmid he served in the R.A.M.C.; unlike MacDiarmid, he did it twice, in different wars. Scotland's experience in the mounting of theatrical productions may be superior to its ability to sustain a living tradition of playwriting, but Bridie's plays were often compared to those of Shaw, not necessarily to Shaw's advantage. Bridie wrote over thirty plays, some of them daringly fanciful. Despite flaws in dramaturgy, several earned long London runs. *Tobias and the Angel* (1930), *A Sleeping Clergyman* (1933), *Mr. Bolfry* (1943), *Daphne Laureola* (1949), and *The Queen's Comedy* (1950) are noteworthy.

Gibbon, too, is a pseudonym, in this case for James Leslie Mitchell, who sometimes wrote under his own name about the lives of explorers, and historical novels, the best being *Spartacus* (1933). Born near Auchterless, Aberdeenshire, Gibbon was familiar from the very beginning with farm life and ultimately celebrated it in his most solidly constructed work, *A Scots Quair*. This trilogy, consisting of *Sunset Song* (1932), *Cloud Howe* (1933), and *Grey Granite* (1934), traces the life history of Chris Guthrie, a crofter's daughter, and the decision she finally makes, after much irresolution and even heartbreak, to remain faithful to her Scottish heritage. This work is often interpreted as an allegory because the dilemma of Chris has far-reaching implications. It is superlative fiction. *Sunset Song* may well be the finest Scottish novel of our century.

Muir, born in Deerness, Orkney, and educated at Kirkwall, served as a clerk in Glasgow, a journalist in London, a free-lance writer and translator on the Continent, and then, in his final decades, as a member of the British Council in Edinburgh, Prague, and Rome, and warden of Newbattle Abbey College, Midlothian (1950-55). MacDiarmid became angry at Muir's distrust of Scots as useable literary language, but for the

most part Muir's gentle brand of mysticism, glowingly transparent love of literature, and realistically grounded appreciation of innocence won him a small but devoted audience.

In such works as *The Voyage* (1946), *The Labyrinth* (1949), and *Collected Poems* (1960), he won recognition as a distinctive voice. His forty-three volumes of translations popularized Feuchtwanger, Asch, Broch, and—most importantly—Kafka, in both Great Britain and the United States. His literary criticism was similarly concerned with the making rather than the breaking of reputations; he rendered yeoman service, for example, to the career of D. H. Lawrence. His novels may be less successful than *An Autobiography* (1954) in reshaping the materials of his life, but many discriminating readers have admired both *The Three Brothers* (1931) and *Poor Tom* (1932). He was, taken all in all, a lovable man, a philosopher-critic, and a writer who dignified or made more interesting every topic that he touched.

In this 1878 painting by William McKay, female farm workers, known as bondagers, are harvesting potatoes under the supervision of an overseer who weighs their loads. In the border counties every laborer had to provide a woman to work, too, and if he had no wife he had to hire someone. To express their independence, and for safety, these women often put all their earnings into colorful garments and jewelry. As a result they were looked on with disapproval by married women. The practice of bondaging was not officially abolished until the 1860s, and then not because of the harshness of the women's existence, but because it was assumed that they encouraged immorality.

ART IN MODERN TIMES
by Marilyn Stokstad

AN EARLY UNION of technology, fine arts, and a social conscience characterizes modern Scottish culture. Scottish engineering and technology are exemplified in the works of the great bridge builder, Thomas Telford; the man who lent his name to the road surface called macadam, John Loudon McAdam; and the inventor of the steam hammer, James Nasmyth. Nasmyth, son of Scotland's first great landscape painter Alexander Nasmyth and himself a painter of romantic landscapes, set up a foundation for the support of needy artists with the profits from his invention.

In the twentieth century, hydroelectric projects and North Sea oil rigs dominate our visual image of a modern Scotland. Architecture and sculpture combine in the monumental precision of the shipbuilders along the Clyde or the bridges over the Forth; they are the art of a people whose genius has been to create beauty from necessity and to modify severity with grace.

In the middle of the nineteenth century technology and aesthetics—science, nature, and art—came together in a brand new art form—photography. Appropriately enough, Scottish artists were pioneers

Thomas Telford built roads and bridges through the Highlands as well as his more famous suspension bridges in England and Wales. Dean Bridge, over the water of Leith in Edinburgh, is one of his most graceful structures.

James Nasmyth, son of Alexander, the artist, showed a great proficiency for model-making early in life. In 1836 he established what became the Bridgewater foundry at Manchester, where he developed a whole series of machine tools, the most famous of which was the steam hammer. He also conceived the basic design for the dentist's drill.

285

Nasmyth's inverted or steam hammer engine of 1848.

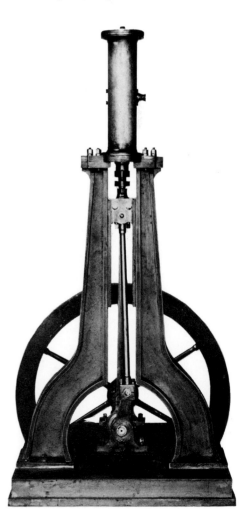

in its development. In the 1830s Louis-Jacques-Mandé Daguerre in France and William Henry Fox Talbot in England "invented" photography at about the same time, although the principles—the use of sun to create images and the action of light on silver nitrate—had been known earlier. Fox Talbot developed a process which he called the calotype (from the Greek word *kalos*, meaning beautiful), and by 1841 he could make a "sun picture" in three minutes. Artists and connoisseurs appreciated the subtle diffused images produced by the calotype process; however, the general public preferred the detailed images possible with the daguerreotypes. Needless to say, most photographers catered to the public demand. That the calotype rather than the daguerreotype was developed as an important artistic medium in Scotland resulted from fortuitous accident.

Fox Talbot, as a fellow of the Royal Society, knew many of the distinguished scientists of the day. One of them was Sir David Brewster, a founder of the British Association for the Advancement of Science and a principal at St. Andrews University. Fox Talbot sent news and details of his invention to Brewster; Brewster passed the information on to a friend, the professor of chemistry at St. Andrews, John Adamson. Adamson in turn taught the process to his younger brother Robert, who by 1842 made the first successful calotypes in Scotland. While his friends considered photography a hobby, and even founded the Calotype Club, Adamson

Photographed by Hill and Adamson about 1845, the Reverend Thomas Chalmers, first moderator of the Free Church of Scotland, had a distinguished career teaching mathematics, moral philosophy, and theology at Edinburgh and St. Andrews universities, alternating with onerous parochial duties as one of the leading evangelical ministers in the church.

286

When Parliament refused to lift its control over spiritual concerns in 1843, some two hundred commissioners, followed by twice as many ministers and professors, seceded from the Church of Scotland. In this act, known as the Disruption, they established their own assembly free of any formal control. To paint this huge group portrait, David Octavius Hill used photographs of the participants.

decided to become a professional photographer. In 1843 he set up a studio in Rock House, Calton Hill, Edinburgh.

Meanwhile, David Octavius Hill was making a reputation as a landscapist with his illustrations for *The Land of Burns*, published in 1840, and although his work was conservative in style, he was interested in new techniques and media, such as lithography. Hill was also an excellent administrator. He was a founder and then secretary of the Society of Artists, which later became the Royal Scottish Academy of Fine Art.

In 1843 the painter Hill and Adamson formed a partnership to make photographic portraits of the Scottish clerics who founded the Free Church of Scotland. Hill intended to produce a commemorative painting in which he would include portraits of everyone attending the historic meeting known as the Disruption, but when he began to sketch the portraits, he realized the enormousness of his task. Hundreds of men could not remain in Edinburgh waiting for a painter to finish their portraits; nevertheless, any representation of a contemporary event would come under intense scrutiny. Furthermore, Hill had made his reputation as a landscape painter, not a portraitist. The new "sun pictures" may have seemed to him to be the answer to his search for speed and verisimilitude.

Adamson had perfected the calotype to make just such records, and Brewster introduced Hill to Adamson. The two artists began to work on the historic project immediately. Hill posed the clerics as he wanted to paint them, and Adamson made calotypes. Hill and Adamson continued to work together after they completed these photographs, which became known as the Disruption series. In four and a half years they produced

Photographers Hill and Adamson pictured the fisherfolk of New Haven (above left) as much for the decorative patterns of their dress and equipment as for the character of their faces. Here is "Sandy (James) Linton, his boat and his bairns."

Scientist, educator, and editor, Sir David Brewster (above right) began his professional life as a philosopher and theologian in the best Enlightenment tradition. His contributions to the science of optics were exceeded by the even greater labors he performed as an editor of scientific journals and encyclopedias, and as a voluminous writer on scientific subjects.

In 1638 Scottish leaders gathered in Greyfriar's churchyard to sign the National Covenant. Hill and Adamson's photographs of Greyfriar's churchyard capture the romantic spirit of the Scot. In those that include living figures along with the Covenanters Tomb and Edinburgh Castle, youth, time, and decay are juxtaposed with the immortality of heroism—the massive and fantastic monuments, the rough stone of the castle and rock, the memorial to the covenanting martyrs, in Scotland's national religious shrine.

more than fifteen hundred calotypes, before Adamson died of tuberculosis in 1848 at the age of twenty-seven.

The contribution of each partner to the production of the finished art work has been debated. When they exhibited calotypes for the first time in the Royal Scottish Academy of Art in 1844, they defined their roles as "Executed by R. Adamson under the artistic direction of D. O. Hill." Although Adamson credited himself only with the technical production, he must have contributed more, for Hill working alone or with other partners never achieved the aesthetic quality that the partnership with Adamson had stimulated. From the portraits of the elite of Edinburgh to the fishermen and women of New Haven, Hill and Adamson captured the faces of Scotland. The camera's eye was used with a painter's finesse.

After Adamson's death, Hill worked for the benefit of Scottish artists in the academy, and also for the foundation of the National Gallery of Scotland. He did some photography in the early sixties, but never with his earlier success. In 1866, he finally completed the huge Disruption painting.

The original Deed of Demission had been signed by only 155 ministers, but many others signed later. Since the Free Church had become very successful, twenty years after the act everyone wanted to be included in the painting. Hill even added people who had not been present but whom he thought should have been. He also aged some of the portraits by adding gray whiskers and balding heads. Hill admitted the anachronisms, but wanted to make his painting seem to be a current event. When it was finally exhibited, the painting was both praised for realism and criticized for dullness. It still hangs in the offices of the Free Church. When Hill died in 1870, he was known as a painter and administrator; the calotypes made with Adamson, for which he is famous today, were almost forgotten.

Together Hill and Adamson produced some of the finest examples of the nineteenth-century photographer's art. In portraits they follow in the grand tradition of Ramsay and Raeburn. In pose, gesture, and mood they characterize their sitters as individuals and as interacting personalities. They enlivened and enriched the setting in a way seldom achieved with the sharp, detailed daguerreotype images. Through the simultaneous use of dramatic chiaroscuro and the specific realism of the camera eye, they rival Baroque painters. Only the bold use of rich color is missing from the calotype portraits; however, so sensitive is the use of subtle gradation of darks and lights that the richness of color is implied.

While photography at first did not have the status accorded painting, it had enthusiastic patrons in Scotland and, as elsewhere, became the medium for the recording of images of self and surroundings. Portrait photography supplanted the portrait painter; topographical photography, the landscape artist. Photographers opened the world to the eager eyes of the middle classes in the nineteenth century, nowhere more effectively than through the stereopticon, that magical device which had such a prominent place in parlors well into the twentieth century. George Washington Wilson of Aberdeen recorded the landscape and the monuments of Scotland with directness and a surprising lack of sentimentality. Of course he photographed the country made famous by Scott and Burns, but he also recorded the streets of the cities, the busy ports, the herring fleet, the cottages and the industries that made Scotland a living country, not a monument to nostalgia.

Meanwhile painters working within the established traditions of western European painting—David Wilkie and William Dyce, the Reverend John Thomson and Patrick Nasmyth, Thomas Faed, and Noel Paton—gave Scotland another kind of record of itself. Among these

In spite of the secession in 1843 of a significant number of adherents, the Church of Scotland continued in a traditional form. A royal nominee, the high commissioner, acted as the presiding officer and convener of the General Assembly. The formal procession here pictured shows the high commissioner on his way to open the annual general assembly on May 24, 1883.

artists, William McTaggart stands out for his masterly interpretation of the Scottish landscape. McTaggart's early paintings were sentimental and anecdotal, paralleling the sentiments of the Kailyard school of literature, but gradually his innate preference for understatement enabled him to free himself from the sentimental narrative painting demanded by the public. He began to paint simple figures in landscape, and by 1883 he was painting almost exclusively in the open air.

In his studies of light and color McTaggart developed his own form of Impressionism. Although he had visited Paris in the 1870s and 80s, and Monet's work had been shown in London and Glasgow, he seems to have developed his own *plein-air* technique independently. McTaggart continued to enliven his landscape with figures and to attach descriptive titles to his work, such as *The Sailing of the Emigrant Ship* (1895); however, sunlight and rain, the action of the sea, the wind in the grass, become the subjects of his work. The soft diffused light of northern Europe, not the striking sunlight of the south, permeates his painting. McTaggart's exuberant brushwork, vivid color, and high emotional tone create a very personal Impressionist style. In *The Coming of St. Columba* (1898), the figures become transparent, the ship has a miniature monumentality, and the rocks, waves, and clouds tremble. The painting, created for the thirteen hundredth anniversary of the landing of the missionary on the island of Iona, had a special attraction for McTaggart. According to his biographer James Caw, when the painter looked at this work in later years, he would say, "What a day for such a mission." The glory of nature fascinated him; McTaggart painted not a historical event but the jubilation of the land and sea at the arrival of the saint.

McTaggart founded a school of landscape painting in Scotland; not the least of his followers was his own grandson William MacTaggart. The "Glasgow Boys" in the west and the elegant Edinburgh artists were equally beholden to the great colorist. Rich color, firm structure, and decorative inventiveness characterize Scottish art in the early twentieth century. The painting makes little reference to the great French, German, and Catalan masters who so profoundly influenced the course of twentieth-century painting elsewhere.

Scottish art achieved international status again at the end of the nineteenth century through the work of artists known as "the Glasgow Four"—Charles Rennie Mackintosh, Herbert MacNair, and two extraordinary sisters, Margaret and Frances Macdonald. Their collaboration was at times so complete that, like Hill and Adamson, the partnership rather than the individual seems to be the "creator." From the moment they first exhibited their work in 1896, the Glasgow Four were recognized as originators of a style that has come to be known as Scottish Art Nouveau. The Four, led by Mackintosh, were so admired by the German, Viennese, and Dutch that they may be credited with significantly influencing the development of early modern art and architecture.

Mackintosh began his career as an architect. In 1891 he won a traveling scholarship and visited France, Italy, and Belgium. On his return to Glasgow he and his friend MacNair attended classes at the Glasgow School of Art, where they met Margaret and Frances Macdonald. In 1894 the Macdonald sisters opened their studio and began to produce a wide variety of decorative arts and illustration. Mackintosh and MacNair established a studio the next year. Frances married MacNair in 1899, and Margaret married Mackintosh in 1900. Although their close collaboration ended in 1899 when the newly wed MacNairs moved to Liverpool, the Four continued to exhibit together.

The work of the Four attracted international attention in 1896 when the Arts and Crafts Society in London included their work in its exhibition.

In spite of its elegance and novelty, their work did not meet with critical success. The Four had adopted the fine craftsmanship, directness, and simplicity extolled by adherents of the Arts and Crafts Movement without William Morris's and his followers' reliance on specific medieval or folk-art sources, or on their own socialist dogma. Instead, inspired by the ideal of "art-for-art's-sake" and the Aesthetic Movement, the Four introduced elements from Japanese art, Celtic manuscripts, and continental Art Nouveau into architectural interiors and decorative arts, the emphatic rectilinearity and verticality of which are inspired by Scottish Gothic or Baronial art. Adherents of the two movements—Arts and Crafts and Aestheticism—with their opposing philosophies (socialism vs. art-for-art's-sake), were not prepared to see any virtue in the other's art; thus the Glasgow Four, by borrowing from both, ran the risk of being condemned by both. Only one critic, Gleason White, the editor of the newly founded (1893) magazine *The Studio*, admired their work and wrote enthusiastically about it.

The Macdonald sisters' art is comparable in quality to the best contemporary continental work. Similar themes and elements characterized their decorative designs: elongated emaciated figures, entangling vines, floating celestial bodies, medieval shape-changing creatures. To this vocabulary they added a greater verticality, rectilinearity, linearity, and two-dimensionality. As graphic artists the Macdonald sisters are worthy rivals to Aubrey Beardsley, a leader of the Aesthetic Movement and for its first year the art editor of *The Yellow Book*. In July, 1896, *The Yellow Book* dedicated an issue (volume ten) to Scottish artists and published a watercolor by Frances Macdonald called *Ill Omen* or *Girl in the East Wind with Ravens Passing the Moon* (1893). The sisters' art was branded the "Spook School" for its deliberately obscure and haunting themes, its aura of mystery and even morbidity, and its use of elongated stylized forms and blue tonalities, all apparent in *Ill Omen*.

Mackintosh, the architect and leader of the Four, did not let them slip into the trap of Celtic revival and nature mysticism that captured the Edinburgh artists and others, especially those in the circle of Patric Geddes and the *Evergreen*. Instead, a structural, architectural strength dominates even the most decorative design. Mackintosh's work gained immediate acceptance in the 1900 Vienna Secession, won second prize in the Darmstadt House competition in 1901, and acclaim in the Turin International Exhibition of 1902. He participated in exhibitions in Munich, Dresden, Venice, and even in a 1913 exhibition in Moscow arranged by the ballet impresario Diaghilev. World War I forced the cancellation of a great exhibition planned for Paris in 1914. Mies van der Rohe and the Bauhaus artists in Germany, the artists of De Stijl in Holland, all recognized their debt to the Glasgow Four and the style they dubbed "Mackintoshismus."

In 1893 Mackintosh won the competition for a new School of Art building in Glasgow. The building was erected in two phases, the main block of studios and offices in 1897–99, with the library wing completed in 1909. Borrowing the severe, vertical, asymmetrical forms of Scottish Baronial architecture, Mackintosh pierced the flat walls with huge studio and library windows reminiscent of Elizabethan houses. Then he enriched and enlivened the principal facade with delicate elongated ironwork distantly inspired by plant forms.

During these years he also received commissions for houses and interior designs, including the remarkable Hill House in Helensburgh for Walter Blackie (1902) and four tearooms in Glasgow for Kate Cranston (1897–1912). In the tearooms and private houses, Mackintosh and his wife created furniture, textiles, and interiors that were both functional

This is Charles Rennie Mackintosh's 1901 design for the Daily Record Building in Glasgow. The elegance and sophistication of Mackintosh's work often appears more clearly in his drawings than in the buildings standing today. His inspiration from Scottish baronial architecture is evident in the towering facade capped by dormers and turret-like forms.

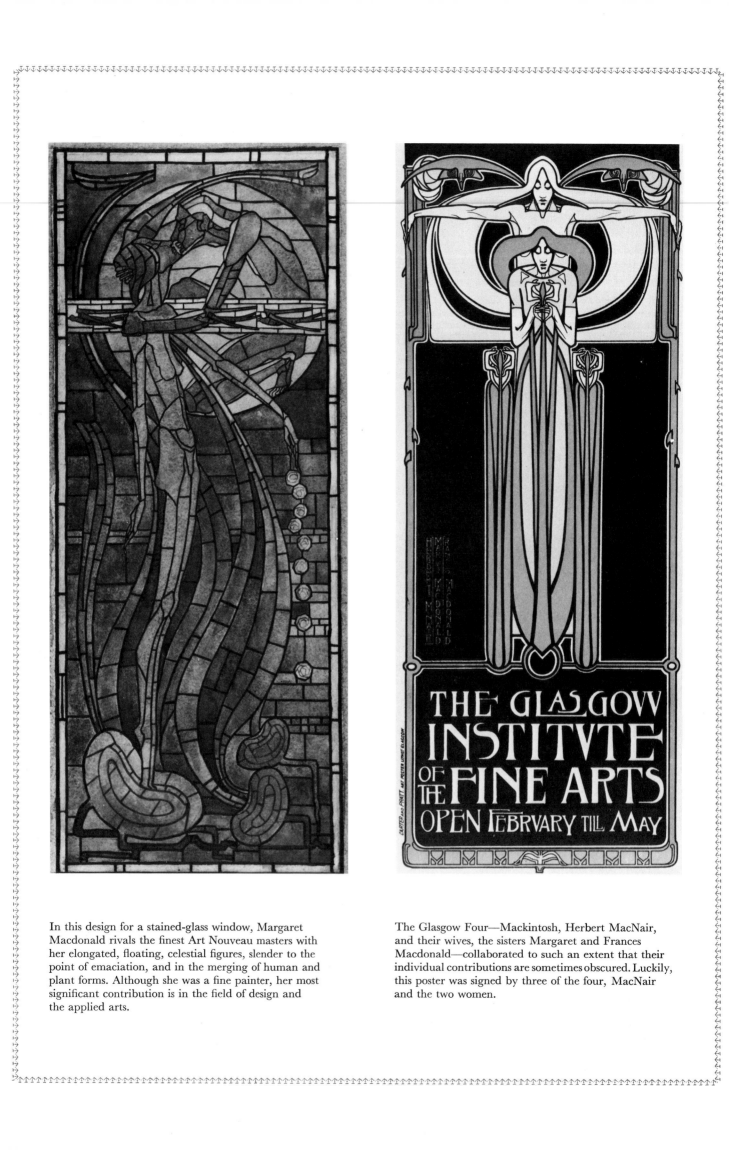

In this design for a stained-glass window, Margaret Macdonald rivals the finest Art Nouveau masters with her elongated, floating, celestial figures, slender to the point of emaciation, and in the merging of human and plant forms. Although she was a fine painter, her most significant contribution is in the field of design and the applied arts.

The Glasgow Four—Mackintosh, Herbert MacNair, and their wives, the sisters Margaret and Frances Macdonald—collaborated to such an extent that their individual contributions are sometimes obscured. Luckily, this poster was signed by three of the four, MacNair and the two women.

and aesthetically satisfying. A slightly exotic, light, pristine atmosphere removed the patrons from the dirty working world of Glasgow. The designers conceived the architectural interior as a total space and coordinated both the enclosing walls and the contents of the room. Furniture, often stark white or black and sometimes stenciled with Art Nouveau designs, became part of the architectural form; chairs, posts, beams, and light fixtures controlled and shaped the spaces.

The hallmark of this decorative style is a carefully balanced rectilinearity in which the verticals often terminate in squash buds or flowers of tightly laced petals. The emphatic verticality of design, the balanced rectilinear character of the composition, the suggestive touches of organic ornament, a new color harmony of luminous grays and lavenders, pale green and yellow, silvery tones heightened with neutral black or gold, are distinctive characteristics of the style; and yet, with this emphasis on verticality and on subtle light and color, the Glasgow Four stand firmly within the tradition of Scottish architecture and aesthetics.

Scottish concern for the total environment, seen in the work of the Four, extends from the interior living space to the exterior environment. Early in their history the Scots became famous as gardeners. They created gardens even where the earth itself had to be carried in basket

293

Charles Rennie Mackintosh's most lasting achievement is the Glasgow School of Art. The main block with the studios and offices was erected between 1897 and 1899, and the library wing was completed in 1909.

In the library of the Glasgow School of Art, Mackintosh combined the simplicity and fine craftsmanship of the Arts and Crafts movement with his own sense of the rectilinear and vertical character of Scottish medieval design to produce an original style that was acclaimed throughout Europe.

An attic sculpture studio at the Glasgow art school is flooded with light.

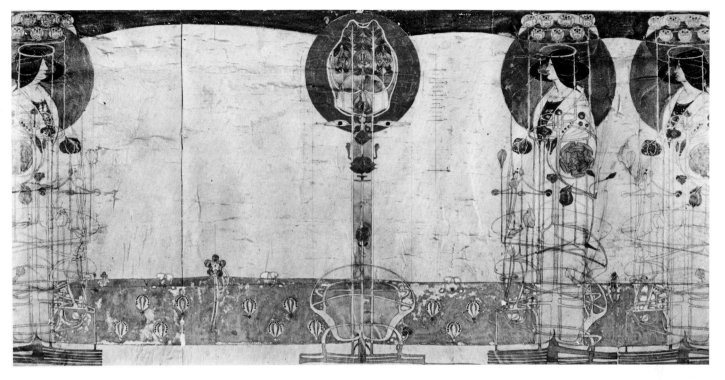

Mackintosh designed interiors for each of the four tearooms run by Miss Cranston in Glasgow. The first, in Buchanan Street, opened in 1897 with decorations by Mackintosh and furniture by George Walton. In the drawing for a Buchanan Street mural above, Mackintosh's characteristic rectilinear patterns turn the Continental Art Nouveau themes of elegant women entwined by roses into an architectural composition distinctively Scottish. In the interior (below) the pattern on the curtains becomes more abstract.

Mackintosh's formal entrance hall for Hill House.

by basket. The skill developed, from Pitmedden—laid out in the French style in the seventeenth century by Sir Alexander Seton—and Sir William Bruce's Kinross, where the gardens have been replanted, to the gardens that surround the Castles of Culzean, Crathes, Falkland, and Brodick. Scottish concern with education and science is reflected in the Garden School at Threave, or the Botanical Gardens in Edinburgh created for scholarly study as well as public enjoyment.

The preservation of national monuments, historic sites, and natural beauty has been given special attention in Scotland in the twentieth century. Most notable of many projects is the one that the National Trust for Scotland inaugurated for preservation of the vernacular architecture of the sixteenth, seventeenth, and eighteenth centuries, which had survived into the twentieth century in Scottish towns. These small domestic buildings are easily lost, for they have little association with historic events or great heroes; yet such architecture describes the life of a people more effectively than any book or pictures.

In 1936 the marquess of Bute and the architect Ian Lindsay began a nationwide survey of domestic architecture. By the time World War II put an end to such activities, they had surveyed 100 burghs and listed

Charles Rennie Mackintosh's domestic masterpiece is the remarkable Hill House in Helensburgh, built for the publisher Walter Blackie in 1902. The exterior, with its sheer rising walls and towerlike element, is inspired by Scottish baronial castles; the light-filled interior belies this somewhat forbidding front. In collaboration with his wife, Margaret Macdonald, Mackintosh designed every detail, conceiving of the interior as a total environment. They developed a new harmony of white and silvery pastels accented with black or gold and upon which the rectangular patterns that emphasize vertical lines are humanized with buds and flowers.

Entrance hall, Hill House (opposite).

Drawing room, Hill House, with plaster panel by Margaret Macdonald.

Master bedroom, Hill House.

A perfect example of nineteenth-century genre painting, this picture, when shown
in 1859, was accompanied by this extract from a letter from Canada: "We have
no church here but our loghouse, or the wide forest; and a grand kirk and forest
makes—not even the auld cathedral has such pillars, space, nor so high a roof; so
we e'en take turns about on Sunday in reading the Bible. We are all well except
Jeannie, and as happy as can be, considering the country and ties we have left.
Poor Jeannie is sadly changed; her only song is, 'Why left I my hame?' But for
her illness our lot ought not to be an unhappy one." The artist, Thomas Faed, was
a master of the form, whose work met with great success on both sides of the
Atlantic. Even Ruskin, while not considering this a first-rate painting, admired its
"gentle pathos." Faed's skillful paintings of costume, still life, and setting constitute
documents of social history.

In an entirely different style, William McTaggart celebrated the 1300th anniversary of the arrival of St. Columba at Iona. The great Scottish Impressionist painter created a work without regard for specific details, but in which he captures the mood of jubilation at the saint's appearance. As McTaggart himself said, "What a day for such a mission."

Contemporary artist Elizabeth Blackadder created this *Still Life with Chinese Puzzle* in 1979. Blackadder assembles the precious bits and pieces of visual life in her tabletop compositions, but handles them in a rather more abstract than realistic manner. A fine sense of architectonic composition anchors the images in an amorphous space.

Elizabeth Blackadder's sensitive watercolor studies of plants combine the exacting vision of the botanist with the subtle sense of balance of the still-life painter. A member of both the Royal Academy and the Royal Scottish Academy, she has emerged as one of Scotland's most important painters.

There is more to Scottish weaving than tartans and tweeds. The Dovecot Studios, founded in 1912 by the Bute family, began as a Scottish variation of the work of William Morris. Since World War II, the studio has woven tapestries from paintings by leading contemporary artists. In this tapestry Elizabeth Blackadder's sophisticated composition of floating forms—flowers, textiles, and still-life objects—was transformed by the skill of the master weavers of the Dovecot Studios, Jean Taylor, Annie Wright, and an apprentice, John Wright, in 1980.

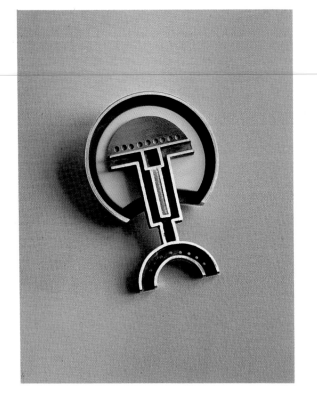

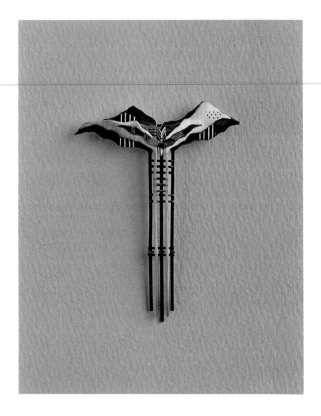

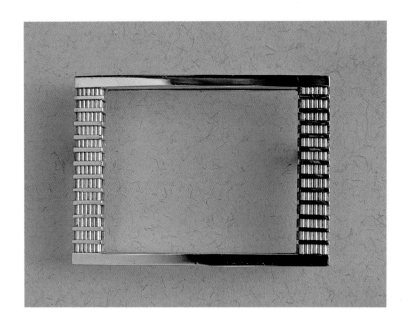

Contemporary Scottish silver and jewelry design shows its debt to the Glasgow Four rather than to the romantic, baronial past. Roger Millar created the brooch at upper left of sterling silver and plexiglas in 1980. Millar studied at the Glasgow College of Art and then at the Royal College of Art, London. Judy McCaig, who trained at the Duncan of Jordanstone College of Art in Dundee, made the brooch at upper right using eighteen-carat gold, sterling silver, and copper. Dorothy Hogg's creation, above, is a brooch of ten-carat gold and sterling silver. In the work of all these artists, stark simplicity and elegant proportions reflect a long and distinctive Scottish tradition.

1,149 buildings as being of architectural and cultural importance. To preserve these buildings the National Trust established the Little Houses Improvement Scheme. A revolving fund was set up to buy, restore, and adapt the properties to twentieth-century standards of convenience. The houses were then sold to owners who agreed to maintain the historic appearance and general character of the buildings and surroundings. The money thus earned was used to buy and rehabilitate more houses. In the 1960s the program was extended to include the "restoring purchaser" plan, in which the new owner agreed to restore the building according to the specifications established by the Trust, with the assistance of architects skilled in historical preservation. The Little Houses Scheme achieved international fame as a practical and relatively inexpensive method of preserving vernacular architecture, and in 1975 it was designated as an official project for the International European Architectural Heritage Year by the Council of Europe. While preserving the past and the historic architecture of the country, Scotland has led the way in providing modern housing for many people who love good old buildings.

Among contemporary artists, the Scottish-born sculptor Eduardo Paolozzi has achieved an important international reputation. Here is his *Hermaphroditic Idol No. 1* of 1962, constructed of aluminum.

Contemporary Scottish crafts defy
the stereotype of thistles and tartans.
Inspired by the painted furniture of
earlier days, Will Maclean has
created an ominous plate rack which
continues a metaphor of sea life, art,
and technology that he has explored
in other mixed-media works of art.

306

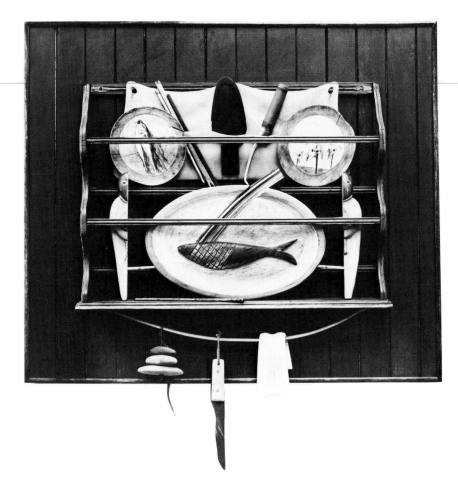

In addition to preserving the past, Scotland has looked ahead as
well. After World War II, in an effort to bring the country back into
the mainstream of European culture, to reestablish contacts abroad, and
to support the arts at home, Rudolf Bing, Harvey Wood, and Sir John
Falconer established the Edinburgh International Festival of Music and
Drama (1947), the first of the great international festivals organized
after the war. The idea was an immediate success and soon expanded to
include the visual arts and film. By the end of the 1970s, over three
hundred groups were participating in the festival.

Though the recent Scottish contribution to the creative arts has not
been on the same international scale, some names stand out. William
Gillies, a student and then teacher at the Edinburgh College of Art,
together with other Edinburgh artists between the wars, created poetic
and sensuous painting that combined traditional landscape, the haunting
mood of earlier symbolists, and the sensitive color of the Scottish
impressionists. A fine draftsman working in the tradition of the Four,
Gillies, who died in 1973, emphasized lyrical qualities in his work.
Other Scottish artists working in Glasgow, Aberdeen, and other centers,
especially since World War II, followed the international trends set in
New York and London. Eduardo Paolozzi, for example, a sculptor and
printmaker of international stature, was a founder of Pop Art in England.
Few remember that he was born in Leith.

Among the many fine women artists in Scotland, Elizabeth
Blackadder, born in 1931 at Falkirk, emerged as a major still-life painter
at mid-century. Blackadder uses traditional feminine themes and materials,

Andrew Turnbull created this monumental bronze and stone sculpture entitled simply *Head* in 1957. It is now in the United States, in the Joseph H. Hirshhorn Museum and Sculpture Garden in Washington, D.C.

references to handicrafts and applied arts, to create compositions with an architectonic sense of structure. Her delicate colors and floating images are deceptive, for they are tied in space by the firm lines of an architectonic composition. Her haunting paintings are highly intellectualized, yet emotionally cool.

William Maclean creates art for the technological age, symbolized by Scotland's hydroelectric works, offshore drilling rigs, radar stations, and atomic installations. A seaman before he became a painter, Maclean produces works that imply the entrapping of water and its energies and perhaps even the twentieth-century despoiling of nature. His speared and trapped fish become a modern metaphor for man's callous treatment of his environment; his austere, intricate multiple images suggest a surrealist's confrontation of art and technology.

What, finally, may be said of the Scottish tradition in the arts? A stripped-down art and architecture as hard as the rock and the climate; the art of a country with a knowledge of essentials based on limited resources; an art of light and color appreciated by people who live in northern zones, where the rebirth of the sun in the spring is an ever-recurring miracle—when the white nights of summer replace the wind, rain, and dark of winter. Romantic brutality, elegance touching austerity: these form the Scottish vision.

THE YEAR 1851 is a great landmark in the history of Britain. The Great Exhibition of that year, fathered by the Prince Regent, marked the ascendancy of England in the international arena, the primacy of England in industrial development, the triumph of England in creating a worldwide empire and begetting governments and nations modeled on its parliamentary democracy. Yet though stocktaking in the south of Great Britain could result only in pride and a sense of accomplishment, the verdict in the north would have been far different. The depopulation following the clearances, which restructured the farms to focus on sheep farming on a large scale, and the potato famine induced by the potato blight beginning in 1846 and 1847 seemed to strip the Highlands of its population. Another Scottish Diaspora had begun.

The Disruption in the church in 1843 and the decade of conflict which followed put the whole nation in turmoil. Further, the growing concentration of heavy industry on the Clyde created unsanitary, overcrowded, and wretched living conditions for the workers who manned the new industries. Yet the second half of the nineteenth century is in many respects the Golden Age of modern Scotland—the period in which it reached a point of economic prosperity and world prominence that has not been equaled before or since. Victorian Scotland was a time of accomplishment. It was also a time of self-doubt and a reawakening of nationalist sentiment.

Though the second half of the nineteenth century was the most prosperous period in Scottish history, the fruits of the economic improvement were shared by few. As elsewhere in the first century of industrialization, those who provided the labor functioned at a near subsistence level. But the impact on this small, traditionally impoverished country was impressive. It began with the revolution in transportation, both internal and external.

Internally we can identify three main phases—roads, canals, and railroads. The road network in Scotland, as in England, had been primitive. This situation began to be remedied in the 1760s; as much as three thousand miles had been constructed by 1780. Turnpike trusts, private companies formed to construct the roads for the tariffs or fees they would generate, were the principal means. Yet the return was generally not commensurate with the investment. By 1821 the poor condition of the roads was being noted with concern. It was not until after the introduction of the automobile dating from the turn of the twentieth century and the increasing use of asphalt pavement that this situation was finally rectified. The vast expansion of private cars plus tourism in the mid-twentieth century had a similar effect, though the remedy, more four-lane, divided highways, has yet to be implemented on any wide scale.

Canals were also an eighteenth-century innovation. Due in part to the formidable topographical difficulties, their employment was never so widespread as in England. Nevertheless, a link between the Forth and Clyde was completed in 1790 followed by a direct link to Edinburgh in 1822. These were the most successful ventures. Others, such as the long-dreamed-of Caledonian Canal, which bisected the country (also completed in 1822), never proved to be a commercial success. Indeed, the Caledonian and the major road improvements of the early nineteenth century were made possible only by heavy government subsidies. Before long they had been superseded by the railroads.

Railways were commonly found wherever coal was mined by the early nineteenth century. When steam power was first introduced in 1826, its initial impetus was to transport coal. The first line to engage in substantial passenger traffic was that which ran between Glasgow and Monkland. The real boom did not start until the 1840s and continued for several decades

309

An engineering marvel in its time and still one of the most striking and picturesque bridges today, the Forth Railway Bridge (overleaf) is shown under construction in a photograph of 1888–89 by G. W. Wilson. The bridge epitomizes the revolution in transport and communication wrought by the railway in Scotland.

thereafter, but development of a railway network was a crucial factor in the expansion of the Scottish economy. Not only did it provide rapid and extensive communication in the Lowlands, the industrial and population center, it also linked the Highlands with the fiscal and political center of the country. Even more important it provided long-overdue, efficient land communication with England and the markets to the south.

Railways, shipping, heavy industry, and coal and iron became the mainstays of the Scottish economy in the second half of the century. New processes in smelting, which also provided the means of utilizing Scottish raw materials, pushed the steel industry up to high production figures by the 1880s. The main purpose to which this steel was put, other than export, was the construction of steamships.

The first impetus to the expansion of Glasgow and the Clyde estuary came in the eighteenth century with the opening of the colonial trade to Scotland following the union of 1707. Initially the trade concentrated upon the processing and marketing of agricultural products, notably tobacco and sugar. With the decline of this trade after American independence, the merchants turned to shipbuilding. Glasgow shipwrights made important contributions to the design and construction of first steam power, beginning with the *Comet* in 1812, and later steel ships.

The proximity and exploitation of the coal and iron industry greatly facilitated this development, though all the Lowland ports, both east and west, shared in this enterprise initially. For example, the *Cutty Sark* was built in Dumbarton in 1869, rival to the proud clipper ships of Aberdeen. However, the dredging and improvements made to the Clyde channel

The elegant and beautifully designed locks of the Caledonian Canal at Fort Augustus, Inverness-shire, were rendered redundant by a more efficient railway system.

soon gave it preeminence over its competitors. As wood ships gave way to iron, and iron to steel, the industry kept pace and made important contributions at each step. From 1812 to 1860 60 percent of all steam tonnage built in Great Britain issued from the Clyde. At mid-century the· development of the screw propeller and the compound marine steam engine increased the Clyde's share of production to 70 percent of British iron tonnage from 1851 to 1870. Successive inventions of the triple and quadruple expansion engine and finally the steam turbine combined with the burgeoning steel industry insured the Clyde's supremacy until the end of World War I.

If heavy industry was the most important feature of Scottish commerce, there were still other contributions of importance. By mid-century the cotton industry had begun a steady decline due to competition. Linen, another staple, also suffered from lack of raw materials and English competition. These were supplanted by jute, sent back by the Scottish merchants in India. Dundee became an important center of this trade, producing sacking and linoleum among its more important manufactures.

Agriculture enjoyed only modest successes. The introduction of mechanized farming resulted in new economies and favored the creation of bigger farms. The extension of the railways encouraged perishable crops. Improvements in cattle breeding led to Scottish cattle finding a ready market. Farming practices, developed in the Low Countries in the seventeenth century and England in the eighteenth, were now implemented, resulting in larger herds being maintained over the winter. This meant an improved supply of meat and provided welcome export income. After the turn of the century, the importation of cheap grain from North America caused a slow but steady decline. However, the diversity of grain products grown also helped to moderate the impact of cheap American imports.

The eastern Lowlands supported a number of industries, the most important being fishing. By 1911 Aberdeen was the largest fishing port in Scotland and the third largest in Britain. Whaling was another industry that enjoyed a limited success until over-fishing and the more technically competitive Norwegians combined to force out the more primitive Scottish fleet. The import of raw materials to sustain the industrial base and the export of the commodities of the factories and farms combined to create substantial shipping requirements. Among the better known firms which were established one must number the Cunard line (1840) and the Peninsular Steam Company (1837), which was the precursor of the famed P. and O. line, the Peninsular and Oriental.

These changes in the economy wrought great changes in the society and made new demands upon the government. The railways and canals were often the work of Irish navvies who came over and settled, joined by their families. Their presence in the major cities changed the whole composition of society. The Roman Catholic church now became a major force because of the Irish immigrants. The Irish were concentrated mostly in Glasgow and the western coalfields. Besides providing a major percentage of the heavy construction crews, they also provided a ready supply of seasonal harvest workers. Mine owners and factory superintendents employed them as strikebreakers. This economic challenge to the working-class Scots, coupled with the traditional religious antagonism, left its mark both in Scotland and in the Ireland left behind by the emigrants.

The success of the new industry and the crowding of new workers into the cities resulted in blighted living conditions that plague parts of Scotland to this day. The census of 1861 gave evidence that one-third of the population lived in one-room dwellings, often windowless. In 1911 the percentage of families in one- or two-room houses was nearly 50 percent. The old-style tenement with many stories was a favored and cheap form of

313

housing. There was little understanding and even less regard for public health. According to 1850 records, infant mortality was so high that 50 percent of the children died before the age of five.

If the unsanitary living conditions, like the execrable working conditions in the mines, were most destructive to children, some small measure of compensation can be found in the changes taking place in the educational system. One of the consequences of the Disruption in the church was the breakdown of the delivery of services for which the church had exclusive responsibility. Among the casualties were the old poor relief system and the church-run school system. The breakaway establishments created their own schools. The government was forced to extend state aid to all schools judged efficient. A national school system was set up in 1872 under a newly created Scottish Education Department. Popularly elected school boards managed education at the local level.

Perhaps the area in which Scotland attracted the most attention so far as the British public was concerned was in the political arena. From the time of the union, Scottish members both in the House of Lords and in the House of Commons were considered government nominees. The Reform Act of 1832 swept away the old electoral machinery and increased the electorate more than tenfold. Yet the structure was still unresponsive, and the increase in commoners from forty-five to fifty-three still did not give anything like proportional representation to Scotland. During the next few decades a growing sense of nationalism awakened Scottish consciousness to its neglect in the national government. But the most immediate cause for agitation was the preoccupation of the executive and the Parliament with the problem of Ireland. As Irish issues grew steadily more dominant, the Scots' anger at their neglect waxed ever greater.

The Tories were the first to seize on this discontent and pressed successfully for an increase in the proportion of Scottish members. The Second Reform Act of 1867 raised the total number of seats to sixty, a partial but nevertheless real response. In 1872, adoption of the secret ballot increased the independence of the voters, lessening the threat of reprisal from intrusive landowners. But it was Liberals, rather than Conservatives, who had passed the 1867 act, that benefited from the reforms. The act increased their share of the Scottish representation, and they regularly elected 75 percent or more of the Scottish members.

William Ewart Gladstone, born in 1809 and of pure Scottish descent, became a personal hero to the Scots. His political duels with Disraeli and his electioneering in the Midlothian campaigns of 1879 and 1880 became the prototype of the appeal of a national party leader. The evident discontent of the Scots gradually evoked a measured response from Westminster. In 1874 Disraeli abolished patronage in the church, but the measure served only to alienate the landowners without gaining him any new adherents. Demanding the same kind of attention the Irish were receiving, the crofters successfully secured an act in 1886 which gave security to tenants and provided for a commission to fix fair rents. Archibald, fifth earl of Rosebery, the leader of Scottish Liberalism and, later, Gladstone's successor as prime minister, urged the reform of local government. A third reform act in 1884 raised the total number of Scottish constituencies to seventy-two. The financial issue was resolved in 1888, when it was agreed that exchequer funds would be allocated on the basis of Scotland's contribution to the national income, a percentage determined to be 11/80ths of that allocated to England.

The two parties were now vying for Scottish votes. In 1885, during his short-lived minority government, Robert, third marquess of Salisbury, created a secretary of state for Scotland, one of the demands of the growing radical movement. However, the new minister was based at Westminster

James Keir Hardie, here portrayed by the Scottish genre painter H. J. Dobson in 1893, began his career as a temperance worker and labor agitator. In the 1880s he organized the mine workers into a union. In 1888 he became chairman of the first Independent Labour party. From 1892 to 1895, and again from 1900 until his death in 1915, he led the Labour party in the House of Commons.

rather than at Edinburgh so that Scotland still lacked a senior resident executive. Still, the office slowly acquired something like the authority so ardently desired by its promoters. The establishment of democratically elected country councils in 1889 and the consolidation of local government authorities in 1892, both under the control of the secretary, helped build the office into one of real substance so that by the end of the century the Scottish office became the real focus of government in Scotland.

Scotland was in the forefront of the most important new political party movement to be launched in this period in the person of James Keir Hardie, the founder of the Independent Labour party in 1893, modeled on his Scottish efforts of 1888. Hardie is one of the most impressive and interesting figures in modern British politics. He raised himself up from a background of desperate poverty to become first a union organizer and then a member of Parliament.

During the three decades that followed the resignation of Gladstone in 1894, Scotland saw four more of its own sons become prime minister: Rosebery (1894–95), Arthur Balfour (1902–5), Henry Campbell-Bannerman (1906–8), and Andrew Bonar Law (1922–23). Rosebery and Campbell-Bannerman both were Moderates and reformers, but neither was able to hold office long enough or had the strength to make major changes. In spite of this failure the concerns of Scotland attracted essential attention from the Liberal prime minister Henry Asquith. The Liberals had always drawn the bulk of their strength from the Celtic fringe, Scotland, Wales, and Ireland. With the departure of the Unionists in the late 1880s this support became essential if the Liberals were to remain in office. Thus Asquith introduced home rule bills for both Ireland and Scotland, but they were shelved with the outbreak of World War I.

The situation of Scotland in 1914 when the war broke out may be quickly summarized. By an increase in the number of representatives and also of those who acted as electors coupled with the dependence of the Liberal party on Scotland to maintain its majority in Parliament, Scotland now had the ear of the government. And there was a need for this attention. The economy in the west was overdependent on shipbuilding. Good iron ores were worked out, and coal was rapidly becoming depleted. Worse, the shipyards were failing to keep up with their competitors in technology. With the development of the diesel engine, Germany took the lead in innovation and design away from Britain. World War I only exacerbated this situation.

The disproportionate emphasis upon heavy industry and concentration of population in the Lowlands, some 80 percent in the ten Lowland counties, became still greater as Scotland was called upon to make new sacrifices in the cause of the war. The shipbuilding and engineering industries were grossly overexpanded to accommodate the insatiable demand for ships. The single purpose to which its industrial capacity was committed caused Scotland to lose its steel trade in Japan and Australia to the United States and to be cut off from virtually all its export trade to the colonies and the neutrals. The necessity to provide foodstuffs for a population now dependent on imports for subsistence left agriculture overextended and in bad condition at the end of the war.

The effects were soon apparent. The mines, which had been taken over by the government, no longer had the capacity or efficiency to compete successfully with the Continent. Bitter labor disputes and lowered wages contributed to this decline. The shipyards found their order books empty as wartime-inspired demands ended. Another victim of the economic depression was the railways, which merged in 1923 with English-controlled lines. With the transfer of locomotive works and repair shops to the north of England, another source of employment was removed, and the locomotive engineering industry of Glasgow withered away.

The loss of markets, the reduction of working capital, and the increasing obsolescence of its plants were English as well as Scottish phenomena, but the more limited range of products and overreliance on a few industries for the bulk of employment made the situation much worse in Scotland. By 1933 more than 30 percent of those with some form of government unemployment insurance were out of work. Because of the shortage of capital, the lack of professional and imaginative management, and the age of its plants, there was little attempt to renovate the factories or convert production to new, more salable commodities. Scotland fell into a decline, a state of lassitude from which it has begun to recover only with the North Sea oil boom in the past decade.

World War I and its aftermath also contributed to increasing labor unrest and political tension. The split in the Liberal party caused by the successful challenge of David Lloyd George to Henry Asquith in 1916 for the prime ministership loosened still further the Labour party's grip on the electorate. The depression following the war gave encouragement to the Labour party and even more radical alternatives. Clydeside was regarded as a red stronghold. Radical shop stewards took over the leadership of the workers from more traditional labor organizers and led a

strike for a thirty-hour week. At a January, 1919, riot in Glasgow, the newly familiar Communist flag was displayed, and troops had to be sent in.

There were some compensations from the war. A shortage of ministers led to a union of the Church of Scotland and the United Free Church in 1929. An act of 1918 replaced appointed school boards with elected education authorities. But the demoralization remained. In 1924 a socialist M.P. introduced a home rule bill in the Parliament, and he was supported by the full Scottish labor representation. This had the beneficial effect of causing the ministry to promote the Scottish secretary to full cabinet rank in 1926. In 1929 parish councils and the several small administration bodies with local government responsibilities were abolished and local administration now became the responsibility of either county or borough councils with the authority to supervise the full range of local government offices. In 1939 those departments concerned solely with Scottish business were returned to Edinburgh, restoring something of the air of a capital to that city. But these measures did not solve the continuing economic depression.

The extraordinary demands of war gave some new impetus to both industry and government in the early 1940s. Tom Johnston, who served as

New Lanark, with its stone mills and houses, was founded in 1784 by David Dale and Richard Arkwright. In the early nineteenth century Robert Owen tried to create a socialist community here, where the first experiments in early childhood education were carried out. The village has been restored and remains today one of the best preserved examples of the Industrial Revolution's impact on architecture. The village is set in the woods along the banks of the Clyde near the market town of Lanark, home of the medieval hero, William Wallace.

Ninian Johnston's designs for housing in Woodside in Glasgow illustrate not only contemporary Scottish architecture of distinction but the importance given to urban development and the creation of a livable environment in a city once known for its dismal living conditions. The renewal of Scottish cities as well as the preservation of the people's architectural heritage is the challenge of the last quarter of the twentieth century.

secretary of state during World War II, insisted on forming a council of state for Scotland, composed of all living ex-secretaries. A North of Scotland Hydroelectric Board was created in 1943, the Scottish Council on Industry in 1942, a separate Scottish Tourist Board, and other new or expanded programs were established. But the economic impact of the war was much as before. The relative remoteness of the Clyde and the underutilized capacity of the mills and yards were once more pressed into service.

The after-effects were also a repetition of the previous conflict. The most radical changes, however, occurred as a result of the Labour party's victory at the polls in 1945. So far as Scotland was concerned, the changes were mostly ill-advised. Ambitious commitments were made to retain the adherence of the electorate, but few materialized. The Labour and successor governments attempted to subsidize and encourage the movement of business headquarters and diversified industries to Scotland from England by the promise of reduced taxes and other incentives, but had little success. Promises of government investments in industry and public housing failed to materialize. Heavy industry returned to the doldrums (though shipbuilding enjoyed a brief decade of prosperity), coal was nationalized, but too late to renovate or modernize worked-out fields, and steel lacked the technology and advanced equipment to compete successfully either nationally or internationally. The nationalizing of major service industries, railways, road transport, and utilities only increased absentee management when the headquarters moved to London.

The postwar period has essentially been one of continuing depression. Though the need to replace equipment lost in the war brought a brief period of activity to the local shipyards, locomotive manufacturers, and others, industry generally stagnated. Unemployment was twice that of England, and it soon became apparent by the mid-1950s that Scotland was not in a position to compete in world markets. The disillusionment of the voters was reflected by a swing to the Conservatives. In 1963 a Scot once again served briefly as premier, when the earl of Home renounced his peerage to take office as Sir Alec Douglas-Home, replacing an ailing Harold Macmillan. When elections were held the next year, Labour won by a narrow majority, once more reflecting voter dissatisfaction.

The malaise that affected Scotland had now spread throughout the British Isles. The Coal Board was forced to shut down still more exhausted mines. The shipyards were given a respite from closing only by government intervention. The depressed industrial areas of Scotland were competing with similarly affected areas in Northern Ireland, Northern England, and Wales for government subsidies.

The weakened pound, devalued at the end of the war, again in 1962, yet again in 1967, and then allowed to float in the 1970s, was the most obvious indicator of the sad state into which the British economy had fallen. The ambitious Labour program to nationalize heavy industry and utilities had drained an already depleted treasury. A national health plan introduced by Labour after the war coupled with other social service programs left the government without sufficient capital to make the major improvements needed in the public housing and public building sectors. The confiscatory rate of taxation and consequent shortage of capital meant that the private sector was unable to take up the slack. Housing in such areas as the Gorbals in Scotland became an international scandal. Scotland was declared to have one of the poorest public health records of any advanced country in the world with the highest known incidence of lung cancer. The future did not offer much hope.

What can only be regarded as a miracle occurred in the late 1960s. With the discovery of oil and gas in the Netherlands at Groningen in 1959, the countries bordering the North Sea began an intensive search. Their efforts were rewarded, notably in Norway and Scotland. As the Scottish discoveries have proven particularly rich, this long impoverished and poor relation of England has now taken on a Cinderella-like role. Champions of Scottish nationalism and home rule, if not independence, were quick to take advantage of the opportunity. They began to gain adherents as they campaigned on a platform to obtain autonomy from England and manage these resources for Scotland alone.

The exigencies of parliamentary politics and the frail majorities of Labour governments in the past decade have led Harold Wilson and more recently James Callaghan to pledge support for a greater degree of Scottish autonomy and even to permit a referendum on the formation of a Scottish Parliament. The nationalists, counting on the negative reaction when Britain joined the Common Market in 1972 and their pledge to keep oil profits for home use, expected to carry the day. But they were defeated in the referendum. Disenchanted with the empty rhetoric of Labour pledges, the Scots helped to defeat Callaghan's party in the 1979 elections, when Britain returned the Conservatives to power under the first woman prime minister in European history, Margaret Thatcher.

She had committed her government firmly to stem the advance of Socialism, abjure the incessant demands for a planned and managed economy, and revive and nurture the tradition of independence in the

The drilling platform, Ocean Prospector, of the Shell Oil Company, illustrates the importance of North Sea oil in Scotland's growing economic independence.

320

private sector. By rapidly introducing her own budget measures she sought by means of a tax cut to employ the profit motive as a means of encouraging greater productivity. At the same time Scotland was rebuffed, in the desire of at least some natives, in its efforts to earn a greater degree of autonomy from England. How the central government will manage Scotland, and what means will be taken to influence Scottish opinion and placate nationalist ambitions remain to be seen. With the wealth of North Sea oil a constant vision, Scotland again dreams of a new prosperity and her own government—a new Golden Age.

Bibliographies

Chapter 1:   *Scottish Stereotypes*

Chiari, Joseph. *Impressions of People and Literature* (Edinburgh and London, 1948).
Craigie, W.A.; Buchan, John; Giles, Peter; and Bulloch, J. M. *The Scottish Tongue: A Series of Lectures on the Vernacular Language of Lowland Scotland* (London, 1924).
Crosland, T.W.H. *The Unspeakable Scot* (London and New York, 1902).
Finlay, Ian. *Scotland* (London, 1957).
Hamilton, Iain. *Scotland the Brave* (London, 1957).
Hanley, Clifford. *A Skinful of Scotch* (London, 1965).
Harvey, William. *Scottish Life and Character in Anecdote and Story* (London and Stirling, 1900).
Laffin, John. *Scotland the Brave: The Story of the Scottish Soldier* (London, 1963).
Lauder, Harry. *A Minstrel in France* (London, 1918).
———. *Roamin' in the Gloamin'* (Philadelphia and London, 1928).
McCallum, Neil. *It's an Old Scottish Custom* (London, 1951).
McLaren, Moray. *Understanding the Scots: A Guide for South Britons and Other Foreigners* (New York, 1972).
Mr. Punch's Scottish Humour (London, n.d.).
Muir, Edwin. *Scots and Their Country* (London, 1966).
Notestein, Wallace. *The Scot in History: A Study of the Interplay of Character and History* (New Haven, 1947).
Shell Guide to Scotland (London, 1965).

Chapter 2:   *From the Beginnings to 1058*

Childe, V.G. *Scotland Before the Scots* (London, 1946).
Cruden, Stewart. *The Early Christian and Pictish Monuments of Scotland* (Edinburgh, 1964).
Dickinson, W. Croft. *A New History of Scotland* (London, 1963).
———. *Scotland from the Earliest Times to 1603*. 3rd ed. Revised and edited by A.A.M. Duncan (Oxford, 1977).
Henderson, Isabel. *The Picts* (London, 1967).
MacKie, Euan W. *Scotland: An Archaeological Guide from Earliest Times to the 12th Century A.D.* (Park Ridge, N.J., 1975).
Mackie, J.D. *A History of Scotland* (Harmondsworth and Baltimore, 1964; rev. ed., 1969).
Piggott, Stuart, ed. *The Prehistoric Peoples of Scotland* (London, 1962).
——— and Henderson, Keith. *Scotland Before History* (London, 1958).
——— and Simpson, W.D. *Illustrated Guides to Ancient Monuments*. Vol. VI, *Scotland* (Edinburgh, 1967; 6th ed., 1970).
Reachem, Richard. *A Guide to Prehistoric Scotland* (London, 1963).
Rivet, A.L.F. *The Iron Age in Northern Britain* (Edinburgh, 1966).
Robertson, Anne S. *The Antonine Wall* (Glasgow, 1972).
Simpson, W.D. *The Ancient Stones of Scotland* (London, 1965).
———. *St. Ninian and the Origin of the Christian Church in Scotland* (Edinburgh, 1940).
Thom, Alexander. *Megalithic Sites in Britain* (London, 1967).
Thomas, Charles. *The Early Christian Archaeology of North Britain* (London, 1969).
Wainwright, R.T., ed. *The Problem of the Picts* (Edinburgh, 1955).

Chapter 3:   *Medieval Scotland: 1058–1488*

Barrow, G.W.S. *The Kingdom of the Scots* (London, 1973).
———. *Robert Bruce and the Community of the Realm of Scotland* (London, 1968).
Burleigh, J.H.S. *Church History of Scotland* (London, 1960).
Coulton, G.G. *Scottish Abbeys and Social Life* (Cambridge, Eng., 1933).
Croft, William; Donaldson, Gordon; and Milne, Isabel Arnot. *A Source Book of Scottish History*. 3 vols. 2d ed. (Edinburgh, 1954, 1961).
Cruden, Stewart. *The Scottish Castle* (Edinburgh, 1960).
Dickinson, W. Croft. *Scotland from the Earliest Times to 1603*. 3d ed. Revised and edited by A.A.M. Duncan (Oxford, 1977).

Dunbar, John. *The Historic Architecture of Scotland* (London, 1966; new ed., 1978).
Duncan, A.A.M. *Scotland, The Making of the Kingdom*. Vol. 1. Edinburgh History of Scotland (Edinburgh and New York, 1971).
Easson, D.E. *Medieval Religious Houses: Scotland* (London, 1957).
Fergusson, Sir James. *William Wallace* (Stirling, 1948).
Hannah, Ian C. *The Story of Scotland in Stone* (Edinburgh, 1934).
MacGibbon, David, and Ross, Thomas. *The Castellated and Domestic Architecture of Scotland*. 5 vols. (Edinburgh, 1887–92).
———. *The Ecclesiastical Architecture of Scotland*. 3 vols. (Edinburgh, 1896–97).
Mackenzie, W.M. *The Medieval Castle in Scotland* (London, 1927).
Mackie, J.D. *A History of Scotland* (Harmondsworth and Baltimore, 1964).
Mitchison, Rosalind. *History of Scotland* (New York, 1970).
Nicholson, Ranald. *Scotland: The Later Middle Ages*. Vol. 2. Edinburgh History of Scotland (Edinburgh and New York, 1974).

Chapter 3:   *Literature of the Middle Ages*

Aitken, A.J.; McIntosh, Angus; and Palsson, Hermann, eds. *Edinburgh Studies in English and Scots* (London, 1971).
Brewer, Derek Stanley, ed. *Chaucer and the Chaucerians* (University, Ala., 1966).
Craigie, Sir William Alexander. *The Scottish Alliterative Poems*. Proceedings of the British Academy, vol. 28 (London, 1942).
Henderson, Thomas Finlayson. *Scottish Vernacular Literature: A Succinct History* (London, 1900).
Irving, David. *The History of Scottish Poetry* (Edinburgh, 1861).
Kinghorn, Alexander Manson. "The Medieval Makars." *Texas Studies in Language and Literature*, 1, 1959.
Lewis, Clive Staples. *English Literature in the Sixteenth Century Excluding Drama*. Oxford History of English Literature, vol. 3 (Oxford, 1954).
Mackenzie, Agnes Mure. *An Historical Survey of Scottish Literature to 1714* (London, 1933).
Smith, George Gregory. *Scottish Literature: Character and Influence* (London, 1919).
———. *The Transition Period: Periods of English Literature* (Edinburgh, 1903).
Speirs, John. *The Scots Literary Tradition: An Essay in Criticism* (London, 1940; rev. ed., 1962).
Walker, Hugh. *Three Centuries of Scottish Literature*. 2 vols. (Glasgow, 1893).
Watt, Lauchlan Maclean. *Scottish Life and Poetry* (London, 1912).
Wittig, Kurt. *The Scottish Tradition in Literature* (Edinburgh and London, 1958).

Chapter 4:   *Renaissance and Reformation: 1488–1603*

Apted, M.R. *The Painted Ceilings of Scotland, 1550–1650* (Edinburgh, 1966).
Cruden, Stewart. *The Scottish Castle* (Edinburgh, 1960).
Dickinson, W. Croft. *Scotland from the Earliest Times to 1603*. 3d ed. Revised and edited by A.A.M. Duncan (Oxford, 1977).
Donaldson, Gordon. *Scotland: James V to James VII*. Vol. 3. Edinburgh History of Scotland (Edinburgh and New York, 1965).
———. *Scottish Kings*. 2nd ed. (London, 1977).
——— and Morpeth, R.S. *Dictionary of Scottish History* (Edinburgh, 1977).
———. *Who's Who in Scottish History* (Oxford, 1973).
Dunbar, John. *The Historic Architecture of Scotland* (London, 1966; new ed., 1978).
Lewis, Clive Staples. *English Literature in the Sixteenth Century Excluding Drama*. Oxford History of English Literature, vol. 3 (Oxford, 1954).
Mackie, R.L. *King James IV of Scotland* (Edinburgh, 1958).
Menzies, Gordon, ed. "National Spirit and Native Culture." In *The Scottish Nation* (London, 1972).

Nicholson, Ranald. *Scotland: The Later Middle Ages.* Vol. 2. Edinburgh History of Scotland (Edinburgh and New York, 1974).

Petsch, Helmut. *Architecture in Scotland* (New York, 1971).

Steer, K.A., and Bannerman, J.W.M. *Late Medieval Monumental Sculpture in the West Highlands* (Edinburgh, 1977).

Chapter 5: *From the Union of the Crowns to the Union of the Parliaments: 1603–1707*

Buchan, John. *Montrose* (London, 1958).

Ferguson, William. *Scotland's Relations with England: A Survey to 1707* (Edinburgh, 1977).

Flinn, Michael, et al. *Scottish Population History from the 17th Century to the 1930s* (Cambridge, Eng., and New York, 1977).

Foster, W.R. *Bishop and Presbytery* (London, 1958).

Lenman, Bruce. *An Economic History of Modern Scotland 1660–1976* (London, 1977).

Lythe, S.G.E. *The Economy of Scotland 1550–1625* (Edinburgh, 1960).

Mackinnon, James. *The Union of England and Scotland* (London, 1896).

Mathew, David. *Scotland Under Charles I* (London, 1955).

Smout, Thomas C. *A History of the Scottish People, 1560–1830* (London, 1969).

———. *Scottish Trade on the Eve of Union 1660–1707* (Edinburgh, 1963).

Stevenson, David. *The Scottish Revolution, 1637–1644* (Newton Abbot, Eng., 1973).

Thomson, Edith, E.B. *The Parliament of Scotland, 1690–1702* (London, 1929).

Chapter 6: *"That Part of the United Kingdom Known as Scotland": 1707–1850*

Burleigh, J.H.S. *Church History of Scotland* (London, 1960).

Campbell, J.L., ed. *Highland Songs of the Forty-Five* (Edinburgh, 1933).

Campbell, R.H. *Scotland Since 1707: The Rise of an Industrial Society* (Oxford, 1960).

Carlyle, Alexander. *Autobiography.* Edited by J.H. Burton (Edinburgh and London, 1860).

Cockburn, Henry. *Journal 1831–1854.* 2 vols. (Edinburgh, 1874).

———. *Memorials of His Time 1779–1830.* Edited by Harry A. Cockburn (Edinburgh and London, 1910).

Davie, G.E. *The Democratic Intellect: Scotland and Her Universities in the Nineteenth Century* (Edinburgh, 1961).

Ferguson, William. *Scotland: 1689 to the Present* (Edinburgh and London, 1978).

Furber, Holden. *Henry Dundas, First Viscount Melville 1742–1811* (Oxford, 1931).

Gray, Malcolm. *The Highland Economy 1750–1850* (Edinburgh, 1957).

Hamilton, Henry. *An Economic History of Scotland in the Eighteenth Century* (Oxford, 1963).

———. *The Industrial Revolution in Scotland* (Oxford, 1932).

Handley, James E. *Scottish Farming in the Eighteenth Century* (London, 1953).

Hunter, James. *The Making of the Crofting Community* (Edinburgh, 1976).

Kyded, J.G. *Scottish Population Statistics* (Edinburgh, 1952).

Lenman, Bruce. *An Economic History of Modern Scotland 1660–1976* (London, 1977).

Meikle, Henry. *Scotland and the French Revolution* (Glasgow, 1912).

Riley, P.W.J. *The English Ministers and Scotland 1707–1727* (London, 1964).

Saunders, L.J. *Scottish Democracy 1815–1840: The Social and Intellectual Background* (Edinburgh, 1940).

Somerville, Thomas. *My Own Life and Times 1741–1814* (Edinburgh, 1861).

Chapter 7: *The Scottish Enlightenment*

Allardyce, Alexander, ed. *Scotland and Scotsmen in the Eighteenth Century, from the Mss. of John Ramsay* (Edinburgh and London, 1888).

Barber, W.H.; Brumfitt, J.H.; Leigh, R.A.; Shackleton, R.; and Taylor, S.S.B., eds. *The Age of the Enlightenment: Studies Presented to Theodore Besterman* (Edinburgh and London, 1967).

Besterman, Theodore, ed. *Transactions of the Second International Congress on the Enlightenment IV.* Vol. 58. Studies on Voltaire and the Eighteenth Century (Geneva, 1967).

Buckle, Henry T. *On Scotland and the Scotch Intellect.* Edited by H.J. Hanham (Chicago and London, 1970).

Campbell, R.H. *Scotland Since 1707: The Rise of an Industrial Society* (Oxford, 1960).

Chitnis, Anand C. *The Scottish Enlightenment: A Social History* (London, 1976).

Clement, A.G., and Robertson, Robert H.S. *Scotland's Scientific Heritage* (Edinburgh and London, 1961).

Donaldson, Gordon. *Scotland: The Shaping of a Nation* (London and Vancouver, 1974).

Ferguson, William. *Scotland: 1689 to the Present* (Edinburgh and London, 1978).

Graham, Henry Grey. *The Social Life of Scotland in the Eighteenth Century* (London, 1937).

Harvie, Christopher. *Scotland and Nationalism: Scottish Society and Politics, 1707–1977* (London, 1977).

Lehmann, William C. *Scottish and Scotch-Irish Contributions to Early American Life and Culture* (Port Washington, N.Y., and London, 1978).

Mackie, J.D. *A History of Scotland* (Harmondsworth and Baltimore, 1964).

Macpherson, Hector. *The Intellectual Development of Scotland* (London, 1912).

Orel, Harold. *English Romantic Poets and the Enlightenment: Nine Essays on a Literary Relationship.* Vol. 103. Studies on Voltaire and the Eighteenth Century (Banbury, Oxfordshire, Eng., 1973).

Plant, Marjorie. *The Domestic Life of Scotland in the Eighteenth Century* (Edinburgh, 1952).

Chapter 7: *Art During the Enlightenment*

Adam, Robert and James. *The Works in Architecture of Robert and James Adam* (London, 1778–1812; reprinted 1900–1902).

Andrews, Keith, and Brotchie, J.R. *Scottish Drawings.* The National Gallery of Scotland (Edinburgh, 1960).

Baxandall, David. *Raeburn Bicentenary Exhibition.* Arts Council of Great Britain, Scottish Committee (Edinburgh, 1956).

Boggs, Jean S. *Three Centuries of Scottish Painting.* The National Gallery of Canada (Ottawa, 1968).

Bolton, Arthur. *The Architecture of Robert and James Adam* (London and New York, 1922).

Caw, Sir James L. *Scottish Painting, Past and Present, 1620–1908* (Edinburgh, 1908; reprinted 1975).

Cursiter, Stanley. *Scottish Art to the Close of the Nineteenth Century* (London, 1949).

Docharty, George, and Donald, Anne. *British Oil Paintings.* Glasgow Art Gallery (Glasgow, 1971).

Dunbar, John. *The Historic Architecture of Scotland* (London, 1966; new ed., 1978).

Finlay, Ian. *Scottish Art* (London, 1941).

Fleming, John. *Robert Adam and His Circle in Edinburgh and Rome* (London and Cambridge, Mass., 1962).

Forman, Sheila. *Scottish Country Houses and Castles* (Glasgow, 1967).

Harris, Eileen. *The Furniture of Robert Adam* (London, 1963).

Hutchison, Robin. *Scott and His Circle.* Scottish National Portrait Gallery (Edinburgh, 1964).

Irwin, David. "Gavin Hamilton: Archaeologist, Painter and Dealer." *Art Bulletin,* 44, 1962, pp. 87–102.

Irwin, David and Francina. *Scottish Painters at Home and Abroad, 1700–1900* (London, 1975).

Lindsay, Ian. *Georgian Edinburgh.* 2d ed. Revised and expanded by David Walker (Edinburgh, 1973).

——— and Cosh, Mary. *Inverary and the Dukes of Argyll* (Edinburgh, 1973).

McWilliam, Colin. *Georgian Edinburgh, an Illustrated Record of the Eight Main Areas of the New Town Development, 1750–1850* (Edinburgh, n.d.).

Pevsner, Sir Nikolaus. *Academies of Art Past and Present* (Cambridge, Eng., 1940).

Ramsay, Allan. *The Investigator: I. On Ridicule, II. On Elizabeth Canning, III. On Naturalisation, IV. On Taste* (London, 1762; 1st ed., 1755).

Skinner, Basil. *Scots in Italy in the Eighteenth Century*. Scottish National Portrait Gallery (Edinburgh, 1966).

Smart, Alastair. *The Life and Art of Allan Ramsay* (London, 1953).

Stillman, Damie. *The Decorative Work of Robert Adam* (London, 1966).

Thompson, Colin. *Pictures for Scotland: The National Gallery of Scotland and Its Collections* (Edinburgh, 1972).

—— and Brigstocke, Hugh. *National Gallery of Scotland: Catalogue of Painting and Sculpture* (Edinburgh, 1957; revised in *Shorter Catalogue*, 1970; 2d ed., 1978).

Thompson, Colin, and Hutchison, Robin. *Allan Ramsay, His Masters and Rivals*. The National Gallery of Scotland (Edinburgh, 1963).

Waterhouse, Ellis. *Painting in Britain 1530–1790* (Harmondsworth, 1953).

Young, A. McLaren. *Glasgow University's Pictures* (Glasgow, 1973).

Youngson, A.J. *The Making of Classical Edinburgh* (Edinburgh, 1966).

Chapter 8:   *The Scot Around the World*

Blaikie, William Garden. *The Personal Life of David Livingstone* (London, 1880).

Burton, John Hill. *The Scot Abroad*. 2 vols. (Edinburgh and London, 1864).

Campbell, D., and Maclean, R.A. *Beyond the Atlantic Roar: A Study of the Nova Scotia Scots* (Toronto, 1974).

Coupland, Sir Reginald. *Welsh and Scottish Nationalism: A Study* (London, 1954).

Devine, T.M. *The Tobacco Lords* (Edinburgh, 1975).

Dickson, R.J. *The Ulster Emigration to Colonial America: 1718–1775* (London, 1966).

Dobson, J.O. *Ronald Ross: Dragon Slayer* (London, 1934).

Donaldson, Gordon. *The Scots Overseas* (London, 1966).

Erickson, Charlotte. *Invisible Immigrants: The Adaption of English and Scottish Immigrants in Nineteenth-Century America* (Leicester, 1972).

Fischer, T.A. *The Scots in Sweden* (Edinburgh, 1907).

Flinn, Michael, et al. *Scottish Population History from the 17th Century to the 1930s* (Cambridge, Eng., and New York, 1977).

Ghosh, Suresh Chandra. *Dalhousie in India, 1848–56* (New Delhi, 1975).

Gibb, Andrew Dewar. *Scottish Empire* (London, 1937).

Graham, Ian Charles C. *Colonists from Scotland: Emigration to North America, 1707–1783* (Ithaca, N.Y., 1956).

Graham, R.B. Cunninghame. *The Essential R.B. Cunninghame Graham*. Selected by Paul Bloomfield (London, 1952).

Holt, Basil. *Greatheart of the Border: A Life of John Brownlee, Pioneer Missionary in South Africa* (King William's Town, South Africa, 1976).

Hook, Andrew. *Scotland and America: A Study of Cultural Relations 1750–1835* (Glasgow and London, 1975).

Insh, George Pratt. *The Company of Scotland Trading to Africa and the Indies* (London, 1932).

——. *Scottish Colonial Schemes 1620–1686* (Glasgow, 1922).

Kerr, W.G. *Scottish Capital on the American Credit Frontier* (Austin, Tex., 1976).

Leacock, Stephen. *Canada: The Foundations of Its Future* (Montreal, 1941).

Lehmann, William C. *Scottish and Scotch-Irish Contributions to Early American Life and Culture* (Port Washington, N.Y., and London, 1978).

Lupton, Kenneth. *Mungo Park the African Traveller* (Oxford and Ibadan, 1979).

MacCormick, Neil, ed. *The Scottish Debate: Essays on Scottish Nationalism* (Glasgow and New York, 1970).

McCullough, John Herries. *The Scot in England* (London, 1935).

McKenzie, N.R. *The Gael Fares Forth* (Wellington, N.Z., 1935).

Macmillan, W.M. *My South African Years: An Autobiography* (Cape Town, 1975).

Meiring, Jane. *Thomas Pringle: His Life and Times* (Cape Town, 1968).

Moir, Fred L.M. *After Livingstone: An African Trade Romance* (London, 1923).

Moir, John S. *Enduring Witness: A History of the Presbyterian Church in Canada* (Toronto, 1975).

Niven, Frederick. *Coloured Spectacles* (London, 1938).

Prebble, John. *The Darien Disaster* (London, 1968).

Pringle, Thomas. *Poems Illustrative of South Africa*. Edited by John Robert Wahl (Cape Town, 1970).

Reid, W. Stanford, ed., *The Scottish Tradition in Canada* (Toronto, 1976).

Roberts, Stephen H. *The Squatting Age in Australia, 1835–47* (Melbourne, 1935).

Shepperson, George. "The American Revolution and Scotland." *Scotia: American-Canadian Journal of Scottish Studies* (Norfolk, Va.), 1, no. 1, 1977, pp. 3–17.

——. "David Livingstone the Scot." *Scottish Historical Review* (Edinburgh), 39, no. 128, 1960, pp. 113–21.

Stevenson, Robert Louis. *Vailima Papers* (London, 1924).

Vogt, Martha. "Scots in Hispanic California." *Scottish Historical Review* (Aberdeen), 52, no. 154, 1973, pp. 137–48.

Waite, P.B. *Macdonald: His Life and Work* (Toronto, New York, and London, 1975).

Wall, Joseph Frazier. *Andrew Carnegie* (New York, 1970).

Whyte, Donald, ed. *A Dictionary of Scottish Emigrants to the U.S.A.* (Baltimore, 1972).

William and Mary Quarterly (special "Scotland and America" issue), 11, no. 2, 1954.

Young, Douglas. "A Sketch History of Scottish Nationalism." In *The Scottish Debate*, edited by Neil MacCormick (Glasgow and New York, 1970).

Chapter 9:   *Romantic Images of Scotland—Words and Music*

Caw, Sir James L. *Scottish Painting, Past and Present, 1620–1908* (Edinburgh, 1908; reprinted 1975).

Hardie, William. *Scottish Painting, 1873–1939* (London, 1976).

Holloway, James, and Errington, Lindsay. *The Discovery of Scotland: The Appreciation of Scottish Scenery Through Two Centuries of Painting*. Catalogue, National Gallery of Scotland, October 12–November 30, 1978.

Irwin, David and Francina. *Scottish Painters at Home and Abroad, 1700–1900* (London, 1975).

Strong, Roy. *And when did you last see your father? The Victorian Painter and British History* (London, 1978).

Chapter 9:   *Romantic Images in Art*

Boswell, James. *The Journal of a Tour to the Hebrides* (London, 1773, and later editions).

Coats, B.H. *Travellers' Tales of Scotland* (1913).

Cox, Edward G. *A Reference Guide to the Literature of Travel: Great Britain*. Vol. 3 (Seattle, 1949).

Duff, David Skene. *Victoria in the Highland: The Personal Journal of Her Majesty Queen Victoria* (London, 1968).

Ford, Richard. *Dramatisations of Scott's Novels: A Catalogue* (1979).

Forsyth, Robert. *The Beauties of Scotland*. 5 vols. (Edinburgh, 1805–8).

Grant, Anne. *Letters from the Mountains*. 3 vols. (London, 1806).

Hill, George Birkbeck. *Footsteps of Dr. Johnson (Scotland)* (London, 1890).

Johnson, Samuel. *A Journey to the Western Islands of Scotland* (Dublin, 1773, and later editions).

Lindsay, Maurice. *The Discovery of Scotland* (London, 1964).

Mitchell, Arthur. *List of Travels and Tours in Scotland, 1296–1900* (Edinburgh, 1902).

Mitchell, Jerome. *The Walter Scott Operas* (University, Ala., 1977).

Smout, Thomas C. *A History of the Scottish People, 1560–1830* (London, 1969).

Chapters 9 and 10:   *Nineteenth- and Twentieth-Century Literature*

Batho, Edith Clara. *The Ettrick Shepherd* (Cambridge, Eng., 1927).

Blake, George. *Barrie and the Kailyard School* (London, 1951).

Buthlay, Kenneth. *Hugh MacDiarmid (C.M. Grieve)* (Edinburgh and London, 1964).

Butter, Peter. *Edwin Muir: Man and Poet* (Edinburgh and London, 1962).

Campbell, Ian. *Thomas Carlyle* (London, 1974).

Cockburn, Henry Thomas. *Life of Lord Jeffrey, with a Selection from His Correspondence* (Edinburgh, 1852).

Daiches, David. *Robert Louis Stevenson* (Glasgow, 1947).

Dunbar, Janet. *J.M. Barrie: The Man Behind the Image* (London, 1970).

Eigner, Edwin M. *Robert Louis Stevenson and the Romantic Tradition* (Princeton, N.J., 1966).

Glen, Duncan. *Hugh MacDiarmid (Christopher Murray Grieve) and the Scottish Renaissance* (Edinburgh, 1964).

Gordon, Ian Alistair. *John Galt: The Life of a Writer* (Edinburgh, 1972).

Grieve, Christopher Murray. *Contemporary Scottish Studies: First Series* (London, 1926).

Hart, Francis Russell. *Lockhart as Romantic Biographer* (Edinburgh, 1971).

———. *The Scottish Novel from Smollett to Spark* (Cambridge, Mass., 1978).

Huberman, Elizabeth. *The Poetry of Edwin Muir: The Field of Good and Ill* (New York, 1971).

Kinsley, James, ed. *Scottish Poetry: A Critical Survey* (London, 1955).

Lindsay, Maurice. *History of Scottish Literature* (London, 1977).

Lochhead, Marion. *John Gibson Lockhart* (London, 1954).

Lyell, Frank Hallam. *A Study of the Novels of John Galt* (Princeton, N.J., 1942).

Millar, John Hepburn. *A Literary History of Scotland* (New York, 1903).

Muir, Edwin. *Scott and Scotland: The Predicament of the Scottish Writer* (New York, 1938).

Oliphant, Margaret. *William Blackwood and His Sons* (Edinburgh, 1897).

Power, William. *Literature and Oatmeal* (London, 1935).

Scott, Alexander. *The MacDiarmid Makars 1923–1972* (Preston, 1972).

———. *Still Life: William Soutar 1848–1943* (London, 1958).

Seigel, Jules Paul, ed. *Carlyle: The Critical Heritage* (London and New York, 1971).

Simpson, Louis Aston Marantz. *James Hogg: A Critical Study* (New York, 1962).

Townsend, James Benjamin. *John Davidson: Poet of Armageddon* (New Haven, Conn., 1961).

Veitch, James. *George Douglas Brown* (London, 1952).

Wilson, David Alec. *Life of Thomas Carlyle*. 5 vols. (London, 1923–31).

Chapter 10:   *Art in Modern Times*

Billcliffe, Roger. *Architectural Sketches and Flower Drawings by Charles Rennie Mackintosh* (London, 1977).

———. *Mackintosh Water Colours* (London, 1978).

Bliss, Douglas. *Charles Rennie Mackintosh and the Glasgow School of Art* (Glasgow, 1961).

Bruce, David. *Sun Pictures: The Hill-Adamson Calotypes* (London, 1973).

Caw, Sir James L. *William McTaggart: A Biography and an Appreciation* (Glasgow, 1917).

Cursiter, Stanley. *Scottish Painters*. British Arts Council (n.d.).

Dickson, T. Elder. *W.G. Gillies*. Scottish Arts Council (Edinburgh, 1970).

Flower Drawings by Charles Rennie Mackintosh. Hunterian Museum, University of Glasgow (Glasgow, 1977).

Ford, Colin, and Strong, Roy. *An Early Victorian Album: The Photographic Masterpieces (1843–1847) of David Octavius Hill and Robert Adamson* (New York, 1976).

Gage, Edward. *The Eye in the Wind: Scottish Painting Since 1945* (London, 1977).

Hardie, William. *Scottish Painting, 1837–1939* (London, 1976).

Howarth, Thomas. *Charles Rennie Mackintosh and the Modern Movement* (London, 1952).

Kitchen, Paddy. *A Most Unsettling Person* (London, 1975).

Michaelson, Katherin. *David Octavius Hill (1802–1870) and Robert Adamson (1821–1848)* (Edinburgh, 1970).

Minto, C.S. *Victorian and Edwardian Scotland from Old Photographs* (New York, 1970).

Young, A. McLaren. *Glasgow University's Pictures* (Glasgow, 1973).

Chapter 10:   *The National Revival*

Burleigh, J.H.S. *Church History of Scotland* (London, 1960).

Coupland, Sir Reginald. *Welsh and Scottish Nationalism: A Study* (London, 1954).

Hanham, H.J. *Scottish Nationalism* (Cambridge, Mass., 1969).

Highet, John. *The Scottish Churches* (London, 1960).

Hutcheson, A. MacGregor, and Hogg, A., eds. *Scotland and Oil* (Edinburgh and New York, 1975).

Kellas, J.G. *The Scottish Political System* (Cambridge, Eng., 1973).

Lenman, Bruce. *An Economic History of Modern Scotland 1660–1976* (London, 1977).

Pottinger, George. *The Secretaries of State for Scotland, 1926–76* (New York, 1979).

Index

Acknowledgments

Among the many people in Scotland and the United States who have assisted and supported our study and teaching of Scottish culture special thanks are due to Margaret and John Bricke, Hugh Brigstocke, Robert Cobb, Howard Creel Collinson, Richard Eversole, Joel Gold, Helena Hayward, Anne Hyde, Colby Kullman, Helen Lowenthal, Timothy Lloyd, John Macauley, Robert McColl, Roderick McDonald, J. Hammond McNish, Colin McWilliam, Alexandra Mason, Thurston Maxwell Moore, Edward Ruhe, Delbert Shankel, George Baxter Smith, Janey St. George, Jeanne Stump, John Weir, and George Worth and staff members of the Attingham Park Summer School, The National Gallery of Scotland, The National Museum of Antiquities, The National Gallery of Modern Art, The Scottish National Portrait Gallery, The National Buildings Record, and The Royal Commission on the Ancient and Historical Monuments of Scotland. Robert Morton, Director of Special Projects at Abrams, and Emily Berns, Assistant to Mr. Morton, provided sound advice and excellent editorial support.

Photographs were assembled and captions edited by Janey St. George, Marilyn Stokstad, and Henry L. Snyder.

Illustration Credits

The authors and publisher wish to thank the following for permitting the reproduction of the photographs, paintings, prints, and drawings in this book:

T. & R. Annan & Sons Ltd., Glasgow *294 above, 295 below*; Aberdeen University Library *259, 289, 310–11*; Academy of Natural Sciences of Philadelphia *242 above*; Aerofilms Ltd. *169*; Anglo-American Art Museum, Louisiana State University, Baton Rouge *275*; Elizabeth Blackadder *302*; Elizabeth Blackadder and the Dovecot Studios *303*; The Bodleian Library, Oxford *66*; The British Council, ©David Farrell, Gloucester *305*; The British Library, London *47* (Add. MS.39761, f.93v); *71 below* (Cotton MS.Ch.XIX.4); *74 below* (Add. MS.48027 Cotton MS.Nero–D.vi.f.61v); *116 above left* (MS. Add.4802); British Museum, London *121, 147, 157, 165, 204 below*; British Tourist Authority *10, 19, 22, 60 above, 60–61, 156 below, 210–11, 216*; Cambridge University Library, courtesy of the Syndics *42 above* (MS.Ii.6.32 ff.29v–30r); Cooper-Hewitt Museum of Decorative Arts and Design, Smithsonian Institution, New York *241 above left and below*; Corpus Christi College, Cambridge, courtesy of the Masters and Fellows *73 left*; Culver Pictures, Inc., New York *27, 234–35*; George Barnard Davis *2–3, 6–7, 8, 212–13*; Henry Barnard Davis *238 below*; Duke of Buccleuch and Queensberry, K. T., and The Scottish National Portrait Gallery, Edinburgh *136, 268*; Duke of Buccleuch and Queensberry, K.T., ©R. Clapperton *137*; Duke of Roxburghe and the National Library of Scotland *65*; Earl of Ancaster, ©The National Museum of Antiquities of Scotland, Edinburgh *138 middle and below*; Eldon and Cornelia Fields *4–5, 58 below, 58–59 above, 62 above left, 98–99, 99 above, 170–71, 172 below, 175 below, 211 above*; Free Church of Scotland and The National Galleries of Scotland, Edinburgh *286 below*; John Freeman Group, London *228*; M. Gibb and The Royal Commission on the Ancient and Historical Monuments of Scotland, Edinburgh *312*; Glasgow Art Gallery and Museum *99 below, 102–103, 126*; Her Britannic Majesty's Stationery Office, reproduced with the permission of the Controller, British Crown Copyright *14, 73 right*; Her Britannic Majesty's Stationery Office, reproduced with the permission of the Controller, and the Public Record Office, London *112*; Joseph H. Hirshhorn Museum and Sculpture Garden, Smithsonian Institution, Washington D.C. *307*; Hunterian Art Gallery, University of Glasgow *191*; Hunterian Art Gallery, University of Glasgow, Mackintosh Collection *291–92*; Michael Lynn Jackson *63*; Kunstgewerbemuseum, Zürich *295 above*; Timothy Lloyd *304*; Lord Chamberlain's Office, London, ©Her Majesty the Queen *110 left, 113 above, 263 above;* The Right Honorable Lord Home of the Hirsel *74 above*; Philip McKnight *62 below*; The Metropolitan Museum of Art, New York, Gift of Irwin Untermyer *107 above*; The Montreal Museum of Fine Arts, presented by Lord Mount Stephen, 896.52 *300*; Musée du Louvre, Paris *125*; Museum of the City of New York *241 above right*; National Galleries of Scotland, Edinburgh *15 above, 108 below, 155, 161, 179 above, 206 below, 222 above, 226 above, 230–31, 233, 244, 248 right, 249, 251, 260 below, 262, 266 above, 283, 315*; National Galleries of Scotland, Edinburgh, on loan from William Nicol *269, 315*; National Gallery of Scotland, Edinburgh *80, 89, 111, 138 above, 184, 204 above, 225, 226 below, 232 above, 266 middle and below, 300*; The National Museum of Antiquities of Scotland, Edinburgh *20, 31, 34, 39–40, 42 below, 43 below left and right, 44 below, 50, 59 below, 62 above right, 71 above, 75, 90, 93, 107 middle and below, 109 right, 120, 133, 159 above left and right, middle left*; The National Portrait Gallery, London *162, 260 above, 285 above, 286 above, 287*; National Portrait Gallery, Smithsonian Institution, Washington, D.C. *243 right*; The National Trust for Places of Historic Interest or Natural Beauty, London *105, 110 right*; The National Trust for Scotland, Edinburgh *118, 122, 185, 206 above, 220–21, 222 below, 223*; The William Rockhill Nelson Gallery of Art—Atkins Museum of Fine Arts, Kansas City *15 below* (Burnap Collection); *217, 227*; *280* (Gift of Mr. Robert Fizzell); Harold Orel *57, 100–101, 171, 209, 214 above, 215*; The Paisley Museum, Art Galleries and Observatory *70*; The Perth Museum and Art Gallery *232 below*; private collection, courtesy of The Scottish National Portrait Gallery, Edinburgh *207*; private collection, photograph by Rupert Roddam *208*; Paul J. Pugliese *24–25*; Recreation and Park Department, San Francisco *243 left*; The Royal Commission on the Ancient and Historical Monuments of Scotland, Edinburgh *82 below, 106 below, 149, 182, 219, 240, 261, 272, 284, 293, 294 below, 317*; The Royal Incorporation of Architects in Scotland *296–99*; The Royal Scottish Academy, Edinburgh, photograph by G. Forrest Wilson *318*; Royal Scottish Museum, Edinburgh, British Crown Copyright *94*; The Science Museum, London *188–89, 285 below*; Scottish Development Agency, Edinburgh, Scottish Crafts Collection *306*; The Scottish Development Department, Edinburgh *33, 41, 44 above, 48, 53–55, 68 below left and right, 78, 106 above* (British Crown Copyright); The Scottish National Portrait Gallery, Edinburgh *17, 108 above, 109 left, 114, 116 above right and below, 129, 130, 132, 139, 142, 147 above right, 152, 156 above left and right, 159 below, 173, 176, 179 below, 192–200, 218, 236, 238 above, 246, 248 left, 263 below, 271, 279, 288*; Scottish Record Office, Edinburgh *147 below*; Carol and Delbert Shankel *67, 174 above*; Shell Oil Company Photographic Service *320*; Henry L. Snyder *100 below, 172 above and middle, 211 below*; Thomas Southall Collection, Lawrence, Kansas *18, 264*; The Helen Foresman Spencer Museum of Art, University of Kansas, Lawrence, Kansas *250*; Kenneth Spencer Research Library, University of Kansas, Department of Special Collections *21, 68 above, 82 above, 134*; Marilyn Stokstad *1, 97, 100 above, 104, 174 below, 175 above, 214 below*; The Tate Gallery, London *108 middle*; U.S. Department of the Interior, National Park Service, Yosemite National Park, California *242 below*; Victoria and Albert Museum, London *113 below, 154, 257*; Vista of Glasgow *92*; Warburg Institute, London *43 above*; Württemburgische Landesbibliothek, Stuttgart *77*; William Young *60 below*.